NO MORE HEROES

GRASSROOTS CHALLENGES TO THE SAVIOR MENTALITY

By Jordan Flaherty

"From systemic racism to climate change, there are no easy fixes to the deep-rooted crises of our time. In this marvelous, enormously instructive book, Jordan Flaherty explores how we too often allow the struggle for change to be undermined by would-be saviors—and how today's grassroots social movements, led by communities on the frontlines of crisis, are charting a far more powerful path forward." —**Naomi Klein**, author of *This Changes Everything* and *The Shock Doctrine*

"Part memoir, part history, part political critique, *No More Heroes* exposes the savior complex for what it really is: imperialism camouflaged as a rescue operation. A perfect gift for the age of Trump." —**Robin D. G. Kelley**, author of *Freedom Dreams*

"Jordan Flaherty is one of America's most committed journalists writing from below and to the left. His work lifts up voices rarely heard in media as he focuses on the tireless, courageous work of marginalized communities building collective power. At a time when many movements are increasingly aligned with the dangerous neoliberal notion of individual saviors, Jordan reminds us there are no masters in the path to love and liberation." —**Harsha Walia**, author of *Undoing Border Imperialism*

"Tying together history, community organizing, scholarly research, mainstream media, and pop culture, *No More Heroes* deftly explores not only the concept of the white savior, 'the leftist version of Manifest Destiny,' but contrasts that with concrete examples of radical visionary community-building, which centers the leadership of the oppressed, especially queer women and trans folks of color. This book can serve as a flashing stop sign to social justice movements so they don't get hit by the freight train of neoliberialism. It demands we answer the question 'which side of justice are you on?' not with words but with self-reflective action. Compelling and accessible, this book may be challenging for folks with privilege—especially cisgendered straight white men—to read as it demands they ask searing questions that may indict them and their behavior, but Flaherty shows clearly that is exactly what privileged people have to do, because oppressed people stare these realities in the face every day—and when we blink, we die." —**Walidah Imarisha**, author of *Angels with Dirty Faces*

"Jordan Flaherty...has learned through personal experience and from listening to those who are marginalized just how dangerous it can be for would-be superheroes (even those with the best intentions) to take up the cause of justice, absent a real grounding in the solidarity and accountability necessary to bring true liberation. This is a unique and compelling contribution to movement literature, written with a humility that is as powerful as it is genuine." —**Tim Wise**, author of *White Like Me*

"In 1977, the Combahee River Collective said 'black women are inherently valuable,' a radical statement because in capitalism no one is believed to be inherently valuable. Even in our movements we are trying to prove that we are individually worthy. *No More Heroes* gives us all another opportunity to do what it will actually take to create liberation in our lifetimes: trust them most impacted, come together across forms of oppression, and most importantly throw away the scarcity-based, fragile individuality that privilege teaches us to defend. Let it go, and embrace the humbling, collective work of getting free." —**Alexis Pauline Gumbs**, author of *Spill*

"Jordan Flaherty's *No More Heroes* is a both fascinating documentation of recent movement history that I enjoyed the hell out of reading, and an example of solidarity journalism at its best. From cautionary tales about rapey manarchist 'saviors' who turn out to be FBI informants, to a breakdown of why most of the people trying to 'save' sex workers actually cause violence and damage, this book is essential literature for movements and people trying to figure out how to do right and not play into the ableist charity and savior models that have been killing us for too long." —**Leah Lakshmi Piepzna-Samarasinha**, author of *Dirty River*

"*No More Heroes* is a vitally useful intervention in the current political moment. Spot-on analysis, gripping examples, and a clear, urgently necessary argument about how we need to re-think harmful 'rescue' frames and the leadership models they foster will make this book immensely useful to contemporary movements. *No More Heroes* helps us understand how our movements' debates about leadership, respectability politics and co-optation relate to long-standing investment in ideas of saving that have got to be dismantled if we are going to build the new world we so desperately need and long for." —**Dean Spade**, author of *Normal Life*

"*No More Heroes* is a much-needed critique of unchecked leadership within causes and social movements. At a time when media latches onto figureheads and sound bites, Jordan Flaherty helps us understand how new movements are able to be democratic, decentralized and effective in changing policy and rewriting discourse." —**Francesca Fiorentini**, Host and Producer of *AJ+*

"From left-wing vanguards, Teach-For-America, and charitable foundations, to the power of military interventions, Jordan Flaherty shows how rhetorics of commercial culture and corporate media re-appear as 'moral' arguments to justify domination. This is an original interrogation of destructive control masquerading as 'help.' A personal and eclectic analysis with interesting background and helpful information." —**Sarah Schulman**, author of *Conflict Is Not Abuse*

"In *No More Heroes*, Jordan Flaherty upends the world. You might think you understand the issues of sex workers, disaster victims, and the poor, but through personal stories from the front lines of these fights, *No More Heroes* demonstrates that our best intended assumptions are often wrong. Read this book before your misguided good intentions do more harm to your pet causes than good." —**Lolis Eric Elie**, Writer, HBO's *Treme*

"If you are earnest in the desire to be a good white ally, if you are a Black male looking to support his sisters in struggle or a cisgendered male trying to find his way in the fight for LGBTQ liberation, you must read this book." —**Max Rameau**, author of *Take Back The Land*

"From Jordan Flaherty, the journalist who broke the story of The Jena Six, comes this thrilling people's history of current movements for revolutionary change. A powerful, engaging, exciting book for anyone concerned about the state of the world." —**Cynthia McKinney**, former Georgia congresswoman

"Longtime movement journalist Jordan Flaherty grounds his analysis of the money, power, and seductive ideology driving the present-day savior impulse in the brutal histories of colonial domination and racism. A wake-up call to decolonize US-based activism and international solidarity work, everyone interested in social change should read this book." —**Anjali Kamat**, independent journalist

No More Heroes: Grassroots Challenges to the Savior Mentality

© 2016 Jordan Flaherty; Foreword © 2016 Roxanne Dunbar-Ortiz

This edition © 2016 AK Press (Chico, Oakland, Edinburgh, Baltimore)

ISBN: 978-1-84935-266-6
E-ISBN: 978-1-84935-267-3
Library of Congress Control Number: 2016941995

AK Press   AK Press
370 Ryan Ave. #100   33 Tower St.
Chico, CA 95973   Edinburgh EH6 7BN
USA   Scotland
www.akpress.org   www.akuk.com
akpress@akpress.org   ak@akedin.demon.co.uk

The above addresses would be delighted to provide you with the latest
AK Press distribution catalog, which features books, pamphlets, zines,
and stylish apparel published and/or distributed by AK Press. Alterna-
tively, visit our websites for the complete catalog, latest news, and secure
ordering.

Cover design by John Yates | stealworks.com

Printed in the USA on acid-free, recycled paper.

CONTENTS

Foreword

by Roxanne Dunbar Ortiz

As an organizer of women's liberation and against the United States war in Southeast Asia, in 1969, I accepted an invitation to meet women representatives of the South Vietnamese National Liberation Front ("Viet Cong") near Montreal, Quebec. There were a hundred or so other such organizers present, mostly women, about half of them young like me, and half from an earlier generation of women's peace organizations. The three NLF representatives, through a translator, spoke clearly, explaining in considerable detail the military situation in South Vietnam: U.S. massive expulsion of people from the countryside into refugee camps, with a "kill everything that moves" program in effect. They told us of their commitment and determination to drive the U.S. invaders out and thanked us for our solidarity and efforts to end the war. When the women opened the discussion, the first speaker, an older U.S. woman, asked how we might contribute funds to the NLF cause. Several other women, including the young, followed up with the same question and offers of checks right then and there. The translator explained the questions and offers to the NLF representative, then talked among themselves, selecting one of their number to respond. She said, "We do not want your money, we do not need your money. We need you to love your own sons who are fighting and dying there and bring them home."

There was considerable confusion among the U.S. American women present, both young and old, a sort of desperate begging to provide material aid. This was the first time that I deeply understood what Jordan Flaherty dubs "the savior mentality." Just having finished graduate school in the field of history, pieces of the puzzle of the apparent contradictions of U.S. imperialism—the populist urge to help the benighted around the world and the method for doing that always including making war on them—fell into place.

The author correctly begins this book with the Christian Crusades in 1096, and jumping across the Atlantic in 1492, as the foundation for the founding of a Republic (the United States) to "rescue" the Native. The very origin story of the United States forms the core of the savior project. In November 1620, English religious dissidents ("Pilgrims") landed on the shore of what is now Cape Cod, Massachusetts. Forty-one of the "Pilgrims," all men, wrote and signed the Mayflower Compact, named after the ship they arrived on. Invoking God's name and declaring themselves loyal subjects of the king, the signatories announced that they had journeyed to North America "to plant the First Colony" and did therefore "Covenant and Combine ourselves together in a Civil Body Politic" to be governed by "just and equal Laws" enacted "for the general good of the Colony, unto which we promise all due submission and obedience." A decade later, when additional English settlers founded the Massachusetts Bay Colony, they adopted an official seal designed in England prior to their journey. The central image depicts a near-naked native holding a harmless, flimsy-looking bow and arrow and inscribed with the plea, "Come over and help us." Nearly three hundred years later, the official seal of the U.S. military veterans of the "Spanish-American War" (the invasion and occupation of Puerto Rico, Cuba, and the Philippines) showed a dark, naked woman kneeling before an armed U.S. soldier and a sailor, with a U.S. battleship in the background. One may trace this recurrent altruistic theme into the early twenty-first century, when the United States still invades countries under the guise of rescue.

Today, U.S. American taxpayers believe they carry an enormous burden of development and crisis financial aid to peoples in need in Africa, Asia, and Latin America, but in reality such aid accounts for only 0.19 percent of the U.S. GDP, and much of that is in kind or in loans. And, as I witnessed in 1969, U.S. Americans rush to contribute dubious calls for charity, often in tandem with U.S. sites of intervention, which then involves U.S. citizens emotionally in the cause, under the guise of "humanitarian intervention."

Following the crushing defeat of the United States military by the Vietnamese and the U.S. emergency withdrawal in 1975, the mainstream press and educational institutions had embraced much of what the antiwar/anti-imperialism movement of the preceding decade had formulated, and a majority of the population opposed future interventions. And, although the U.S. Congress and many politicians made gestures in the form of investigations into the illegal activities of both the FBI and the Central Intelligence Agency for domestic abuses, armed interventions continued covertly in Afghanistan, Africa, the Middle East, the Philippines, Central America, the Caribbean, and Latin America. In the wake of post-war recession, inflation, skyrocketing interest rates, the oil crisis, and general malaise identified with the positive reforms by Governor Jerry Brown in California and President Jimmy Carter, by 1980, Sunbelt quasi-fascism and the military-industrial complex had found the perfect candidate to restore confidence through militarism and extreme nationalism: Ronald Reagan. Yet the interventions in Nicaragua and El Salvador and in Southern Africa were widely opposed in the 1980s, with fears of another Vietnam, but were sapped of energy by intensive Cold War anticommunist propaganda. When Vice-President George H. W. Bush, former CIA chief in the 1970s, took the presidency, he tested the mood by launching a lightning invasion of Panama in December 1989, removing the sitting president and imprisoning him in a federal penitentiary, with little protest, and general mainstream media support.

The following summer plans ("Desert Shield") for the invasion of Iraq began with a troop build up of a half-million U.S. professional volunteers poised to launch the invasion in early 1991 ("Desert Storm"). This was conceived by the Bush administration as a way to end the "Vietnam Syndrome." It was also presented, like the invasion of Panama, as ridding the country of a brutal dictator. The highly publicized story (fabrication) that the administration created of Iraqi soldiers invading a Kuwaiti hospital and pulling the tubes out of premature babies awakened the "savior mentality," eliciting fervent support for the U.S. invasion. It was accompanied by the drumbeat of "Support our Troops," advertised as a reversal of the presumed maltreatment of Vietnam veterans, although no such treatment, least of all hippies spitting on returning vets, was ever documented.

At the same time, the Union of Soviet Socialist Republics collapsed and broke down into independent republics, and the stage was set for the resurgence of U.S. military domination through the North American Treaty Alliance (NATO). The United Nations, cowed by the Bush administration audacity, and absent previous Soviet objections, passed a resolution to "legalize" the U.S. invasion of Iraq.

What followed in the 1990s, as the author recounts, billionaire George Soros bankrolled non-governmental organizations and actors, such as the journalist Samantha Power, to push for a policy of humanitarian intervention, achieving success in the United Nations by 2005, with the institutionalization of the doctrine of "Responsibility to Protect."

This, then, is new U.S. imperialism, supported by both Neoconservatives and Neoliberals, twisting the argument about U.S. military expansion around the world and endless wars as one between "isolationism" and "internationalism," between "generosity" in helping beleaguered populations and "selfishness" in arguing the U.S. can't afford it, with their populist calls to let those people take care of their own demons.

So, the "savior mentality" is key to the continuation of brutal United States militarism and the phantom "war on terror."

In the words of Vietnamese-American war refugee writer Viet Thanh Nguyen: "Armored cosmopolitanism is the new spin on the white man's burden, where the quaint idea of civilizing the world becomes retailored for culturally sensitive capitalists in the service of the United States, the World Trade Organization, and the International Monetary Fund."[1]

Jordan Flaherty demonstrates how this mentality also seeps in and even guides much of our oppositional projects, and that is the point of this book, our own complicity in intervention and the absence of a significant antiwar, anti-imperialist movement.

Introduction

It was a beautiful spring evening in New Orleans when I ran into Brandon Darby at a café in the Marigny neighborhood. After a quick hello, he lowered his voice. "Have you seen the news today?"[1]

"What do you mean?"

Darby was an activist who carried himself with an air of self-importance and liked to brag about his guns and plans for revolution. He often started conversations with questions like this, delivered with a mysterious and urgent air. But this sounded more serious than usual.

"It's Riad. He's dead." He gave an awkward, nervous smile. "I feel kind of bad about it."

I was speechless. Darby went on to tell me that the body of my friend Riad Hamad had been found with his hands and feet bound, floating in a lake. He voiced what sounded like a conspiracy theory, telling me he thought perhaps the government had killed Riad. Less than two years later, Darby would publicly announce his role as an FBI informant who had conspired to imprison Riad and others.

When I think about that night and about Riad's strange and sudden death, I still feel pain and grief. In looking for answers, I return to unanswered questions about the role of Darby in Riad's death. Then I turn inward, looking at my own responsibility in not speaking up as Darby rose to his positions of power and influence in my community.

Darby had a magnetic charm, and social movements have an unfortunate history of following the leadership of charismatic hero figures. I've come to think of this as the savior mentality, the idea that a hero will come and answer our societal problems, like Superman saving Lois Lane or a firefighter rescuing a kitten from a tree. It's a simplistic view of change, taught by religion, popular culture, and our school system.

The idea of a heroic rescue is compelling to me as well, and I've made many mistakes in my attempts to do good over the years. Too often I was one of those who saw and said too little, or who took action without looking into what the long-term effects were likely to be.

Over years of working as a journalist, I have encountered this savior mentality repeatedly. From New Orleans to Phoenix to Anchorage to Gaza, I have seen pain caused by those who say they are coming to help. As I discuss in the coming pages, I have seen idealistic young activists pulled into campaigns on behalf of "saving" sex workers through policing. I've seen them plan international "voluntourism" trips and consider joining Teach For America; all in the name of rescuing those less-fortunate than themselves.

I have also spent time observing and participating in popular uprisings—from Tahrir Square in Egypt to Occupy Wall Street to the Movement for Black Lives—that have consciously challenged this dynamic. I have learned from the people most affected by so-called saviors: the people with the least privilege, who resisted easy solutions and have built grassroots, accountable movements focused on systemic change. From these front lines of social justice struggles, I have learned firsthand the importance of systemic solutions to the problems we face.

I am indebted to the people on the frontlines of these movements, who have seen saviors claim to help them as they make things worse. The best analysis of saviors comes from those who have been on the receiving end of their rescues, and my goal here is to amplify their voices. I believe that with the privileged position I was born into, it is important to speak up against white supremacy, patriarchy, and other systems that uphold the advantages I have as a white, cisgender male. My purpose in writing this book is not to supplant the voices of those with less privilege, but to create a tool and resource for all of us to challenge these systems and stand together with already existing movements to create a better world.

Chapter One
The History of Saviors

Caitlin Breedlove grew up queer in the Midwest in a mixed-class white immigrant family. In 2003 she moved to Tennessee and worked for three years at the Highlander Center, a movement training space in the hills of rural Tennessee started by radical labor activists in the 1930s. Highlander continued to be an important center during the civil rights movement, training Rosa Parks and many other important leaders and activists.

Suzanne Pharr, a longtime white antiracist organizer, was the director of the Highlander Center when Breedlove arrived, and she helped mentor Breedlove in avoiding the pitfalls of the savior mentality. "There are a lot of smart white girls with great ideas," she told Breedlove. "Be more than that." Pharr taught her to listen and build trust with communities of color, rather than seeking to lead them. "People are being told what to do and where to do it every day of their lives. They don't need another person coming in and telling them how to do it," said Pharr.

The assumption that you have something to contribute to communities you know nothing about is "an incredibly entitled notion," adds Breedlove. "To think that you can save someone you really must think highly of yourself."[1]

Breedlove went on to spend nine years as codirector of the LGBT racial justice organization Southerners On New Ground (SONG). The organization seeks liberation for all people, building power among working-class LGBT communities in the South, uniting across class, age, race, ability, gender, immigration status, and sexuality. Through working in grassroots queer communities, she helped the organization grow to three thousand members and one hundred member-leaders. They fought repressive and racist laws, such as an anti-immigrant bill in Georgia, and changed attitudes through one-on-one conversations, media work, and direct action. Breedlove left SONG in 2015 to become campaign director of Standing on the Side of Love, a social justice campaign of the Unitarian Universalist Association.

Mentorship from elders like Pharr was central to Breedlove's growth as an organizer, along with time outside of traditional movement spaces, like conversations in working-class gay bars in small southern towns. Breedlove says that activists with privilege should ask how they are centering or decentering themselves, which "means getting feedback from people you don't have power over." In other words, if you run an organization, you need to hear feedback from people who aren't on staff and have no reason to hesitate in being honest with you. "How are you aligned with people who are quietly getting things done, who sometimes are white?" adds Breedlove. "Not 'How you are aligned with the loudest voice of the Good White People Club?'"

Breedlove's codirector in SONG was Paulina Helm-Hernandez, a queer Latina organizer and artist. In a reflection on their shared lessons of nine years of working together, Helm-Hernandez said, "I think white people in movement building need to make a call about whether they will be individual activists or if they are really ready to commit to collective organizing. The latter means that you don't have to always be the final vote on the strategy, pace, timing, tone, and approach. Put another way, it means you have to learn how to share political imagination, power, and work without having to always be in charge." At the same time, she says, "I don't want them to go to those antiracist trainings where they get declawed and told that they should just sit quietly in meetings and then follow people of color around asking them what to do. I want them to have their claws. They need them ... we are in a region, a moment, a country where those claws are needed for the enemies who are killing us."

"Doing workshops with other white people is not enough," adds Helm-Hernandez. "You need backbone. You need practice, you need to take risks, be uncomfortable, and stand side-by-side with leaders of color and do what needs to be done. You have to be willing to trust leaders of color who have the track record, integrity, and vision to get things done."[2]

It is crucial for people with privilege to work and struggle and take risks and have difficult conversations within their own communities. "I want to have more conversations with other white people about reparations," says Breedlove. "Why? Am I an expert? No. Because it is a way to engage with Black liberation that's not about being the good white person in the room."

Many people with privilege are actually bored, estranged, and disconnected, Breedlove says, seeking what they perceive as the excitement of belonging to an oppressed group. As a queer woman, she's encountered this dynamic from straight people. "I've found straight people in my life who covet the depth of emotional intimacy that those of us who are queer have forged in the struggle because we've been through a lot together, and there's a form of intimacy, and I wouldn't trade that for anything."

This desire for "the high and passion and urgency and realness of what marginalized people need to do to thrive and survive" leads to cultural appropriation and insensitivity, she says. "The well-intentioned are always reaching out. 'What is your culture? Tell me about all your inner pain.' It's forced intimacy. It's not wanting to turn the reporting back on yourself."

"How can you ask yourself a different set of questions?" asks Breedlove. "What's missing for you? Why are you trying to help everyone else? What are the actions for social justice and movement building that don't center you as a protagonist?"

For people born into privilege, decentering yourself can feel difficult. It involves giving up a certain amount of privilege, and when you're accustomed to privilege, equality feels like oppression.[3] Being born with privilege, it's easy to become so used to that privilege that we think of it as the natural order of things. Stepping outside of that privilege feels unnatural, but it's a crucial step to challenging systems of inequality.

"What we need is strategies that don't make us look as good, don't make us as visible," says Breedlove. "Most savior types are speaking of themselves as martyrs but are actually doing exactly what they want to do, because a lot of the work that needs to be done is pretty boring." We sometimes expect everyone to feel sorry for us for taking on a lot of leadership, while we are actually avoiding the work we really don't want to do, like the behind-the-scenes work of child care or answering phones that often falls on women and people of color. Instead, we need to ask ourselves the hard question of what it would mean to take chances, to risk losing our privilege for the cause of shared liberation.

This work of undoing the savior mentality is not easy. Its history runs deep.

In AD 1096, Pope Urban II launched the Crusades— three centuries of massacres of Jews, Muslims, and other non-believers that ultimately left up to three million people dead. He masked his call for violence in the language of peace: "Let therefore hatred depart from among you, let your quarrels end, let wars cease, and let all dissensions and controversies slumber. Enter upon the road to the Holy Sepulchre; wrest that land from the wicked race, and subject it to yourselves."[4] That is the savior at its worst, with lies of peace and generosity masking violent self-interest. It is as old as conquest and as enduring as colonialism.

Christopher Columbus brought boats filled with saviors to the Americas, on a mission to "save" whomever he encountered by conversion to Christianity. Like saviors today, he spoke of generosity and freedom. "I knew that they were a people who could be more easily freed and converted to our holy faith by love than by force," he wrote, as he launched history's bloodiest genocide.[5]

The most violent massacres are often portrayed as the efforts of virtuous men to rescue women and children. In 1781 Thomas Jefferson said Native women left to their own societies "are submitted to unjust drudgery. This I believe is the case with every barbarous people. It is civilization alone which replaces women in the enjoyment of their equality."[6] Later ethnic cleansing came in the form of "rescuing" Native Americans by forcing them into "boarding schools" that would violently erase their language, culture, and history. "A great general has said that the only good Indian is a dead one," said Richard Pratt, the founder of the first of these schools. "In a sense, I agree with the sentiment, but only in this: that all the Indian there is in the race should be dead. Kill the Indian in him, and save the man."[7]

Hundreds of years after Columbus, war and colonialism are still depicted as a form of rescue, as necessary to bring freedom. In 1999, embracing what Noam Chomsky later called the "New Military Humanism," the *New York Times* described President Clinton's bombing of Serbia as the actions of an "idealistic New World bent on ending inhumanity."[8] In 2001 George W. Bush continued this connection by making the argument for invading Afghanistan (as later with Iraq), on human rights grounds. He also made his connection to earlier campaigns of violence against the Muslim world clear when he referred to his so-called War on Terror as a "crusade." Channeling Jefferson, Laura Bush called for support for an invasion of Afghanistan by saying, "The fight against terrorism is also a fight for the rights and dignity of women."[9]

Less than two years later, as the administration was pushing to invade Iraq, Vice President Cheney famously bragged, "We will, in fact, be greeted as liberators." Bush described his push toward war as a way to rescue the Iraqi people. "I have a deep desire for peace [and] freedom for the Iraqi people," he said, adding that the United States "never has any intention to conquer anybody." A few months after the invasion, Bush declared triumphantly, "The Iraqi people are now free and are learning the habits of freedom and the responsibilities that come with freedom." The next year, Cheney declared, "Freedom still has enemies in Iraq—terrorists who are targeting the very success and freedom that we're providing to that country."

Nearly the entire world stood against this invasion. But some U.S. liberals, stating concern about the Taliban and other (mostly Muslim) state forces that they saw as repressive to women (and perhaps also seeing the potential for funding and access to the corridors of power), allied themselves with Bush's foreign policy. In 2004, feminist academics Phyllis Chesler and Donna M. Hughes, writing in the *Washington Post*, declared the need to "rethink" feminism and join with U.S. imperialism. "Many feminists are out of touch with the realities of the war that has been declared against the secular, Judeo-Christian, modern West," they wrote. "They are still romanticizing and cheering for Third World anti-colonialist movements, without a realistic view of what will happen to the global status of women if the Islamists win. Many feminists continue to condemn the United States, a country in which, for the most part, their ideas have triumphed."[10]

In addition to throwing their lot in with Bush's wars and equating criticism of Israel with racism, the authors called for an alliance with the religious right against sex work, and they added, "Too often [feminists] have viewed organized religion only as a dangerous form of patriarchy, when it can also be a system of law and ethics that benefits women."

During the Obama administration, Hillary Clinton and Samantha Power embodied the new imperialist feminism. Power was a close advisor to Obama during his 2008 campaign, went on to be appointed to Obama's National Security Council, and in 2013 became U.S. ambassador to the United Nations. She is pro–human rights, feminist, and pro-LGBT while also pro-Israel and pro-imperialist. She is a champion of so-called "humanitarian intervention," from the 1995 NATO bombing of Serbia to the U.S.-led "no-fly" zone in Libya in 2011. Power is even friendly with war criminal Henry Kissinger, who she publicly bonded with over baseball and foreign policy.[11]

Hillary Clinton has long cloaked herself in both feminism and hawkish foreign policy, from her 2003 support of the Bush war on Iraq to her pro-war 2008 and 2016 campaigns for president.

Activist and author Harsha Walia calls this kind of feminism "a handmaiden to cultural imperialism, essentializing communities of color as innately barbaric." Walia is critical of human rights work that uses the label of feminism to mask imperialism. "Women and queers are supposedly devoid of any agency—forced to veil, subjected to honor killings, coerced into arranged marriages. In the post-9/11 context, cultural imperialism is evident in debates about gender and Islam that force a singular feminism—secular, sexually expressive, and liberal autonomist—on women and queers of color."[12]

Saviorism was conceived in a Christian theology that has been a guiding principle in the Americas for at least five hundred years, but to be a savior one need not be religious or American. We in the United States have perfected saviorism in the same way that we made colonialism ours. And while most progressives today would recoil at the actions of colonialists from Columbus to Cheney, there is a clear line from the brutality of America's founding to the soft violence of unchallenged privilege and the many charitable projects that it entails.

Today's saviors are kinder and gentler than the era of the Crusades. They are no longer launching mass genocide and calling it a gift. But they still hold on to that inherited tradition by believing in their own superiority and refusing to listen to those they say they want to serve. This book is about the saviors of today and how our social movements can and must break with this inheritance of violence. The path of Caitlin Breedlove, of listening and learning and engaging in accountable collective action, is one solution. Breedlove is just one of many principled activists creating alternatives to our current poisonous system.

The prototypical savior is a person who has been raised in privilege and taught implicitly or explicitly (or both) that they possess the answers and skills needed to rescue others, no matter the situation. The message that they are the experts in all things has been reinforced since birth. They are taught that saving others is the burden they must bear.

Having privilege means not having to ever notice your own power or the systems that gave you that power. "Growing up in segregated environments (schools, workplaces, neighborhoods, media images and historical perspectives), white interests and perspectives are almost always central," writes antiracist scholar Robin DiAngelo. "An inability to see or consider significance in the perspectives of people of color results."[13]

The savior mentality means that you want to help others but are not open to guidance from those you want to help. Saviors fundamentally believe they are better than the people they are rescuing. Saviors want to support the struggle of communities that are not their own, but they believe they must remain in charge. The savior always wants to lead, never to follow. When the people they have chosen to rescue tell them they are not helping, they think those people are mistaken. It is almost taken as evidence that they need *more* help.

The savior mentality is not about individual failings. It is the logical result of a racist, colonialist, capitalist, hetero-patriarchal system setting us against each other. And being a savior is not a fixed identity. Under the struggle to survive within capitalism, most of us are forced into decisions that contradict our ideals. Many people are involved in liberation movements in their free time while their day job is at a charity or other nonprofit that does not challenge the status quo. We can be a savior one day and an ally the next.

The savior mentality always looks for solutions by working within our current system, because deeper change might push us out of the picture. This focus on quick fixes is also partly a product of an outrage-oriented media. We pay attention to an issue for one day, and we want to hear that someone will be fired or arrested. If that happens, we move on.

Saviors adopt trendy labels such as *social entrepreneur* or *change agent*. They preach the religion of kinder capitalism, the idea that you can get rich while also helping others, that the pursuit of profit, described with buzzwords like *engagement*, *innovation*, and *sharing economy*, will improve everyone's lives through efficiency. However, I stand with nineteenth-century novelist Honoré de Balzac, who wrote that behind every fortune is a concealed crime. I don't believe you can get rich while doing good—wealth and justice are mutually exclusive. The more wealth exists in the world, the less justice.

"There's a term, *social entrepreneurship*, that I see tossed around a lot these days," says poverty lawyer Dean Spade. "That what we just need is the right person to graduate from Harvard, maybe Harvard Business School, and have this vision about how to change poverty, how to end poverty. That kind of imagination, that there's just the smart right-thinking charismatic individual, and that's how change is made, is completely the opposite of everything we know about movements. We know that real expertise and leadership around transforming poverty is going to come from masses of poor people in coordinated movement together solving these problems and creating a new world."[14]

This paucity of imagination has led to a bleaker life for all of us. If all of our "solutions" are just tinkering within the system, how can we truly imagine, let alone build, a better world? It's also disempowering—it teaches that most people will have no role in affecting the problems that afflict them.

For some, the journey to more accountable activism can be difficult. People with privilege often respond with defensiveness when their privilege is pointed out. Robin DiAngelo coined the term *white fragility* to describe white reactions to criticism from people of color, including "the outward display of emotions such as anger, fear, and guilt, and behaviors such as argumentation, silence, and leaving the stress-inducing situation." All of which, she notes, serves to "reinstate white racial equilibrium."[15] White people have a hard time talking about what racism is. When someone is a member of the Klan or says racial slurs, we call that racism. But when we discuss race we often don't discuss systems that maintain inequality and injustice. Scholar and prison abolitionist Ruth Wilson Gilmore defines racism as "the state-sanctioned or extralegal production and

exploitation of group-differentiated vulnerability to premature death."[16] It's not about feelings and words; it's about the
devastation visited upon communities of color by systems like
capitalism and white supremacy.

Novelist and activist Sarah Schulman describes privilege
as seeing your dominance as "simultaneously nonexistent and
as the natural deserving order . . . the self-deceived premise that
one's power is acquired by being deserved and has no machinery
of enforcement."[17] Those who have power hate accountability,
she adds, in favor of "vagueness, lack of delineation of how things
work, the idea that people do not have to keep their promises."[18]

The privilege of the able-bodied leads to people with disabilities being pushed out of our movements and our society.
Saviors often see people with disabilities as fundamentally
less than a full person, of needing help, rather than having
wisdom and experience to learn from. Rather than deserving political power and autonomy, they are supposed to be
grateful for telethons and sympathy. The disability justice
movement is mostly led by people of color, and advocates
for change on an intersectional model, as opposed to the
mostly white-led disability rights movement. ("Intersectionality" refers to a way of looking at interlocking identities and
oppressions and was coined by scholar Kimberlé Crenshaw
in 1989). Disability justice says we all must move forward
together or it's not really justice. It issues a challenge to the
able-bodied. As poet, author, and disability justice activist
Leah Lakshmi Piepzna-Samarasinha has said, "You need to
change the way your life is and the way movements are so we
can actually be part of that radical imagination."[19]

People with privilege are raised to see their own experience as central and objective. We can't imagine a story in which
we are not the protagonist. We can't imagine a different, better
economic system. We can't imagine a world without white, cisgendered, male dominance.

Saviors are not interested in examining their own privilege. We don't want to see that the systems of race and class and
gender that keep us in comfort where we are—in the "right"

jobs and neighborhoods and schools—are the same systems that created the problems we say we want to solve.

Charity is often seen as the wealthy helping the less fortunate. But the roots of modern charity have a sinister undertone, rooted in maintaining inequality. Charitable gifts in the postcolonial Americas came with biological warfare. In 1763 Lord Jeffrey Amherst plotted to give blankets infected with smallpox to Native Americans, writing to a colonel at Fort Pitt, "You will do well to try to inoculate the Indians by means of blankets, as well as to try every other method that can serve to extirpate this execrable race."[20] Of course, most of today's charitable enterprises do not have such murderous intentions. But in many ways they have not come that far from the days of Amherst—generous on the surface, but with deadly consequences.

The Progressive Era in U.S. politics, from the late nineteenth century through the early twentieth century, represented a rise in charitable giving and a more active role for the federal government in blunting the sharpest abuses of capitalism (passing labor reforms like the minimum wage law, for example, and antitrust statutes). But this era, when colonial expansion was publicly defended through the philosophy of manifest destiny, also modeled the condescending kindness we see in the worst kinds of charity today. This was also the era of forced sterilizations and hospitalizations of people with disabilities. In other words, military invasions in the "best interests" of those being invaded abroad and interventions into the lives of poor people at home, also to "help."

Entities like the Charity Organization Societies provided aid to the poor while catering to wealthy sensibilities. The New York branch's *Hand-Book for Friendly Visitors among the Poor* divided the "worthy cases needing relief" from the "shiftless cases needing counsel, stimulus, and work." In words that have been echoed by charitable givers a million times since, the handbook advises, "It is well for the visitor to bear in mind the important distinction between poverty resulting from misfortune and that resulting from ignorance or vice."[21]

Philanthropy is portrayed as generous, but where did that money come from? Have the Rockefeller and Ford charities washed the blood off of their family names, and should we allow them to? The more than $700 billion held by U.S. foundations is twice stolen. It was stolen the first time by making profit from the work of others (employees or even slaves) and from the earth's resources. The money was stolen a second time when the wealthy avoided taxes by funneling their fortunes through foundations, which allow them to dictate how the money will be spent.[22]

As rapper and mogul Jay-Z wrote in his book *Decoded*: "To some degree charity is a racket in a capitalist system, a way of making our obligations to each other optional, and of keeping poor people feeling a sense of indebtedness to the rich, even if the rich spend every other day exploiting those same people."[23]

When charities and other nonprofits seek to "save" poor people, they often end up perpetuating unjust hierarchies. Sixty percent of U.S. nonprofits see their mission as serving people of color. Sixty-three percent say that diversity is a key value of their organization. Yet 93 percent of nonprofit chief executives, 92 percent of their boards, and 82 percent of their staff are white. Thirty percent of nonprofit boards are all-white.[24] These statistics suggest that the people directing and funding these organizations have absorbed the idea that people of color are not the experts in what they need.

Despite mission statements that nobly describe commitment to racial justice, many of these "liberal" or humanitarian organizations are just a couple staffing changes (or less) from having the look of a white supremacist organization. And if you don't think any people of color are qualified to work on your project to help people of color, are you sure you're not a white supremacist? What is your definition of white supremacy if it does not include undervaluing the work, intelligence, and experience of people of color?

In my experience with unpaid and less formalized grassroots activism, it is often those who have the most leisure time—which is generally those with the most privilege—who end up being in leadership positions. Especially when there are no official leaders.[25] And after they "generously" give their time, they are the first to use that experience on their resume, on a research project, or just to brag about to their friends. "The poor have long provided cultural currency to the rich," writes scholar Gabriel Winant. "The social attitudes and political ideology of elites have understood the ghetto as a credibility gold mine."[26]

Charity is often an expression of a belief that current injustices will continue forever. "The oppressors, who oppress, exploit, and rape by virtue of their power, cannot find in this power the strength to liberate either the oppressed or themselves," writes Paulo Friere in *Pedagogy of the Oppressed*. "In order to have the continued opportunity to express their 'generosity,' the oppressors must perpetuate injustice as well." Friere continues, "An unjust social order is the permanent fount of this 'generosity,' which is nourished by death, despair, and poverty. That is why the dispensers of false generosity become desperate at the slightest threat to its source. True generosity consists precisely in fighting to destroy the causes that nourish false charity."[27]

This injustice arises with even with basic acts of generosity, such as serving free food. Author and scholar Janet Poppendieck writes that soup kitchens help a right-wing agenda of shrinking government. "By harnessing a wealth of volunteer effort and donations, [food distribution programs make] private programs appear cheaper and more cost effective than their public counterparts, thus reinforcing an ideology of voluntarism that obscures the fundamental destruction of rights," she writes. "And, because food programs are logistically demanding, their maintenance absorbs the attention and energy of many of the people most concerned about the poor, distracting them from the larger issues of distributional politics. It is not an accident that poverty grows deeper as our charitable responses to it multiply."[28]

Referencing scholar Jennifer Wolch, Ruth Wilson Gilmore calls this nonprofit infrastructure of care the "shadow state."

She notes that each of these organizations operate "without significant political clout, forbidden by law to advocate for systemic change, and bound by public rules and non-profit charters to stick to its mission or get out of business and suffer legal consequences if it strays along the way."[29]

Poppendieck writes that in New York City there were thirty emergency food providers in 1979, and more than fifteen times as many just eight years later. By 1991 that number had climbed to 730, and by 1997 nearly a thousand.[30] During this time, the Reagan, Bush, and Clinton administrations were slashing government benefits for the poor, and the rise of non-profit services like food pantries contributed to "society's failure to grapple in meaningful ways with poverty."

"Massive charitable endeavor serves to relieve pressure for more fundamental solutions," writes Poppendieck. "It works pervasively on the cultural level by serving as sort of a 'moral safety valve'; it reduces the discomfort evoked by visible destitution in our midst by creating the illusion of effective action and offering us myriad ways of participating in it. It creates a culture of charity that normalizes destitution and legitimates personal generosity as a response to major social and economic dislocation."[31]

Of course, when food, housing, and other basic needs become a gift instead of a right, they are subject to all of the prejudices of the generous. The gift can be taken back from those who are not deserving or grateful enough. Those who are too decadent or perverse or lazy or rebellious may not qualify to receive the gift in the first place.

Many organizations that help provide housing to homeless people speak of "housing readiness," in which people must show they are "ready" to have homes. But what about the reverse of that question? Is anyone ready for homelessness? Should any of us have to be? If we recognize housing as a right, that eliminates the question of whether people are "ready" to receive it.

George H. W. Bush launched his "thousand points of light" volunteer program in 1989 to encourage voluntarism like that seen in food pantries. George W. Bush, in 2002, continued that legacy, saying, "My call . . . is for every American to commit at least two years, 4,000 hours over the rest of your lifetime, to the service of your neighbors and your nation." While the president declared the importance of volunteering, his advisor Grover Norquist spoke of shrinking government small enough that he could "drown it in the bathtub."[32] The conservative celebration of volunteers aligns with the policy goal of destruction of the social safety net. The more private citizens volunteer, the less the government has to spend.

As Louisiana environmental justice advocate Monique Harden noted to me, when George W. Bush visited New Orleans after Hurricane Katrina, he came dressed casually, with his sleeves rolled up, and posed for a photo-op helping rebuild a house. While this may have read like a commitment to rebuild the city, it actually sent a very different message: the rebuilding of the devastated Gulf Coast was not a government obligation but an individual burden. The president would chip in as a volunteer and hammer some nails, but the full resources of the U.S. government would not be required. The president showing up at a volunteer site was a public relations tool to put a kind face on this cruel philosophy. "A conservative recovery agenda," said Harden, "means not everyone gets to recover."

It's also worth noting that the most valuable "charity" work is rarely recognized or rewarded. It's the mutual aid that oppressed communities show each other as they help each other survive. This work rarely makes it onto resumes or into the news or in tax deductions, but it is part of most poor people's daily struggle.

A lack of structural analysis on the part of nonprofits didn't just happen; it was the result of deliberate planning by the wealthy and powerful. INCITE! Women of Color Against Violence make this point in their crucial book *The Revolution Will Not Be Funded: Beyond the Non-Profit Industrial Complex*, which thoroughly examines the ways in which movements and charities have their agendas set by the wealthy who fund them, rather than by the poor and working class people they claim to serve.[33] For example, prioritizing the funding of policy and legal reform rather than organizing, to redirect "activist efforts from radical change to social reform," writes author and scholar Andrea Smith in the book's introduction. Even funding leadership development is a tool to keep power hierarchically controlled by elites within oppressed communities and to have influence over those elites.

INCITE's use of the term *non-profit industrial complex* deliberately references *prison industrial complex*, the term for the interconnected web of government and corporate interests that perpetuate mass incarceration, surveillance, and state violence. "While the PIC [prison industrial complex] overtly represses dissent the NPIC [non-profit industrial complex] manages and controls dissent by incorporating it into the state apparatus," writes Smith. "Essentially, foundations provide a cover for white supremacy. . . . People of color deserve individual relief but people of color organized to end white supremacy become a menace to society."[34]

This nonprofit industrial complex pushes competition within our movements. If there is an organization based in the community we want to work in, doing the work we want to do, we are not taught to find ways to support them. Instead we are taught to see that organization as an obstacle.

"The idea that these same elite institutions that are invested in maintaining capitalism are going to be the ones that produce the knowledge that solves poverty is very much what philanthropy invests in," says Dean Spade, the founder of Sylvia Rivera Law Project. "That's who runs philanthropy, that's who gives to philanthropy, and that's who is employed, as program officers, often as foundation heads."[35] Often these foundations directly employ family members of the wealthy person who started it, paying more in salaries than they give away—another way that the wealth is kept in the same circles.

From their positions of wealth and power, the foundations attach conditions to their generosity, often dictating what social movements will look like and what goals they will pursue. Radical redistribution of wealth, for example, might be seen as "unrealistic" and therefore not worthy of funding. Instead these wealthy benefactors might encourage the recipients of their largesse not to seek a change in tax law that would eliminate the exception enjoyed by foundations. This happened in 2009, when President Obama proposed lowering the cap on tax deductions for charitable contributions from 50 percent of income to 28 percent, the level it was at during the Reagan administration. Foundations and nonprofits formed a united front to fight the proposal.[36]

Spade notes that U.S. nonprofits have corrupted movements by demanding non-systemic changes and upholding a status quo. "Through the rise of the nonprofit form, certain logics that support criminalization, militarization and wealth disparity have penetrated and transformed spaces that were once locations of fomenting resistance to state violence," he says. "Increasingly, neoliberalism means that social issues taken up by nonprofits are separated from a broader commitment to social justice; nonprofits take part in producing and maintaining a racialized-gendered maldistribution of life chances while pursuing their 'good work.'"[37]

Spade sees this shift in many post-1970s movements. "The analytical frameworks of the social movements of the 1960s and 1970s, which focused on broad, population-level disparities, [were] replaced by individual discrimination-based understandings of racism, homophobia, ableism, and sexism, both in law and popular culture," he writes. "The result, thus far, has been legal reforms that mostly maintain—and often bolster—systems of maldistribution and control in the name of equality, individuality, and even diversity."[38] The kind of reform led by those who have privilege does not offer real change. It uses buzzwords like *diversity* and may address individual complaints, but leaves the cause of the problems untouched, even unmentioned.

Aside from foundation funding, how do movements lose a focus on systemic change? The post-1970s period saw a dropoff in radicalism among nonprofit workers and union members during a period in which communist and socialist groups saw a drop in membership—both from disillusionment among their members and from massive state repression that imprisoned movement leaders. While these revolutionary organizations also had internal conflicts or contradictions, they did help keep an anticapitalist analysis front and center. At the same time that this foregrounding of alternatives to capitalism disappeared, neoliberal economics pushed hours higher and wages lower, while stranding more young people in debt and leaving people with less free time for activism and more fear caused by precarious economic conditions.

The savior's behavior is raced and gendered and classed. Hollywood teaches us to cheer for the lone hero riding in to save the day. People with race and gender privilege are taught by white supremacy and patriarchy that they have a certain authority to impart to the world. As Sarah Hagi has written, "Lord, give me the confidence of a mediocre white man."[39]

The social myth of the savior leads to reflexive praise of police, soldiers, and prosecutors. We use "fighting crime" as a synonym for doing good and "getting help" as a synonym for calling the police. Neighborhoods are called "good" when they lose their diversity and "safe" when the original inhabitants feel unsafe.[40] Systemic abuses are ignored or characterized as aberrations within a system intended for good. Those who abuse from positions of power are viewed bad apples. When police kill another young Black man, we say that the criminal justice system isn't working instead of noting that it is working just the way it was constructed. The lack of popular outlets for systemic solutions also affects many people without privilege. It can push working-class people to join the army or become police out of a genuine desire to help people, making them further invested in systems of violence and control.

From a young age, children are told that change comes from saviors, not mass movements. Students are mostly taught the "great man" theory of history—a simplistic nineteenth-century idea popularized by Thomas Carlyle, who wrote in 1840 that "the history of the world is but the biography of great men."[41] In this view, President Lincoln ended slavery, while the revolts led by enslaved people are rarely mentioned. Benevolent capitalists, rather than struggles of organized labor, are responsible for the gains of working people. The civil rights movement won victories due to the efforts of Martin Luther King Jr. (or perhaps by some combination of Presidents Kennedy and Johnson), not because of the millions of unnamed Black people who struggled and died for liberation.

Students are certainly not taught that slavery did not end—that the Thirteenth Amendment allowed slavery to continue if one was convicted of a crime—or that the central accomplishments of the civil rights movement have been slowly chipped away, as rights to vote and equal education are "reformed" away by voter ID laws and underfunded school districts.[42]

Karl Marx critiqued this view of history back in 1846. "Civil society is the true source and theatre of all history," he wrote, "and how absurd is the conception of history held hitherto, which neglects the real relationships and confines itself to high-sounding dramas of princes and states."[43] Or, as Howard Zinn wrote, the "power of the people on top depends on the obedience of the people below. When people stop obeying, they have no power."[44]

It's by design that this myth of great men shaping history is taught in our schools. Similarly it was no aberration when Arizona conservatives passed a law banning books that "bred ethnic resentment," including many written by Latino authors. Conservative politicians were decades ahead of progressives in grasping the importance of winning school board elections and controlling curricula. As George Orwell wrote in *1984*, "Who controls the past controls the future." The United States was born through genocide and built by slavery. But we are collectively unwilling to teach future generations about the crimes through which our nation was born. Germans have paid nearly one hundred billion dollars to Jewish people in reparations.[45] In the United States, discussions about reparations for slavery or for the genocide against Native Americans remain off limits for most politicians and even the most liberal of commentators. German schools teach about the Holocaust perpetrated by their forebears. But a 1957 history textbook used in Virginia described slavery this way: "Life among the Negroes of Virginia in slavery times was generally happy. The Negroes went about in a cheerful manner making a living for themselves and for those for whom they worked. They were not so unhappy as some Northerners thought they were."[46] This whitewashing has hardly gone away—in fact, it's making a comeback. As recently as 2015, Texas textbooks referred to enslaved Africans as "workers" to avoid describing the ugly reality of the slave trade.[47]

There are very few museums that confront the history of slavery and the legalized discrimination of the Jim Crow era in this country. "The endnote in most . . . museums is that civil rights triumphs and America is wonderful," notes historian Paul Finkelman. "We are a nation that has always readily embraced the good of the past and discarded the bad. This does not always lead to the most productive of dialogues on matters that deserve and require them."[48]

American history is much more eager to learn lessons from the crimes of others. Across the United States there are European Holocaust museums and memorials but scarcely a mention of the genocide of Africans and Native Americans, a brutality that continues today in reservations and in cities like Ferguson, Missouri. Or in the words of rapper Chuck D from Public Enemy, "The cost of the Holocaust / I'm talking about the one still going on."[49]

"If the Germans built a museum dedicated to American slavery before one about their own Holocaust, you'd think they were trying to hide something," notes historian Eric Foner. "As Americans, we haven't yet figured out how to come to terms with slavery. To some, it's ancient history. To others, it's history that isn't quite history."[50]

While ignoring the crimes that built this nation, we celebrate the heroic individualist capitalist in our media and schools. Even those of us who have a radical critique of capi-talism often find it hard to transcend the ethos of individuality that comes with being raised in this country.

People in movements today, even when they talk about financial divides, rarely examine how those divides manifest interpersonally. We might share statistics about inequality, but how often does that discussion include information about our-selves? It is seen as impolite to talk about our own money. As a result, both the very rich and very poor in the United States call themselves middle class. Kids brought up in the wealthi-est homes are often taught to hide their class advantage, and especially if they enter social movements they must hide their privilege. Activists may protest a bank, not realizing that their friend's father is the bank president.

Researchers and other scholars say they seek to help by bringing their skills to the study of an "underprivileged" community. But in almost every situation the community has no say in the research goals or process and never even sees the final product.

Writing about research on sex work, a masters candidate and former sex worker named Sarah M. wrote advice that should serve for anyone considering this kind of research. "If I can't provide a direct, material benefit to the subjects of my investigation—if the money or the time or the will just isn't there (and it often isn't)—if my research is going to be all take and no give—I don't do it. Period. I think, 'Oh hey, it'd be nice to know <blah>,' and then *I find something else to study*."

"'Nothing about us without us' means that sex workers are *so over* research that uses our knowledge without paying us back," she adds. "That investigates their lives without asking them what needs to be found out, or that talks about them behind their backs, protected from critique by an academic publisher's paywall."[51]

That phrase "nothing about us without us," which came into use during the global disability rights movement of the 1980s, is a great guiding principle for movements. In examples I explore later in this book, FBI informant Brandon Darby rose to the leadership of an organization with thousands of volunteers despite having no relevant experience and no base in the community he was supposedly helping. Through the KONY 2012 campaign, a group of young white men from San Diego were suddenly hailed as experts on Africa.

In most cases, failure never even slows saviors down. They are experts in "failing up." Though they may leave wreckage in their wake, they win praise and jobs as analysts and advisors. No one in power seems to notice or care what they left behind. In the social circles of entrepreneurs, failing means that you take risks, and failure is worn as a mark of pride. But one of the marks of having less privilege is that failure means something different. When poor people or people of color fail, they are confirming expectations.

Social change often comes from the young, and every cause wants to capture the attention of the idealistic next generation. As I discus later in this book, student groups dedicated to fighting "sex trafficking" have spread to campuses across the country, and Teach for America recruits at all the top colleges and universities.

Projects like fighting trafficking and teaching kids seem unambiguously good at first glance. But as I discuss later, charitable efforts that proceed without a demand for systemic change strengthen the system by providing an apolitical means of addressing the symptoms while ignoring the underlying issue. These "consensus" efforts are often the first introduction to activism for idealistic young people. Then, when these future activists discover that these projects are shams or at best misdirected, they may give up on the possibility of change altogether. When I speak with people who are not involved in social justice work at all, I find that their inaction comes not from thinking that nothing is wrong. Instead it often results from not seeing a systemic solution offered or from feeling alienated by the organizations that represent themselves as change makers.

An alternate solution to social problems lies in the words of the Zapatistas, who popularized the slogan *Preguntando caminamos*, or "Walking, we ask questions." In other words, don't be so afraid to take action that you are immobilized. But, as you take action, listen to the voices of those most affected, and be ready to change course based on their feedback. As author and activist John Holloway has said, "To think of moving forward through questions rather than answers means a different sort of politics, a different sort of organization."[52]

Today a new generation of activists, from the Arab Spring and Occupy to the Movement for Black Lives, is rejecting charity and saviorism, challenging traditional forms of activism, and building a movement led by and accountable to those communities most affected by injustice. This book praises and documents some of the work of this generation of activists.

There are missteps and mistakes in these new movements too, as people learn by taking action. I think I make fewer mistakes now, or at least different ones, but I hold past mistakes close to my heart, as a reminder to keep asking questions. As Ngọc Loan Trân wrote on the *Black Girl Dangerous* blog, "We have to remind ourselves that we once didn't know."[53] Just calling this behavior out and moving on makes little difference. I think it is the responsibility of those of us who come from privilege, and therefore are susceptible to saviorism, to engage in the hard work of building accountability to others and ourselves. This book maps a path from the savior mentality to shared liberation.

Chapter Two
We Are the World, We Are the Children

In 2015 I visited Dinétah, the homeland of the Diné (Navajo) people, spread across parts of what is also known as New Mexico, Colorado, Utah, and Arizona. In the last forty years an estimated ten thousand to twenty thousand Diné have been forcibly relocated off of that land by the federal government, working in collaboration with coal mining corporations. This is, of course, on top of centuries of genocide and displacement.

I met with Diné youth and elders who are fighting to maintain their land, homes, and culture, while the U.S. government is still trying to push them out. "They try to take every little thing that they can," explains Selest Manning of Indigenous Youth for Cultural Survival, one of the organizations in the Diné community. "Basically just to get rid of us. If we don't have our necessary things to survive, we won't."

Manning is still in her early twenties but already committed to the struggle. For her, resistance can be as basic as learning their language or helping elders stay on their land. She and a few other young activists organized a gathering in late 2015 for elders to pass along cultural knowledge to the next generation. "It's not even about us anymore," Manning told me. "It's about the next seven generations now, and that's why we're here."

In Dinétah, I also spoke with Berkley Carnine, a cisgender white woman activist who works in solidarity with the Diné community. Carnine's views on social change were shaped in 2008, at age twenty-six, by her experience with the Anne Braden Program of the Catalyst Project, an antiracist training organization in the Bay Area. The Anne Braden Program is a four-month-long organizer development program for radical white activists. As part of her training, Carnine was placed with Generation Five, an organization whose mission is to end childhood sexual abuse in five generations. In response to many nonprofits that see their work as continuing forever, Generation Five want to be successful enough that they no longer need to exist. "They have incredible analysis of trauma, how and why that gets perpetuated, and the modes of individual and collective healing that are necessary to shift that," Carnine told me. "They also had a pretty core analysis of colonialism and the sexual violence that has been deeply rooted in colonialism."

Connecting personal and systemic violence sparked new understanding in Carnine. "I was understanding things that have been harmful for me and seeing how and why I couldn't feel okay in the world, because I was benefiting from the bodily harm and violence that was being done on such a broad and massive scale against people of color." She started asking, "What is the trauma I carry from violence against me, but also what [are] trauma and patterns of abuse that I carry because of the violence that was done *for* me?"

After the training ended, she moved to Arizona and was inspired by the indigenous resistance happening in an area known as Black Mesa. Carnine joined Black Mesa Indigenous Support (BMIS), a group of mostly non-indigenous activists "working in solidarity with Native people upholding their responsibility in protecting land." Since 2012 she has lived in nearby Flagstaff. She helps to train and coordinate the efforts of non-indigenous solidarity activists who wish to stand with the Diné resistance.

Carnine sees her work as part of an overall decolonization process, resisting the structures of settler colonialism our society is based in. She says that sometimes people from our settler culture interpret decolonization as meaning "making spaces more inclusive of Indigenous people," which she says reproduces the assumption "that settlers are the rightful inheritors of the space to begin with." Carnine says that true decolonization requires something more radical than being inclusive.

"Decolonizing the mind is about unlearning colonial mentalities and modes of relating based in western logic, exploitation, domination, entitlement, and individualism, based in disconnection from each other and the land," Carnine says. "Also, this means doing the work of learning our various histories and understanding how our ancestors were first colonized to become colonizers." This analysis of the importance of challenging your own privilege before you can stand with others is key for anyone doing international solidarity.

Colonialism has historically been enforced by military violence, but today's conquests are often masked as charity. And international aid has become the first line of engagement. We engage with the world as saviors and leave devastation behind. In most cases we do not seek to listen and follow, like Carnine, but instead to lead and dominate.

In 1843 President Andrew Jackson famously called U.S. territorial expansion "extending the area of freedom," an ideology also known as Manifest Destiny (as in a destiny of white people to dominate the rest of the world). A half-century later, *Jungle Book* author Rudyard Kipling would make this racist call even more explicit with his poem "White Man's Burden":

Take up the White Man's burden—
Send forth the best ye breed—
Go send your sons to exile
To serve your captives' need
To wait in heavy harness
On fluttered folk and wild—
Your new-caught, sullen peoples,
Half devil and half child

Since Jackson's day, U.S. foreign policy has changed in tone but not mission. We still define ourselves as rulers of the world. We're just more polite about it. U.S. international aid is contingent on accepting our country's moral instruction and political guidance. Our cultural assumption is that our wealth and power imbue us with moral authority. Our government provides development aid and loans through the United States Agency for International Development (USAID), the International Monetary Fund, and the World Bank, but that aid comes with demands for neoliberal restructuring. We donate to rebuild after disasters, but U.S. disaster relief comes with instructions to buy U.S. products. We engage with the world as helpers but only on our own terms, in ways that benefit us.

Our government gives money to fight AIDS around the world, but it has traditionally been given with restrictions against preventative measures like needle exchange programs or efforts on behalf of sex workers. In 2003 the Bush administration passed the President's Emergency Plan for AIDS Relief (PEPFAR), which required organizations receiving funding to sign the Anti-Prostitution Loyalty Oath (APLO). All organizations receiving PEPFAR funding had to explicitly oppose prostitution in their policies. This meant they could not even give a condom to a sex worker, much less support sex worker–led movements.

"From Sachs to Kristof to Invisible Children to TED, the fastest growth industry in the U.S. is the White Savior Industrial Complex," wrote Teju Cole in a series of tweets later reprinted in the *Atlantic*. Cole was criticizing a general trend but also specifically targeting neoliberal economist Jeffrey Sachs, *New York Times* columnist Nicholas Kristof, and a charity called Invisible Children, best known for their *KONY 2012* video. Cole went on:

- The white savior supports brutal policies in the morning, founds charities in the afternoon, and receives awards in the evening.

- The banality of evil transmutes into the banality of sentimentality. The world is nothing but a problem to be solved by enthusiasm.

- The White Savior Industrial Complex is not about justice. It is about having a big emotional experience that validates privilege.

- Feverish worry over that awful African warlord. But close to 1.5 million Iraqis died from an American war of choice. Worry about that.

- I deeply respect American sentimentality; the way one respects a wounded hippo. You must keep an eye on it, for you know it is deadly.[1]

Cole notes that the savior individual is often from the United States but focused on the world, particularly Africa. The savior sees dark skin and translates that to helplessness. And saviors see their own white skin as validation of the gifts they bring.

Author Binyavanga Wainaina, in a satirical essay titled "How to Write about Africa," identified the patterns he has seen in non-Africans writing about Africa. His words are a stinging reminder of the ways in which colonial attitudes persist. Although his essay is directed at writers, it applies well to the many Westerners who have enriched their resumes and assuaged their consciences with charity work in communities that are not their own—from remote African villages to U.S. inner cities. Via social media these young white people spice up their vacations, posting photos of themselves with the darker-skinned children they have helped as evidence of their goodwill. "Establish early on that your liberalism is impeccable," writes Wainaina, "and mention near the beginning how much you love Africa, how you fell in love with the place and can't live without her. Africa is the only continent you can love—take advantage of this. If you are a man, thrust yourself into her warm virgin forests. If you are a woman, treat

Africa as a man who wears a bush jacket and disappears off
into the sunset. Africa is to be pitied, worshipped or dominat-
ed. Whichever angle you take, be sure to leave the strong im-
pression that without your intervention and your important
book, Africa is doomed."[2]

At elite schools, students are recruited for the Peace
Corps, which sends them after graduation to countries they
know little about, to do unpaid work that takes jobs away from
locals or that helps maintain corrupt or authoritarian governments.[3] Sometimes this work even entails feeding information
back to U.S. intelligence services.[4] Outside the elites, young
people are recruited by the military, often with similar claims
of helping others in faraway lands.

Many of the most offensive charitable campaigns involve
white people "saving" Africa, but they never mention the history of colonial exploitation that led to poverty in Africa in the
first place. The classic of the entertainment industry's "savior
pop" genre is the 1984 Bob Geldof song, sung by a forgettable
assemblage of eighties pop stars, "Do They Know It's Christ-
mas," which also includes the tellingly offensive line "Thank
God it's them instead of you."

The song (and Live Aid, the subsequent project it birthed)
raised over $100 million for famine relief. But when journal-
ists dug deeper, they noted that the issues leading to the famine
could not be solved through charity. Massive numbers of people in Ethiopia were dying. However, the primary cause was
not a lack of food or bad weather leading to reduced crops.
People were starving because of the political decisions of Ethi-
opian dictator Mengistu Haile Mariam.

As one reporter noted at the time, "Ethiopia, which has
the largest standing army in Africa, is embroiled in four internal wars . . . government troops have systematically scorched
the farmlands, destroying crops and killing oxen." Ethiopia was
yet another proxy war in the global Cold War, with Russian
and U.S. interests both engaged. Any aid organization working
within the country had to work within this dynamic, often ac-
tively supporting government resettlement programs. "People

are dying in Ethiopia because of starvation. But throwing money and food at the problem without consideration of the politics that is keeping people and food apart is inexcusable," concluded the report.[5]

The Save Darfur Coalition was founded in 2004 to raise awareness of human rights abuses in the Darfur region of western Sudan and recruited heavily on college campuses. The actions or crimes of the Sudanese government are almost beside the point. As Columbia University professor and author Mahmood Mamdani points out, the focus on Darfur was used to obscure crimes committed by the United States, Israel, and U.S.-supported dictators in the region, even though these were the crimes citizens were paying for from their tax dollars. Unlike Bush administration atrocities, liberals could condemn Sudan without endangering the overall project of empire. In a debate at Columbia University, Mamdani was harshly critical of this project. "The facts that this movement gives out are completely decontextualized," he says. "Go to a Save Darfur website. What you will find on this website is a documentation of atrocities. No history, no politics, nothing [that] tells you why there is violence. All you see is evidence of killing, raping, ethnic cleansing. I call it a pornography of violence."

"It is meant for the good of the one who views it, not for the good of the one who is being viewed," said Mamdani. "The focus is on naming and shaming. On punishment, on criminal justice. The demand is not reform, the demand is punishment, as if they are lusting for blood. It is, I believe, seamlessly a part of the War on Terror."[6]

These campaigns disseminate a simplistic worldview that disassociates the causes from realities on the ground. Save Darfur tells us to look at this video, sign this petition, and your duty to the world is done. To Mamdani it is the opposite of intellectual engagement. "The peace movement of the 60s turned the world into a classroom; its signature activity was the teach-in," says Mamdani. "Save Darfur has turned the world into an advertising medium."

It relates to its constituency not as an educator, but as an advertiser. It has not created or even tried to create an informed movement but a feel good constituency. Its focus, you can see, is increasingly shifting from college students to high school kids. These are Save Darfur's version of child soldiers. Its leaders are less educators, they are more celebrities from high-profile activities: showbiz and sports. They openly disdain education and debate.[7]

Mamdani says that Save Darfur represents the difference between feel-good charity and true civic engagement. It is a way to "help" others, without addressing your own problems. "Why were my students and my son's classmates . . . being mobilized around Darfur and not around Iraq?" asks Mamdani.

And I realized that Iraq calls on Americans to respond as citizens. A student who thinks of Iraq realizes either he feels or she feels guilty, or he or she feel impotent, that there are limits to American power. When it comes to Darfur, these same students . . . do not relate to Darfuris as citizens but as victims. . . . I realized that Darfur is a charity, Iraq is a tax. In Darfur these same students can feel what they know they are not in Iraq: powerful saviors. In Darfur, the assumption is as throughout the world . . . that if they don't make it right we must go and make it right. The assumption is that the problem is internal, the solution is external. The U.S. has to learn to live in the world, not to occupy it.[8]

At the time, Darfur was often used as a rhetorical weapon against the growing pro-Palestine student movement. "Why are you focusing on Israel?" went the refrain. "Why not focus on the Muslims committing genocide against Africans?" And while real solutions to war and displacement are complicated and involve challenging systemic issues like the legacy of colonialism, Save Darfur offered a comforting, simplistic solution that did not involve challenging the privilege of U.S. citizens. Not coincidentally, the coalition was sponsored by pro-Israeli organizations (the United States Holocaust Memorial Museum and American Jewish World Service) at a time of increasing criticism of the Bush administration's role in the Middle East and the Israeli occupation of Palestine. The campaign provided a Muslim villain for easy condemnation—perfect for an audience that might be uncomfortable with the style of the Bush administration's demonization of Islam but still accepting a basic distrust of Muslims.

In 2009 the *Christian Science Monitor* reported that "activist campaigns mischaracterized and sensationalized" casualty rates in Darfur. "What they tended to leave out was that the majority of the casualties occurred as a result of disease and malnutrition" rather than more directly from war. As a result of activist efforts like Save Darfur, hundreds of millions of dollars of U.S. funding shifted from humanitarian aid (which would have been more useful for combating disease and malnutrition) to military "peacekeeping." The newspaper concluded, "Had the Darfur activists not advocated for a reallocation of funds, more lives would probably have been saved."[9]

Many from inside humanitarian institutions argue that even in the best cases their intervention is flawed. "The scenes of suffering that we tend to call humanitarian crises are almost always symptoms of political circumstances, and there's no apolitical way of responding to them—no way to act without having a political effect," writes journalist and author Philip Gourevitch. "Humanitarianism relieves the warring parties of many of the burdens (administrative and financial) of waging war, diminishing the demands of governing while fighting, cutting the cost of sustaining casualties, and supplying the food, medicine, and logistical support that keep armies going. At its worst—as the Red Cross demonstrated during the Second World War, when the organization offered its services at Nazi death camps, while maintaining absolute confidentiality about the atrocities it was privy to—impartiality in the face of atrocity can be indistinguishable from complicity.[10]

In 2003, the year before Save Darfur was founded, three young white Christian missionaries in their early twenties traveled from San Diego to Uganda in search of a documentary project. They were part of a Christian movement called the Emerging Church. Jason Russell, one of the founders, had first traveled to Africa in 2001, as a missionary in Kenya. After this trip his mission became to embody the gospel by "ending genocide."

What the missionaries found inspired them to not only make a film but also start a charity that would distribute it, mostly to church groups. In 2006 they founded Invisible Children, a nonprofit aimed at raising awareness of war crimes in Uganda, through distributing their film of the same name.

After years of distributing *Invisible Children*, on March 5, 2012, they released a new video, *KONY 2012*. Across the United States thousands of people, many of them youth affiliated with church groups, tweeted the link to the video. Within five days the video had over one hundred million views. That hundred million would be a decent number for a new music video by Beyoncé or the Super Bowl or the Academy Awards, but for a half-hour slickly produced but ponderously paced and simplistic infomercial, it was a phenomenon, the most viral video ever at the time.

The goal was vague but simple: make Ugandan militia leader Joseph Kony famous, and then some nation's military (that of the United States or perhaps an African nation) would respond to the publicity and make his capture a priority, and his reign of terror would come to an end.

In terms of digital outreach, it was a phenomenal success. But as Joshua Keating wrote at the time in *Foreign Policy*, in words that apply to most activist projects launched by saviors, "What are the consequences of unleashing so many exuberant activists armed with so few facts?"[11]

Criticism of the video came hard and fast, much of it from Ugandans and other Africans. "This is another video where I see an outsider trying to be a hero rescuing African children," wrote Ugandan blogger Rosebell Kagumire. "We have seen these stories a lot in Ethiopia, celebrities coming in Somalia, you know, it does not end the problem." She went on:

> How do you tell the story of Africans? It's much more important what the story is, actually, because if you are showing me as voiceless, as hopeless . . . you shouldn't be telling my story if you don't believe that I also have the power to change what is going on. And this video seems to say that the power lies in America, and it does not lie with my government, it does not lie with local initiatives on the ground, that aspect is lacking. . . . It is furthering that narrative about Africans: totally unable to help themselves and needing outside help all the time.[12]

Ironically these saviors had declared war on a man who is the end product of previous generations of white saviors' interventions in Africa. It was the white missionaries who brought the Christianity to Africa that Joseph Kony credited with inspiring him. He even named one of his children George Bush.

While Invisible Children never led to the capture of Kony, it added support to further U.S. military engagement in Africa—the kind of collateral damage saviors often bring. They organized thousands of young people to lobby Congress for more U.S. military engagement—seventeen hundred visited congressional offices in one day, and the next day a bill calling for more U.S. "involvement" in the region had over one hundred sponsors.[13]

Obama appointee Samantha Power's first public address after she became U.S. ambassador to the United Nations was to the Fourth Estate Leadership Summit, an event organized by Invisible Children. Writer Vijay Prashad described Power's military interventionist foreign policy as "KONY-ism," adding that "Power praised the group for its 'new kind of activism' whose 'army of civilian activists' had pushed the Obama administration to tougher action against Joseph Kony, the head of the Lord's Resistance Army (LRA), and whose example had helped Kenyans and Russians and most of all Arabs, who 'barely knew democracy as recently as three years ago,' to use the Internet to hold governments accountable."[14]

Under the strain of international attention, Invisible Children burned out in spectacular fashion. Ten days after KONY 2012 launched, cofounder Jason Russell had a public mental breakdown, ranting naked on the street corner outside his San Diego home, yelling at cars. "My mind couldn't stop thinking about the future," he said later. "I literally thought I was responsible for the future of humanity."[15]

In 2014 the organization began the process of shutting down. "Even though we're announcing this before the capture of Joseph Kony," said CEO Ben Keesey, "the Invisible Children story is one of gigantic progress and huge impact in people's lives."[16]

Their defenders say that Invisible Children and Save Darfur led to more engagement with the problems of the world. But these campaigns do not lend themselves to long-term engagement precisely because, by their nature, they are all about the quick fix. The campaigns encourage emotional reactions instead of critical thinking, and band-aids instead of lasting solutions to systemic problems. They also reinforce old stereotypes about western superiority and about Africa's need for external salvation, by calling for white rescuers.

Western colonial engagement with Africa, even with the best of intentions, rarely ends well. Western Christians in Uganda, perhaps inspired by Invisible Children, have also successfully lobbied for some of the world's most homophobic laws, such as the Uganda Anti-Homosexuality Act of 2014, which called for the death penalty for gays and lesbians.

This is not an issue unique to Invisible Children—you can see it in the fund-raising and membership campaigns of most nonprofits. You are asked to donate and perhaps to sign something but nothing more. However noble and uncomplicated it may seem to offer help to those in need, the kind of help, and how it is delivered, matters. As Harvard law professor David Kennedy has said, "Humanitarianism tempts us to hubris, to an idolatry about our intentions and routines, to the conviction that we know more than we do about what justice can be."[17]

How many people who joined Save Darfur or Invisible Children were left with the idea that all they needed to do was sign a petition or forward a video? How many were later left with the idea that change is impossible, noting that despite the mass involvement, atrocities are still committed in Darfur, and Joseph Kony is still free?

The "white people know best" activism of KONY 2012 can also be seen in the voluntourism industry, a range of businesses that have sprung up to help make the privileged feel useful by rebranding vacations as generosity. "On the Indonesian island of Bali, for example, a burgeoning orphanage industry exists to cater to voluntourists who want to help children," writes Rafia Zakaria.

> Children leave home and move to an orphanage because tourists, who visit the island a couple of times a year, are willing to pay for their education.
>
> These children essentially work as orphans because their parents cannot afford to send them to school. Instead of helping parents cater to the needs of their children, the tourist demand for orphans to sponsor creates an industry that works to make children available for foreigners who wish to help. When the external help dries up, these pretend orphans are forced to beg on the streets for food and money in order to attract orphan tourism.[18]

The staff of voluntourism companies are either cynically aware of these issues from the beginning, or they soon become aware. "To be honest, I have never really felt like I truly helped anyone," writes Alexia Nestora, a former employee of the voluntourism company I-to-I, who blogs as Voluntourism Gal.[19] In almost every case, it would be better to stay at home and send money instead.

The individualist responses of voluntourists or Invisible Children make for easy targets. However, the same issues come up in the larger, more professional organizations like the Red Cross. The relief industry is filled with people, however well meaning, who are seeking easy solutions to systemic problems.

As Tracy Kidder wrote after the 2010 earthquake devastated Haiti, "At least 10,000 private organizations perform supposedly humanitarian missions in Haiti, yet it remains one of the world's poorest countries."[20] And in the midst of this poverty, the aid workers always seem to live in the most comfort. One could be forgiven for coming to the conclusion that the more aid groups are active in a country, the worse things become. At the very least, they do not seem to work with the aim of realizing a world in which they are no longer necessary.

Haiti today is the perfect illustration of the twin legacies of colonialism and neoliberalism. The *Nation* magazine described it as "the NGO Republic of Haiti," a country where nongovernmental organizations have far more wealth and power than the government.

Ever since the Haitian people freed themselves from slavery and French rule in 1791–1804, they have faced economic exploitation from colonial powers. In 1825 French King Charles X demanded that Haiti pay an "independence debt" equal to ten times the country's GDP, a debt they spent over one hundred years repaying. This was followed by U.S. support for brutal dictatorships in the twentieth century, International Monetary Fund and World Bank loans that demanded neoliberal restructuring of the economy, and "gifts" from funds like the Clinton Foundation, which encouraged more sweatshops.

Hillary Clinton's State Department worked hard to overturn a 2009 law passed by the Haitian Parliament that raised the minimum wage to sixty-two cents per hour. According to State Department documents released by Wikileaks, Clinton's State Department worked with USAID and private corporations like Levis and Hanes to cut that wage in half for garment workers.[21] Both Bill Clinton (representing the Clinton

Foundation) and Hillary Clinton (still at the State Department) later pushed for an industrial park in which most workers took home less than two dollars a day.[22]

The 2010 Haiti earthquake could have been an opportunity for wealthy nations to right historical wrongs. Instead it was a chance for further profit and exploitation by business and aid groups. "Between 2005 and 2009, aid in Haiti ranged from approximately 113 to 130 percent of the total revenue available to the government," wrote Kathie Klarreich and Linda Polman. "After the earthquake, the flow of relief and recovery aid significantly exceeded—by more than a factor of four—the government's internal revenue."

"Our priorities are not the same as theirs, but theirs are executed. In theory, NGOs come with something, but not with what the population needs," Joseph Philippe, a Haitian government worker told the *Nation*. "We have no choice but to accept what they bring us. But then, when it doesn't work and it's not what we need, the state is blamed, not the NGOs."[23]

The representative of one of the largest UN organizations in Haiti was asked by *Nation* reporters whether the local government of Haiti has ever told them what to spend donor money on. He replied anonymously, "Never. They are not in the position, because they are financially dependent. Recently, there was a government press conference. There was nothing 'government' about it; we organized it and told them what to say."[24]

In a scathing June 2015 report, *Propublica* wrote that the Red Cross had raised half a billion dollars for Haiti relief, and all that the money had produced was six houses. Progress by the Red Cross was held back by a reliance on U.S. employees who not only did not have the expertise to do more, they could not even speak the language. "Going to meetings with the community when you don't speak the language is not productive," complained one Haitian development professional.[25] But people from the United States always see themselves as experts with something to bring, even if they cannot communicate with the people they are claiming to help.

Somali poet Ali Dhux beautifully described the way aid recipients view aid workers:

> A man tries hard to help you find your lost camels.
> He works more tirelessly than even you,
> But in truth he does not want you to find them, ever.[26]

In other words, when your job is international aid, you have an interest in your job continuing forever and a disincentive to pursue systemic solutions. The United Nations, USAID, Red Cross, and Invisible Children are very different organizations, and the people working there come from a wide range of backgrounds but share (let's assume) altruistic motivations. This is not about any one organization or any one incident or any individual doing that work. Any aid that is not accountable to the community it seeks to serve, and does not address the fundamental systemic issues behind the problems it claims to address, will only reinforce an unjust system.

Another popular innovation from philanthropist-saviors is the microloan. This capitalist innovation was supposed to make money available for poor communities, erase gender disparities, and encourage small local businesses to thrive. Bangladeshi banker Muhammad Yunus won a Nobel Peace Prize in 2006 for inventing the modern microloan.

But studies show that these loans are not as effective in the streets as they are in the minds of people in corporate boardrooms and university economics departments.[27] Instead of heralding a novel way of addressing systemic poverty, microloans are an innovation that give the rich a new way to exploit the very poor, ensnaring communities in a debt economy where none existed before, making more of the world subject to the dictates and violence of finance capital, and making the life of the very poor even more hopeless. In just a few months in 2012, in the Indian state of Andhra Pradesh, more than two hundred victims of a microloan scheme committed suicide. An Associated Press report on the deaths reported, "Originally developed as a nonprofit effort to lift society's most downtrodden, microfinance has increasingly become a for-profit enterprise that serves investors as well as the poor."[28]

So what is the answer? If it's not troops on the ground or humanitarian aid or loans, how can we help people in need? The answer is to support organizations based in the affected area that are accountable to the people they serve. This takes more time than giving to Red Cross or counting on USAID to step in, but it is more likely to achieve results. If we are not challenging our colonial relationships to the so-called developing world, all our charitable efforts just make for a kinder colonialism.

The Palestine liberation struggle offers a political case study of the problems of international aid. While Palestine and Haiti are very different, both are examples of anticolonial rebellions crushed by the false generosity of aid. Billions of dollars have been spent on aid to Palestine since the mid-1990s. Much of that money came from donors, like the United States and Saudi Arabia, which are politically opposed to an independent Palestinian state. In fact, the United States at the same time sent tens of billions of dollars in direct military aid to the Israeli state. Palestinians say that their problems come from the root cause of occupation. Massive amounts of money are spent with the goal of *not addressing* this root cause, and in fact pacifying Palestinians to get them to accept Israeli occupation, and the result is an endless continuation of the bloody and devastating status quo.

In 2009 in Gaza City, I met Dr. Haidar Eid, an associate professor of postcolonial and postmodern literature at Gaza's al-Aqsa University and a leader of the global boycott, divestment, and sanctions (BDS) movement. As we drove through a city still recovering from massacres and bombings during Israel's Operation Cast Lead in the winter of 2008–2009, Eid told me he saw many Westerners who come to Palestine to help but bring their own assumptions of what that help should look like. "This is my problem with white liberal ideology," he says, "that kind of postmodern politics that does not take into consideration the perspective of the other. It talks about the other; it claims to be recognizing the other, in order to assimilate the other. When the other comes up with something that is completely different from what the Western self is defending, the other becomes terrorist. The other becomes unacceptable." In other words, if you do not want what we are offering, there must be something wrong with you.

Another manifestation of the "othering" that Eid critiques is that even progressives from the United States often judge the resistance of other cultures through their own lens. For example, they are hesitant to see anticolonial movements as allies if they are "too Muslim." Eid is critical of Hamas but also sees them as the legitimate elected representative of the Palestinian people and deserving of praise for their principled resistance against Israeli occupation. Many progressives in the United States cannot see this complexity. Postcolonial theorist Edward Said used the term "orientalism" to describe the patronizing attitude that sees Eastern cultures as fundamentally uncivilized and unchanging.

Eid says that aid has been tethered to an endless wait for a frozen peace process to deliver. This "peace industry" taints the entire Palestinian liberation movement, especially the political parties. "Billions of dollars have been poured into the discourse of the two-state solution. The formation of the Palestinian Authority. The Palestine Satellite Channel. TV stations, radio stations, newspapers, telling people 'two-state, two-state.'"

Eid sees the two-state solution as fundamentally racist and impractical. Racist because it shapes borders based on "exclusive ethno-religious identities." Impractical because, like the tribal Bantustan system of the apartheid South African government, it does not offer true independence to the Palestinian people. Eid told me that the Palestinian revolutionary parties, like the Popular Front for Liberation of Palestine, initially resisted this accommodation for just this reason, but were later bought out by international aid, especially through the Oslo peace process, which Eid (quoting Edward Said) says birthed a new "peace industry."

"From 1993 up until now, what [has] happened is that their revolutionary consciousness has been pacified," says Eid.

Eid says that Palestinians do not need aid; they need allies to stand in principled solidarity with the Palestinian struggle. He sees hope in the international grassroots movement, following the lead of Palestinian civil society, which has called for boycott, divestment, and sanctions against Israel. Eid, who earned his PhD studying in South Africa, sees the movement that led to the end of apartheid in South Africa as key for ending colonial occupation in Palestine. "In the mid eighties, more than 75 percent of white South Africans voted for the apartheid system," he explains.

> And everyone was saying it is impossible for Blacks and whites to live together in South Africa, and that the overwhelming majority of whites do not want to live with Blacks. But the same percentage, more than 75 percent of white South Africans, voted for the end of apartheid in 1994. Now doesn't that raise a question? What was the reason behind that type of change? I would go back to the BDS campaign. When every single white South African felt ostracized whenever visiting a foreign country. Nobody wanted to buy South African products. Nobody wanted to shake hands with white South Africans. And that is why, in 1994, they understood that there has got to be an end to this. When Israelis start feeling the same thing, Israelis will be forced to look at the world and say, "What do you exactly want?"

Even human rights NGOs sometimes fall into the trap of not listening to the needs of those they claim to support. Activists with Al Qaws ("The Rainbow"), an LGBTQ organization based in Palestine, are critical of international LGBT human rights organizations, saying they do not see the larger issue of occupation. "'Gay rights' has become the new global measure of whether different nation states and peoples are progressive or not," says Haneen Maikey of Al Qaws. "It's a colonized/colonizer dynamic, this savior complex where LGBTQ activists go to 'save' people in other places. In order for me to convince you to be saved, I need to convince you to hate your community. This disconnects people from their own communities and societies."

> Rights as an approach is not something I personally and al Qaws as a collective relate to. . . . And what does it even mean to demand gay rights—from whom? From the occupier? Or the occupier arm in the West Bank? What does that mean, to get your gay rights without getting your human rights, or dignity, or basic food, work, basic conditions of being a human being? We think in Palestinian society, and without a broader critique, "gay rights" is an unethical approach. . . . The focus on a single issue (homophobia) is tempting, because it is easier than thinking about the complexity of our experiences and how our bodies and sexualities are used and abused by different layers of power.[29]

For members of Al Qaws, the idea of separating homophobia from other systems of oppression is part of the colonial project, and furthers pinkwashing, the use of LGBTQ rights to "cleanse" from discussion other forms of oppression. "You cannot have queer liberation while apartheid, patriarchy, capitalism and other oppressions exist," writes Al Qaws member Ghaith Hilal. "It's important to target the connections of these oppressive forces. Furthermore, pinkwashing is a strategy used by the Brand Israel campaign to garner the support of queers in other parts of the world. It is simply an attempt to make the Zionist project more appealing to queer people. This is another iteration of a familiar and toxic colonial fantasy—that the colonizer can provide something important and necessary that the colonized cannot possibly provide for themselves."[30]

What leads people to give up on change? Is it the slow pace required by asking questions and listening to communities most affected? Or are people driven out of social movements because they are fundamentally disempowered by the inevitable failures of shortsighted campaigns?

If the energy that went into KONY 2012 went toward pressuring a government that the United States has more influence with, like the Israeli state, this could have incredible influence. Through the international BDS movement, the Israeli government would be forced into real negotiations that could bring lasting peace. By focusing on an individual rather than a state or systemic change, Invisible Children set their goals far too low, yet still out of reach.

Whether it's aid for rebuilding in Haiti, human rights advocacy in Palestine, or hunting warlords in Africa, there is ample reason to be suspicious of gifts from wealthier nations. If the aid does not address the structural issues that create injustice, then it only creates a more stable status quo, locking injustice into place.

The U.S. position in the world—in fact, the very existence of the United States—comes from a history of colonial domination. If we want to make amends for that history, kindness is not enough. We need to stop thinking we can "rescue" the world from problems we helped create. Haiti has no money because the United States, France, and other colonial powers stole it. When we buy a twenty-dollar shirt that a Haitian was paid pennies to make, we are continuing to steal from them. When a U.S. aid worker in Haiti is paid a salary equivalent to that of fifty Haitians, we are continuing to steal from them. This is not aid. Aid is reparations. Relief is overthrowing the system of colonial domination, and eliminating debt. Support is standing in solidarity with Haitians and Palestinians and the Diné, all of whom are organizing and fighting and leading their own struggles for an end to colonialism.

Through her struggles around decolonization with Black Mesa Indigenous Support, Berkley Carnine sees many examples of both principled solidarity and the savior mentality, which she defines as "an internalized superiority added to a history of settler colonialism and genocide."

Carnine often sees a pattern among non-Indigenous volunteers. They are confronted with the deep injustice of Native American genocide and don't know how to deal with those feelings. That produces guilt and shame, which then trigger another set of emotions. "I'm feeling bad, and I want to be able to take some action and alleviate that bad feeling. So then the goal becomes not alleviating suffering for others but alleviating one's own suffering."

Carnine grapples with how to fight for change without putting herself at the center. What does it mean to not be from a community but still be accountable to their struggle? She seeks the answer through principled, accountable work as an ally. She has not sought to be a leader or a spokesperson but to help make space for indigenous activists to lead themselves, by taking on tasks like herding sheep that might otherwise take up their time.

"Decolonization is about mutual self-determination between people groups without the colonial state as mediator," adds Carnine in a document written with fellow BMIS organizer Liza Minno Bloom. Among the other steps they advise for activists seeking decolonization:

- Know whose land you're on and "acknowledge that you are on occupied land when you say where you are or where you are from."

- Shift the entitlement inherent in settler experience by asking permission to be on the land.

- Know where your water, heat, electricity and other resources come from.

- Incorporate an analysis of settler colonialism into all of your organizing work, even if you are not working explicitly on Indigenous solidarity.[31]

These examples are a good baseline for any kind of solidarity work.

Chapter Three
The Death of Riad Hamad

I met Brandon Darby in New Orleans in 2004. He was twenty-eight, with a widow's peak, a dimple on his chin, and a cool confidence that belied an intense passion when he got worked up. We talked about Palestinian rights, and he immediately expressed his support for anti-colonial armed resistance. He wanted me to know that he was ready to die for the cause of revolution. He also talked about his friendship with Robert King, who had been one of three imprisoned Black Panthers at Louisiana State Penitentiary at Angola, collectively known as the Angola Three. King had spent twenty-nine years in solitary confinement for a crime he did not commit, was freed in 2001, and eventually moved to Austin, Texas, where Darby lived. Darby told me the militants of the civil rights and Black Power movements inspired him.

Reading the autobiographies of Malcolm X and Assata Shakur radicalized me as a young activist, and as Darby talked about the Black Panthers and Palestinian freedom struggles while smoking cigarettes and drinking a beer he projected a white working-class cool that appealed to me. He had a compelling pattern of speech, expressing radical ideas about revolution or imperialism as if it was the most obvious thing in the world. He would emphasize his passion through repetition, saying quietly, "There's something wrong with a system that would allow this to happen, you know? There's something wrong." He would pause at a common word or phrase, as if offering to define it for you. "The FBI was afraid of the Panthers' free breakfast program," he might say. "You know, *breakfast*?"

Darby was visiting New Orleans and talking about moving there from Austin. That didn't happen, and I didn't hear from him for a while. Then, less than a year later, New Orleans was submerged in the aftermath of Hurricane Katrina, and Darby was back.

His story of returning to New Orleans quickly became legend. He had come in a car with scott crow, an anarchist activist also from Austin. They had come to rescue Robert King. Darby had taken a boat to Robert King's house, faced down state troopers who got in his way, and rescued King from his house. "I knew I had to save King's life, and I wasn't going to let federal authorities or the New Orleans police force stop me," he later said.[1] Then he and crow went to the Algiers neighborhood, where they helped former Black Panther Malik Rahim face down armed white vigilantes. Robert King later disputed elements of this story, but by then the legend had taken on a life of its own.

Darby quickly became a leader of Common Ground, an anarchist-leaning volunteer group that brought thousands of young, mostly white volunteers in to work on rebuilding New Orleans. Founded by Rahim, his partner Sharon Johnson, Darby, and crow, Common Ground began with a well-informed critique of the massive failures of the Red Cross and other aid agencies.[2] Their defined goal was to support local control of the recovery. Their slogan was "Solidarity, Not Charity." From the beginning, Darby was impatient with the non-hierarchical organizing style many of the founders and volunteers came with. "For some, Common Ground might have been about creating a little anarchist utopia," he later said. "For me, it was about helping people have their rights heard and have their homes [restored], and it was about getting things done."[3]

This period in New Orleans crystallized the idea of the savior for me. It is not just about Brandon Darby but also about the people who followed him. Darby is not so much a proto-typical savior as he is the kind of dangerous person who can rise to power when we are seeking saviors. Tens of thousands of people came to New Orleans to save the city, and too many were uninterested in listening or learning. I heard again and again, "There was no organizing here before we came here." Or, "We're going to teach the people here about resistance." A city with hundreds of years of history of resistance to white supremacy faced the indignity of being "taught" how to orga-nize by an endless stream of privileged white twenty-year-olds.

In the first two years, for many who had come to New Orleans to save the city and its people, Darby was like a cult leader. Young volunteers would hang on his every word. He always seemed to be dating several beautiful, idealis-tic, college-aged activist women. With Darby's example, post-Katrina relief was almost a contest of machismo: who could gut houses faster, stay longer in housing without elec-tricity and running water, stand up to police, and lead the Black masses to justice? Scholar Rachel Luft, who worked to support feminist and antiracist responses among volunteers, described this attitude as *disaster masculinity*.[4]

When the city released a planning blueprint that called for the flooded Lower Ninth Ward to be bulldozed and left as a green space, Darby moved into an empty house in the neighborhood and announced that he was going to stay there to represent all the residents who had been displaced, stand-ing against demolitions until the rightful owners could return. "If I'd had an appropriate weapon, I would have attacked my government for what they were doing to people," he said later, declaring that he'd bought an AK-47 and was willing to use it: "There are residents here who have said that you will not take my home from me over my dead body, and we have made a commitment to be in solidarity with those residents."[5]

In a time when most New Orleanians were displaced, Darby's leadership position in Common Ground gave him a platform for media attention. There was a story on *Nightline*; Academy Award–winning director Jonathan Demme filmed a profile of him; he was featured on the *Tavis Smiley Show*, in documentaries, and on local and international TV and radio. Although Darby had no roots in the city or experience, he had rushed into a vacuum and became an internationally known voice of New Orleans. The influx of Common Ground volunteers, many of whom brought media connections from around the United States, helped Darby to grab the spotlight. He took advantage of journalists not up for doing the work to find the authentic voices of the affected communities of New Orleans. Everyone seemed to be enamored by the story of the charismatic white savior.

Darby represented what I think of as the classic tendency of the savior, a sort of leftist version of Manifest Destiny, where a person acts as if he is destined to lead the struggle of poor people, who implicitly are unqualified to lead their own struggle. Darby was always leading in their name. "I don't think I want to be a hero any more than someone who's a firefighter. Are they firefighters because they want to be [heroes]?" Darby later asked a reporter. "Some people are really good with numbers, and they're accountants. My brain thinks of ways to fix things I think are wrong."[6]

Darby was a polarizing figure from the beginning. Many New Orleans organizers were convinced by his disruptive presence that Darby was paid by the federal government to bring dissent to the movement. Even Malik Rahim's own son was suspicious. "It came to the degree that my son just knew that there was something too wrong with Brandon, and he searched Brandon's possessions, because he said, 'This guy is an agent, or he is an informant,'" Rahim said later. "And, let me tell you, it caused a rift between my son and I, so much so that eventually, he left. Because I believed Brandon. I defended him."[7]

These concerns were well-founded. Rahim lived through *COINTELPRO*, the FBI's Counter Intelligence Program, which utilized agents and informants to spy on and sabotage movements from 1956 though the operation's exposure in 1971.[8] The FBI's paid informant program has grown dramatically since the days of *COINTELPRO*, with the number of informants rising from 1,500 in 1975 to 15,000 in 2011. While *COINTELPRO* focused on the civil rights and Black power movements, today the FBI uses undercover agents and paid informants in a range of movements, with the majority apparently focused on Muslim communities. From 2001 to 2011, almost half of all terrorism prosecutions involved the use of a paid informant.[9] In many of these cases, lawyers and advocates have found that the so-called "terrorists" were confused young men, often with mental disabilities, limited intelligence, emotional problems, or desperate life situations who were manipulated by the informant into agreeing to actions they had previously shown no interest in.[10]

By late 2005, Darby was developing relations with the police. In December 2005 he told a reporter that he had "the New Orleans Police Department's hierarchy on speed dial" and had regular meetings with police.[11] Local organizers condemned his provocative behavior, but his leadership position in Common Ground shielded him from accountability.

In the tense post-Katrina era, Darby seemed to be encouraging conflict between different activists and organizations doing reconstruction work. When organizers from the local chapter of INCITE! Women of Color Against Violence announced that they were opening a women's health clinic, Darby announced his own clinic, and with his higher profile was able to secure funding that might otherwise have gone to the local, women of color–led effort.

Darby's friend crow (in an action he later said Darby pushed him to take) wrote a brutal letter attacking People's Hurricane Relief Fund, a coalition of Black-led organizations active in the city, further causing conflict among local organizers. Lily Keber, one of the many new arrivals to New Orleans who dated Darby in 2006, told me that even when Darby was in a bar, "there would always be fights near him. He would never be in the fight, but it was always between two people he had just been talking to."

New Orleans after Hurricane Katrina was a touchstone in social justice history in this country. Tens of thousands of volunteers came to help rebuild the city. In one month, during spring break 2006, about two thousand five hundred volunteers passed through Common Ground, most of them staying in a gutted schoolhouse in the Upper Ninth Ward and washing in outdoor showers. When volunteers saw the devastation in mostly Black areas, while white areas were receiving aid and recovering quickly, and when they saw Black-led organized resistance to this unequal recovery, it was a transformative, inspiring experience. Like the protests in Ferguson nearly ten years later, it was a moment of awakening that spread virally across the United States.

But there were also problems in that gutted schoolhouse: an epidemic of sexual assault, committed by young white males against female and transgender volunteers. And Darby had helped foster a macho culture that dismissed the complaints. "He kicked in the door of a trailer where there were volunteers with guns on them. He did a lot of Wild West shit—Mister Macho Action Hero," says Lisa Fithian, an early leader of Common Ground who was driven out by Darby. For Fithian, there was obvious misogyny involved in the blind support for Darby. "A lot of women had been hurt by this man, and a lot of men had defended him over the years, and it's not okay," she says.[12] Other people in the organization's leadership followed Darby's example. In the macho atmosphere he fostered, talk of patriarchy or sexual assault was seen as a distraction.

At one point, allegations appeared online that Darby had sexually assaulted volunteers. His then-friend Common Ground cofounder scott crow worked to take the online postings down. "I used my connections with Indymedia all around the world to take it down, on server after server after server, because Brandon asked me to," he said later. "I still stand by that, because you know, no physical person ever came forward, and no advocate for a physical person ever came forward and said, 'He physically assaulted me.'"[13]

At the time, I was aware of the dynamic of white volunteers seeming to take over Black neighborhoods (laying roots for the gentrification that was to come over the following years), but I was mostly unaware of the epidemic of sexual assault at Common Ground. The work of feminist organizers and scholars like Rachel Luft, who wrote about the assaults, and Shana griffin, a New Orleans–born organizer with the national organization INCITE!, helped me learn the ways that privilege had blinded me to situations happening right in front of me.

For many of those who worked in Common Ground then, it was a time of crushed hope. It was a time of conflict and broken promises and backstabbing that pushed many idealistic young people away from activism. Tens of thousands of volunteers had come to New Orleans to fight against an historic injustice and help people recover from one of the worst disasters in U.S. history. Too many of them ended up facing sexual assault and bullying and macho leadership. Not just from Darby but even more from the many young men and women who aspired to be like him. Disaster masculinity was not just an issue in Common Ground but in other organizations working on relief and reconstruction. I was personally aware of sexual assault allegations against men in at least two other organizations working on the ground. In both cases the women were pressured to stay silent.

In early 2006 Darby traveled with a delegation from Common Ground to Venezuela, an attempt to raise money for the reconstruction of New Orleans from the Chavez government. The trip collapsed in disarray—once again, conflicts between activists seemed to follow Brandon everywhere he went. According to Darby's narrative, Venezuelans offered to introduce Darby to representatives of leftist guerilla forces from Colombia, and this caused him to rethink his political ideas. He claims he had always been a patriot, but he says that this was the moment he realized he was on the wrong side. Others on the trip dismiss his claims as absurd.

In the summer of 2006 Darby left Common Ground for Austin, and a new disaster caught his eye. In Lebanon, hundreds were being massacred by a brutal Israeli invasion. As Israeli bombs dropped on Lebanon, Darby announced a new project, called "Common Ground Critical Response." According to a press release, a team of activists led by Darby would be using their experience in Katrina relief to aid civilians caught under Israeli bombs. The group would be "sending a rescue and relief team into Southern Lebanon to assist with humanitarian aid efforts. Our team will go into areas that are not currently being served by relief organizations due to the risk involved." The press release quoted Darby as declaring, "Somewhere in that region there is a young girl trapped in rubble. No one is hearing her call, and we want our hands to be there to pull her out. . . . When two groups of powerful men cannot get along, that does not clear the rest of us from our responsibility to ensure that children have water, food, and medical supplies."

Considering Darby's previous outspoken defense of the Palestinian right to resist Israeli colonialism by any means necessary, many of us who knew him noted with interest that now he was not "taking sides." The press release even offered that the project would "send a response team to Israel if aid to the civilian population becomes insufficient," an absurd notion on many levels, not the least of which was that there were more than one thousand Lebanese civilians killed and fewer than fifty Israeli civilian deaths.

The press release added, "In addition to rescue and relief operations in Lebanon, the Critical Response team will develop networks and an infrastructure to enable other American civilians to provide assistance in the region. Furthermore, the organization will provide an independent media presence to show a fair and balanced picture of what is happening on the ground in this region." Darby, who by his own account began informing for the FBI around this point, reached out to local activists for their contacts in the region.[14]

Critical Response never sent a delegation. It's unclear what Darby did with the contacts he received or the funds he raised, or what his real goals were for this project. Perhaps it was part of his work for the FBI or part of his endless quest for publicity. "It fit his hero complex very well," says professor Caroline Heldman, who worked with Darby on the project and is still friends with him. "He'd get attention, he'd be the hero, and it was a cause he believed in." Heldman believes Darby was still pro-Palestinian at this point. "It wasn't until a few years later that I heard him calling himself pro-Israeli," she tells me. However, she also adds that she doesn't really know if he was conservative from the beginning and the entire period was an elaborate hoax.

Two fellow activists, including scott crow, say that around this time—in fall of 2006—Darby tried to convince them to join him in a plan to burn down a right-wing bookstore in Austin.[15]

In 2007 Darby was back in charge at Common Ground New Orleans and no longer talking about Lebanon. Darby responded to continued criticism and efforts to reform the organization by conducting an organizational purge. He said he was sick of identity politics, that people raising concerns about gender were getting "in the way" of the work of Black freedom. He went on to say that his critics were more concerned with political correctness than "getting things done." Dozens of people within the organization had concerns about the influx of mostly white volunteers on surrounding Black communities. Most of those expressing concern were women and queer-identified. Because they sought to address these issues, Darby told them that they had to leave the organization. In his view, he was speaking for the "silenced" Black population of New Orleans (implied to be straight and mostly male). Darby was not the first or last progressive leader I saw dismiss the concerns of women and LGBT folks as side issues that were getting in the way of a larger struggle. It's a common refrain. And it always leads to a smaller, divided movement.

Women, LGBT folks, and many people of color had raised alarms about Darby from the beginning. "Even if no one suspected he was an informant, his domineering and macho behavior should have been all that was needed to call his leadership into question," wrote Courtney Desiree Morris in *make/shift* magazine. "The state has already understood a fact that the Left has struggled to accept: misogynists make great informants." Morris makes the point that divisive behavior is often excused when it comes from white men. Sexism is seen as an issue that is "less important" than the other revolutionary struggles we're involved in. But, says Morris, ignoring these problems makes all movements weaker.

> Before or regardless of whether they are ever recruited by the state to disrupt a movement or destabilize an organization, they've likely become well versed in practices of disruptive behavior. They require almost no training and can start the work immediately. What's more paralyzing to our work than when women and/or queer folks leave our movements because they have been repeatedly lied to, humiliated, physically/verbally/emotionally/sexually abused? Or when you have to postpone conversations about the work so that you can devote group meetings to addressing an individual member's most recent offense? Or when that person spreads misinformation, creating confusion and friction among radical groups? Nothing slows down movement building like a misogynist.[16]

Disproportionately, it is white men who are called geniuses or visionaries. How many women or people of color geniuses and visionaries are ignored? How many more could fit this role if given the same training, mentoring, opportunities, funding, and attention? Once they are given the label of genius, there is even more pressure to allow them to get away with bad behavior, because they have become too vital to our movement. How many others are pushed out of the movement by the behavior of these men?

In the summer of 2007 Darby announced his "retirement" from the all-volunteer organization. Common Ground continues to this day as a more standard NGO mostly removed from its radical roots, but in some ways it never recovered from Darby's leadership.

Back in Austin, Darby was spending time with Riad Hamad and with the FBI. I met Riad in New York City in 2003. I had just returned from reporting in the West Bank and Gaza, and he had a merchandise table at a conference where I was a guest speaker. Hamad told me about the Palestine Children's Welfare Fund, an aid project he directed from his home in Austin. He would buy handcrafts from nonprofits in the West Bank and Gaza, sell them to activists and churches in the United States, and send any profits or extra donations to health clinics, schools, and other charities. Hamad struck me as a bit socially awkward, mostly because he seemed singularly focused on raising money for the children of Palestine. During the conference, Hamad slept in his car on a cold spring night, rather than paying for a New York hotel room.

Fifty years old, Hamad had salt and pepper hair, was married and had two children, and was driven to distraction by injustice in the world. He was an activist in a way that reminds me of many middle-aged activists I've met, driving an old energy-efficient car covered in peace bumper stickers, writing angry letters to the editor of the local paper, showing up at protests and meetings with fliers to hand out. He was a middle school teacher, originally from Lebanon, and kind, generous, and trusting. He was passionate about education—he had three master's degrees—and loved to teach and to learn.

Although he was a full-time teacher, he seemed to spend every spare moment figuring out how to sell more crafts, with a desperation that reminds me of the title character in *Schindler's List* at the end of the film, as if each sale might save a life. He would call me sometimes, just to tell me about some beautiful crafts from Bethlehem he had received, and how they'd be perfect for holiday gifts. "I can send them to you, and you can just send me the money whenever you sell them. I know people will want them. You can go to churches, you can go to mosques, anywhere."

Hamad was Muslim, but he was better known in churches than in mosques. Many of the crafts he imported were from the Palestinian Christians of Bethlehem, such as olive wood crosses, which were popular in the progressive congregations that Hamad spent his time in.

Hamad passed his passion for justice—and tireless work—on to his family. His daughter, Rita, studied economics at Harvard, later earned a medical degree and a master's degree in public health from the UC Berkeley–UC San Francisco Joint Medical Program, and went on to teach at Stanford, where she now is using her medical and economics background to research poverty as a disease.[17]

Darby says that during this time Hamad had a hidden life that he chose to reveal only to him. He says Hamad invited Darby to join him in a money-laundering scam to get money to armed groups in Palestine and Lebanon. We may never know their relationship, as Hamad is dead and Darby is an unreliable narrator, but in my experience Hamad was sweet and trusting to a fault and personally opposed to violence.

Darby says he went to the FBI with his concerns. On February 27, 2008, the FBI raided Hamad's home and took forty boxes of receipts, documents, computers, and music CDs—everything they could get their hands on. Despite all of the confiscated files, in addition to some level of surveillance and Darby's firsthand spying reports, the FBI found no evidence of any terrorism connections. They found the kind of sloppy bookkeeping you might expect from an organization with no paid staff, run out of the director's living room. There is also some speculation that Hamad could have been consciously avoiding some of his tax responsibilities—he had expressed sentiments that U.S. taxes pay for war and said he admired tax resisters—but the government never presented any evidence that Hamad had committed a crime.[18]

Weeks later Hamad was dead. On April 17, 2008, his body was found in Lady Bird Lake. The police called it a suicide. But according to a local TV station, "Park-goers who saw the body said the death did not look accidental. They said the man's face was wrapped with duct tape, and his arms appeared to be tied in front of his body."

Hours later, I saw Darby. After I saw him, I went online and saw the news reports about Hamad's death, and then I called Darby. This was no suicide, Darby told me. He thought

someone, maybe the FBI, had killed Hamad. He sounded gen-
uinely concerned. Was he feeling guilty? I asked him why he
thought the FBI would want to do anything to Hamad, and
Darby deflected.

After Darby hung up, I was overwhelmed by grief and
confusion. I don't know why Darby wanted to talk to me
about Hamad. He often seemed to be running multiple games
at once. He would pretend to have something to say when he
was actually trying to get information. He would brag about
his guns and his willingness to die for the cause, and then ask
me if I had ever done anything illegal. He would give away
secrets about somebody "in confidence," when he was clearly
trying to spread that information as far as possible. He once
called me to tell me about a grant that Common Ground had
received that other organizations had applied for. "They'll be
really upset if they hear," he told me conspiratorially. "So—do
with that information whatever you think is best. You know?
Just thought you should know."

Hamad's memorial was held at Austin's St James Episcopal
Church and featured multidenominational tributes as well as
moving words from his family.[19] "I think of him as a holy man,
really, a kind of saint," said Karen Hartwell, a friend of Hamad's and wife of an Episcopal priest. "Saint Francis, who only
wanted to serve others and not himself."

While Hamad's family and friends mourned, Darby had
already moved on. He joined with a group of Austin activists
traveling to Minnesota to protest against the 2008 Republican
National Convention. According to protesters who were part
of the meetings, Darby had become a mentor to David McK-
ay and Bradley Crowder, two kids from small-town Texas, in
their early twenties, and new to activism. Darby taunted the
young men, asking if they were willing to commit violence for
their cause. "I stated that they all looked like they ate too much
tofu and that they should eat beef so that they could put on
muscle mass. I stated that they weren't going to be able to fight
anybody until they did so," related Darby in an email to the
FBI after an early meeting.

At the Republican convention McKay and Crowder were arrested and charged with planning to throw Molotov cocktails at a lot where police cars were parked. McKay and Crowder and others they traveled with say that Darby bullied the young men into the plan. Darby says he foiled a criminal scheme, and he sued the *New York Times* after they wrote in 2011 that Darby had "encouraged" the plot.

Months after the 2008 convention, during the trial of McKay and Crowder, Darby's name surfaced as an FBI informant and a key witness in the case. Even with that evidence, some of Darby's friends refused to believe it. His then-friend scott crow wrote an open letter expressing support of Darby, calling the revelations that he was working with the FBI "an absolute COINTELPRO lie. . . . If Brandon was conning me, and many others, it would be the biggest lie of my life since I found out the truth about Santa Claus as a child. It is absurd."

"I stand by Brandon Darby," repeated crow multiple times in a passionate email he sent out widely. "I have known him for years. I know his grandmother, his mom and his friends. . . . He and I faced the cops with arms."

If only crow and others had been as willing to stand up for the women sexually assaulted at Common Ground. "Brandon could not have continued to do what he did if he was not backed by Malik and [Common Ground]," said Lisa Fithian. "And Darby could not have continued to do what he did around the RNC if he wasn't backed by crow. So you have to see there is a repeating pattern where the dominant systems and the people within them are in many ways unconsciously continuing to promote this."[20] Darby's own defense of his actions back up this narrative. "If I was so bad, why was I the spokesperson for Common Ground Relief for so long?" he asked a reporter. "Why, after 2006, did they have me come back and ask me to direct the organization and be the spokesperson again?"[21]

The far right embraced Darby, and he rushed into their arms. Suddenly this admirer of the Black Panther Party had become an outspoken fan of Sarah Palin, giving speeches to

Tea Party gatherings about the "secrets" he had learned from inside the left, and how he had been duped but finally saw the light when he realized that he loved his country and that the activists around him were traitors.

In 2012 Darby claimed to be back working with the FBI, investigating child sex trafficking cases. More recently he boasted in late 2015 about taking Donald Trump on a tour of the Texas border. "It is of utmost importance that possible future leaders of our country visit the border region," declared Darby. "Mr. Trump will learn firsthand of the many holes and vulnerabilities that the Los Zetas cartel exploits to enter Texas and oppress their victims."

We may never know what drove Darby, what he really believed, and whether he had a change of heart or not, and it doesn't really matter. The lesson is to be wary of heroes, no matter how brave or charismatic they may seem. Darby left pain and disorder and distrust in his wake on a massive scale. He left scars on the social justice communities of New Orleans and Austin and around the United States. He is a warning of the harm that the idea of a savior can bring. I think of him as a warning to myself as well.

Many of us, especially those of us socialized as men, do not do enough to speak up against other men who have relationships with women they have power over. The young volunteers who came through Common Ground looked up to Brandon. It's a dynamic I have seen often in activist circles, men taking sexual advantage of their position.

And it is not just in activist worlds. Journalist Katie J. M. Baker wrote about sexual harassment scandals shaking the "relatively small field of philosophy." In one case, philosopher Thomas Pogge, who wrote and spoke passionately about global justice and inequality, was accused by several young women of color of taking advantage of his position over them. One student asked, "How could he advocate 'gender-sensitive' solutions to global power imbalances while exploiting the power imbalance between himself and the much younger, non-Western women who idolized him?"

Pogge responded that her arguments "were 'gathered from feminist and petty-bourgeois sources.'"[22]

Those of us raised in the United States, especially white males, are often taught that we know more than others, that we have more to give the world, that we should lead others to salvation. We don't question our position of power and privilege, and we don't ask who has been silenced when we speak.

The life of Che Guevara, the Argentine radical who came from privilege and dedicated his life to third world movements, is an ideal I aspire to. But in practice, not everyone who comes from a life of privilege seeking to help actually does make things better. Sometimes the savior makes things worse. Darby was an extreme example, and he may have been paid to cause dissent, but he was neither the first, nor will he be the last to act this way. Most of those who do the most damage are not paid by the state to disrupt, we just think we know what is best. Or we see the actions of someone like Darby, and we stay silent because we have bought into the idea of a savior, and he seems to look the part.

Chapter Four
Batman Is the Problem

In 1979, boxing legend Muhammad Ali invited film critic Roger Ebert to his home, for the two of them to watch Sylvester Stallone's *Rocky II*. In the film, Stallone's white boxer defeats Carl Weather's Apollo Creed, a character widely thought to be based on Ali.

Ali's entire commentary on the film is compelling, far more memorable than the film itself. As the credits rolled, Ali delivered his final verdict, "For the black man to come out superior would be against America's teachings," he commented. "I have been so great in boxing they had to create an image like Rocky, a white image on the screen, to counteract my image in the ring. America has to have its white images, no matter where it gets them. Jesus, Wonder Woman, Tarzan and Rocky."[1]

Our culture creates and celebrates saviors. Films, books, TV, comics: we are surrounded by the message that we should wait for a hero to save us, and that hero will likely be white and male. Despite the popular perception that Hollywood is the home of liberal attitudes, our popular media often reflect a racist, patriarchal worldview.

We are in the age of the superhero movie. Over half of the top-grossing films of the past twenty years have been adapted from comic books, toys, or young adult novels. Others, like *Star Wars*, might as well have been. Even before the age the blockbuster, the predominant cinematic storyline has almost always centered on an individual. Even films about labor struggles—the ultimate collective effort—are structured like *Norma Rae*—the 1979 Academy Award–winning story of one brave individual who almost single-handedly wins a union for her workplace.

Batman is the perfect capitalist savior hero. He's a wealthy man who uses his wealth to fight the problems of the world one on one. Instead of giving his money away, he spends it on himself and his Batcave and Batmobile, self-assured that he alone is the best solution to the world's problems and that the millions spent on his toys are investments in saving the world. It's no wonder that the definitive modern Batman comic, *The Dark Knight Returns* (also a partial basis for several of the recent Batman films), was written by Frank Miller, one of the most far-right authors in the world of comic books. Miller also wrote *Holy Terror*, a self-proclaimed propaganda comic book in support of Bush's War on Terror. He told an interviewer, "We are in the midst of a long war. The enemy we are up against is pernicious, deceptive, merciless and wants nothing less than our complete and total destruction."[2] Miller later called Occupy Wall Street "nothing but a pack of louts, thieves, and rapists."[3]

The criminal justice system is an ongoing obsession in film and TV, and in the vast majority of these stories, the heroes are the police. Even when the story focuses on corrupt or villainous police, they are almost always caught by other, heroic, officers that we are impelled to root for. Amongst the worst actors in our real life criminal justice system are prosecutors, yet they are almost universally depicted by Hollywood as idealistic and honest. Meanwhile, it is almost unheard of to see a film about a heroic public defender. David Simon's HBO series *The Wire*, which among other virtues was lauded for portraying the complexity of those normally depicted as heroes or villains, had arguably only one cartoonish villain: the defense attorney who worked for the drug dealers.

Too much of today's popular science fiction conveys Margaret Thatcher's dictate that "there is no alternative." Depictions of a better future—or any imagining of a different and better system—are rare. During the social upheavals of the twentieth century, science fiction authors like Octavia Butler, Arthur C. Clarke, and Ursula K. Le Guin often depicted a utopian future where the drudgery of work had been eliminated through technology, and where divisions, such as those of race, class, gender, and nation, had vanished. This filtered into the mainstream imagination through shows like *Star Trek* that imagined a multiracial, peace-oriented (though still hierarchical) future. Even the *Jetsons*, which imagined a whitewashed fifties version of our future, seemed to be a future without war or conflict or much need for work. Now we live in the era of the dystopian imagination, and our most popular entertainment features post-apocalyptic zombie-filled fascist nightmares.

People may be inspired toward change by oppositional messages in mainstream work like *The Hunger Games*, but there is a need for art that challenges the status quo more directly. Today the creative class that bring us our films, theater, television, dance, painting, and the other arts all come from the same insular and wealthy world. Like nonprofit leadership, most careers in film require degrees from elite institutions. For any artist, dissent is risky when your career depends on the whims of the wealthy. "Reimagining the world becomes far more difficult," writes Sarah Schulman. "Reflecting back what power-brokers and institutional administrators think about themselves feels essential to survival."[4]

The 1970s was a decade when movie funders, trying to reach a countercultural youth audience they did not understand, financed films that featured both more complicated heroes (and anti-heroes) as well as films that didn't necessarily have a single protagonist or a three-act narrative structure. These were films made by directors that often came from outside the insular world of Hollywood, films like *Network*, *Midnight Cowboy*, *Harold and Maude*, and *Reds*, which are smart, complicated, revolutionary stories without easy resolutions.

Foreign directors have also had more freedom to create outside of the Hollywood template, like most of the Iranian new wave, which had to deal with censorship when showing romantic relationships but was freed from most commercial concerns. Or British filmmaker Ken Loach's films, collective in goals and structure, like his classic about the socialist and communist volunteers in the Spanish Civil War, *Land and Freedom*. Gillo Pontecorvo's *Battle of Algiers* is a brilliant 1966 Italian-Algerian film that demonstrates through its narrative structure that revolution exists outside of any one leader. It's a film that could never have been made in Hollywood.

John Sayles, who funds his own films through his work on more commercial fare, tells ensemble stories in movies like *Matewan*, *Lone Star*, and *City of Hope*. Peter Watkins's revolutionary agit-prop, exemplified in his futuristic semi-documentary about government repression *Punishment Park*, is brilliantly unique. *Born in Flames*, the classic 1983 underground feminist revolutionary science fiction film by Lizzie Borden, is an example of how a film might explore feminist intersectionality. Through the story of Black feminist revolutionaries in a post-socialist revolution United States, the film dramatizes the intersections of race, class, and gender in a story without any single protagonist. Borden could do this because she was working far outside of the Hollywood funding structure. But these are exceptions. Now more than ever, Hollywood follows the cult of the individual. In fact, screenwriting books and film schools dictate it.[5]

The film industry, like the media in general, is overwhelmingly white and male, and they like to make films where the heroes look like themselves (or how they imagine themselves). The Directors Guild of America found that of the people hired for the first time to direct an episode of a television show between 2009 and 2014, 87 percent were white and 82 percent were male. That same year another study found that women were 12 percent of protagonists in the top-grossing films of 2014—a percentage that had actually gone down since 2002. And women were only 2 percent of film music composers and 5 percent or less in many other technical film positions.

A 2014 report found that people of color made up just 10 percent of the lead roles in recent films. The show *Fresh*

Off The Boat, which premiered in February 2015, is the first U.S. television comedy with East Asian leads in twenty years (the previous program, Margaret Cho's *All-American Girl*, was quickly canceled).

The logic of Hollywood has long dictated that Black stories, even if they are about Africa, must be told through white eyes. How much does Hollywood (and white America) love the story of the white savior in Africa? Since the Edgar Rice Burroughs novel *Tarzan of the Apes* was published in 1914, there have been over two hundred films made about the character. The first adaptation was released in 1918. The most recent was in 2016, which also saw the release of the newest adaption of Rudyard Kipling's racist fantasy, *The Jungle Book*.[6] With so many versions, there is a wide range of how offensive and racist the adaptations can be, but at its heart each film is the story of the noble white man conquering darker lands.

A refined Tarzan for a more intellectual audience, the 1962 Academy Award winner *Lawrence of Arabia* starred Peter O'Toole as the savior of the Arab masses. The 1987 Academy Award winner *Out of Africa* set the modern template for U.S. films about Africa. Watching this film you might think Africa is only populated by white people and wild animals. That same year *Cry Freedom* told the story of South African freedom fighter Steve Biko through the eyes of a white character played by Kevin Kline. *The Last King of Scotland*, in 2006, was about Ugandan president Idi Amin and starred Scottish actor James McAvoy, who sleeps with Idi Amin's wife. Africa didn't even make it into the title of the film.

The 1989 film *Glory* told the story of the first all-Black Civil War regiment, with sweet-faced white actor Matthew Broderick billed as the star. Broderick played regiment leader Col. Robert Gould Shaw, who in real life was a racist who described his regiment as childlike. The movie version of Shaw, of course, would never speak such racist thoughts, even though he was a white man born in the early nineteenth century. Therein lies another problem with Hollywood's insistence on white protagonists: in addition to falsifying history and erasing

Black leadership, it also serves to hide white culpability. "I love *Glory*," writer Phenderson Clark told the *LA Times*. "But the movie would have you believe that Robert Gould Shaw is this white man plopped into the middle of the 1860s without a racist belief. In order to create the white savior, all of these stories have to be changed."[7]

Glory director Edward Zwick has a bit of a white savior fetish. He later made *The Last Samurai* in 2003, starring Tom Cruise as the leader of an army of Japanese rebels fighting an oppressive Tokyo government, and his 2006 *Blood Diamond*, set in Africa, stars Leonardo DiCaprio as a white mercenary with a heart of gold. These military saviors continue through 1990's *Dances with Wolves* (Kevin Costner, savior of Native Americans) and 2003's *Tears of the Sun* (Bruce Willis as the NAVY Seal rescuing white women in Nigeria). The 2009 film *Avatar* brought this model to space, with aliens in the role of Indigenous people needing a white savior.

Even when characters are not white, Hollywood loves to cast a white actor in the role. Many people think blackface ended a hundred years ago. But just in the last few years we've had white actors like Rooney Mara playing the Native American "princess" Tiger Lily in *Pan* (2015), Emma Stone as a mixed-race character with a half-Chinese, half–Native Hawaiian father in *Aloha* (2015), and an endless series of biblical epics with white stars playing characters who would certainly have been African or Arab (including 2014's *Noah* and *Exodus: Gods and Kings*).

White supremacy demands that white people, especially males, be the protagonists, even when a story is not primarily about them. The white hero is a neutral avatar we are supposed to project ourselves onto, even if that "we" includes people of color. Perhaps the most embarrassing modern example is the 1988 Academy Award–winning film *Mississippi Burning*, in which the story of the civil rights movement is reshaped as a story of the heroism of two white male FBI agents. Alan Parker, the white liberal director of *Mississippi Burning*, told *Time*, "The two heroes in the story had to be white. That is a reflection of our society as much as of the film industry. At this point in time, it could not have been made in any other way."[8]

The Blind Side and *The Help* won Academy Awards in 2009 and 2011 because they celebrated good-hearted white people saving Black people. More recently, the 2014 film *Selma* was attacked by white critics and historians for not making President Johnson the hero of the civil rights movement.[9]

In an interview with the *Hollywood Reporter*, one member of the Academy of Motion Picture Arts and Sciences defended her vote against *Selma* for best picture, saying, "As far as the accusations about the Academy being racist? Yes, most members are white males, but they are not the cast of *Deliverance*—they had to get into the Academy to begin with, so they're not cretinous, snaggletoothed hillbillies. When a movie about Black people is good, members vote for it. But if the movie isn't that good, am I supposed to vote for it just because it has Black people in it? I've got to tell you, having the cast show up in T-shirts saying "I can't breathe" [at their New York premiere]—I thought that stuff was offensive. Did they want to be known for making the best movie of the year or for stirring up shit?"[10] This Academy member voted for Clint Eastwood's war fantasy *American Sniper* that year.

Hollywood loves to celebrate soldiers. The warrior-as-savior construct may have met its nadir with *300*, perhaps the most racist film made since the 1915 KKK recruitment film *Birth of a Nation*. Based on a comic by Frank Miller and released in 2006, *300* enacted Miller's racist fantasies of the eugenics and homophobia of ancient Sparta as a metaphor for the need for white men to fight terrorism around the world. Coming as the Bush administration was threatening war on Iran, the film's characters do battle with demonic, evil, polysexual monsters of the Persian Empire. Gerard Butler, in the lead, nearly quotes Bush in talking about stopping the enemy over there before they come here, declaring his fighters as the "world's one hope for reason and justice" versus the "dark will of the Persian kings." He might as well wave a U.S. flag as he declares "No retreat, no surrender. . . . A new age has dawned, an age of freedom."[11]

As one reviewer noted, "If *300* had been made in Germany in the mid-1930s, it would be studied today alongside *The Eternal Jew* as a textbook example of how race-baiting fantasy and nationalist myth can serve as an incitement to total war. . . . Here are just a few of the categories that are not-so-vaguely conflated with the 'bad' (i.e., Persian) side in the movie: Black people. Brown people. Disfigured people. Gay men (not gay in the buff, homoerotic Spartan fashion, but in the effeminate Persian style). Lesbians. Disfigured lesbians."[12]

It was inevitable that Hollywood would seek to tell the story of a white savior fighting to defeat African warlord Joseph Kony. In 2011, *300* star Gerard Butler starred in and produced *Machine Gun Preacher*, based on the true story of a white former drug dealer who finds God and descends on Africa on a mission to both rescue children and teach adults how to fight. As the film was released, some news outlets reported the unsurprising truth about Sam Childers, the preacher. Community leaders from the town in Sudan where Childers ran an orphanage complained that the children there were "malnourished, unhealthy, and unhappy."[13]

"As a community, we want Sam to leave and let other people take over," said one resident. "Let Sam go away so that someone with a good heart, someone who is humane, can come in and take over." The year before, a mostly positive profile of Childers in *Vanity Fair* showed a sinister undercurrent, including some evidence that Childers was engaged in smuggling arms to multiple forces. "You ask me another question about the arms dealing, I'm going to throw you out of the car," Childers told the reporter when he asked too many questions about the shady dealings he witnessed.[14]

But when Danny Glover tried to produce a film about Toussaint Louverture, the leader of the Haitian revolution, he was told by producers in both the United States and Europe that he needed a white lead character. "I went to everybody. You wouldn't believe the number of producers based in

Europe, and in the States, that I went to," said Glover. "Producers said 'It's a nice project, a great project . . . where are the white heroes?'"[15]

Mario Van Peebles reported that when he and his father made *Panther*, their film about the Black Panther Party, "One of the studio heads suggested that we make one of the leading Panthers a white man. Others suggested focusing on a Berkeley white person who would meet five young Black guys, teaches them to read and stand up for themselves, and then they become the Panthers."[16]

Dangerous Minds, the 1995 film in which a high school teacher played by Michelle Pfeiffer saves a group of students of color through the sheer power of her inspirational presence is such a classic of the genre that it's become a cliché. This trope has been revisited again and again. You can find it in the 2007 Hilary Swank film *Freedom Writers*, the 1999 Meryl Streep film *Music of the Heart*, the absurd 1987 James Belushi drama *The Principal*, and at least as far back as the 1955 film *Blackboard Jungle*. My favorite version is a skit on the Fox Show *MadTV* called simply "Nice White Lady," featuring the slogan, "When it comes to teaching inner city minorities, you don't need books and you don't need rules. All you need is a nice white lady."[17] In a way, *Dangerous Minds* and these other films heralded the rise of Teach for America—the teacher as white savior.

If we want to change our world, we also need to change our popular culture. As Walidah Imarisha has written, "Whenever we try to envision a world without war, without violence, without prisons, without capitalism, we are engaging in an exercise of speculative fiction. Organizers and activists struggle tirelessly to create and envision another world, or many other worlds, just as science fiction does." With adrienne maree brown, Imarisha edited *Octavia's Brood*, a collection of science fiction stories written by social justice organizers, mostly people from marginalized communities. They were inspired by Octavia Butler, a Black woman who wrote science fiction that often visualized utopian worlds. And Imarisha coined the phrase *visionary fiction* to "distinguish science fiction that has relevance toward building new, freer worlds from the mainstream strain of science fiction, which most often reinforces dominant narratives of power. Visionary fiction encompasses all of the fantastic, with the arc always bending toward justice. We believe this space is vital for any process of decolonization, because the decolonization of the imagination is the most dangerous and subversive form there is: for it is where all other forms of decolonization are born. Once the imagination is unshackled, liberation is limitless."[18]

There will always be space for dystopian imaginings—some of my favorite fiction falls into that category. But our radical imagination also needs the inspiration of radical art. From this radical, transformative art, it's our job, in the words of Imarisha, to "do the hard work of sculpting reality from our dreams."[19]

Chapter Five
Nicholas Kristof Saves the World

Journalists like to say they are above political bias. Their quest for truth is intrinsically moral and politically neutral. But the field of journalism is as given to bias as any other profession. And journalists are not only shaped by the systems of oppression that shape the rest of our society, they then help to codify and give legitimacy to oppressive systems by accepting those oppressive framings. They shape the worldview that says we need saviors.

Our news media teaches us who is considered valuable by which deaths are reported and how they are reported. Thousands dead overseas are not given the same time and attention as one death at home. "This is the centerpiece of supremacy ideology," writes Sarah Schulman. "The idea that one person's life is more important than another's."[1]

The media shape our view of the world by influencing who is seen as an expert and by shaping where and when the story begins. Does a story of poverty in Haiti begin that morning, or does it begin with the Haitian Revolution and move through debt enforced by colonial nations and pass through dictators supported by the U.S. and others? Rebecca Solnit has written, "The writer's job is not to look through the window someone else built, but to step outside, to question the framework, or dismantle the house and free what's inside, all in service of making visible what was locked out of the view. It is a tendency of journalism to focus on what changed yesterday rather than ask what are the underlying forces and who are the unseen beneficiaries of this moment's status quo."[2]

Rolling Stone writer Matt Taibbi noted that even something as seemingly apolitical as sports coverage is open to the bias of the writer. "Open any newspaper from the Thirties or Forties, check the sports page; the guy who wrote up the box score, did he have a political point of view?" asks Taibbi. "He probably didn't think so. But viewed with 70 or 80 years of hindsight, covering a baseball game where blacks weren't allowed to play without mentioning the fact, that's apology and advocacy. Any journalist with half a brain knows that the biases of our time are always buried in our coverage."[3]

As recently as the 1960s, most U.S. newsrooms were 100 percent white. "As the civil rights movement became a major national story, and as dozens of American inner cities became the sites of urban riots, African-American journalists employed by the Black press finally found a door opening to mainstream media," writes the *Columbia Journalism Review*. "Some of them said they could name the specific riot that resulted in their hiring."[4] If you look at the staff of most daily newspapers today, located in cities that are often majority people of color, the sixties status quo remains unchanged. In New Orleans, where I live, the two major newspapers, the *Advocate* and *nola.com* (formerly the *Times-Picayune*), are still almost entirely white, despite serving a city that is 60 percent African American.

Addressing the *Times-Picayune*'s lack of coverage of police violence in the 1950s and 1960s, professor Leonard N. Moore wrote, "The *Times-Picayune* and its attitude of journalistic negligence . . . by its refusal to cover Black activism, protest and frustration . . . neglected to inform most whites about the frustration that ripped through Black New Orleans."[5]

In 1968 Lyndon B. Johnson's National Advisory Commission on Civil Disorders, the Kerner Commission, wrote that part of what caused the riots that shook the country was that "the media report and write from the standpoint of a white man's world. . . . Fewer than five percent of the people employed by the news business in editorial jobs in the United States today are Negroes." In 2014 the American Society of News Editors reported that the number of Black newsroom employees was 4.78 percent, essentially unchanged after nearly fifty years. Looking at the increased numbers of people of color graduating from journalism schools, the *Columbia Journalism Review* noted, "The number of minorities graduating from journalism programs and applying for jobs doesn't seem to be the problem. . . . The problem is that these candidates are not being hired."[6]

Race, gender, or class identities are of course not the only variables important for a good reporter. But when a community is not represented in the staff of a media outlet, it often means their stories are also left out. When the media had almost no out gay reporters on staff in the 1980s, they did a terrible job of covering the AIDS epidemic.

Former *New York Times* reporter Howard French described his experience of white reporters ignoring communities of color, adding that even when Black reporters are hired, they are still limited to only writing about their own community. "Those black people who make their way into the business are heavily concentrated in stereotypical roles," he writes. "This has meant sport, entertainment and especially what is euphemistically called urban affairs, often meaning reporting on black people. By contrast, there are very few black journalists writing about politics and national security, international news, big business, culture (as opposed to entertainment) or science and technology—they are essentially absent from large swaths of coverage, and even more sparsely represented among the ranks of editors."[7]

All this leads to a view of Black people (and other underrepresented communities) as objects or a curiosity to be reported on rather than as worthy of telling their own story, much less the story of others. French quotes former *Washington Post* reporter Jill Nelson as saying, "When it comes to

black folks, we exist mostly as potential sociological, patho-
logical, or scatological slices of life waiting to be chewed,
digested, and excreted into the requisite number of column
inches in the paper."[8]

French also described the blatant racism he experienced
from the "liberal" reporters of the *Times*. French described a
white senior editor at the paper, a former correspondent in Africa, who "tried to encourage me by saying that between the epi-
sodic hard news provided by the occasional conflict or coup, one
could amuse oneself there scribbling postcards about the exotic
and primitive, or what he called 'oogah-boogah.'" Thirty years
ago, when French started at the *Times*, it had no Black reporters
assigned to the presidential campaign. In 2016 it had one.[9]

In New Orleans, our local media mostly did not report
on the police violence in the days after Hurricane Katrina.
This was a widely known story in Black communities across
the city, but the reporters covering the city did not see it as
a story worth covering. In fact, one photographer with the
Times-Picayune was later found to have helped police cover
up a post-Katrina murder.[10] Even the city district attorney at
the time, Eddie Jordan, saw the local paper as too close to the
police. "They were looking for heroes," he told me later. "They
had a cozy relationship with the police. They got tips from the
police; they were in bed with the police. It was an atmosphere
of tolerance for atrocities from the police. They abdicated their
responsibility to be critical in their reporting. If a few people
got killed, that was a small price to pay."

Progressive funders who wished to support journalism
in New Orleans gave hundreds of thousands of dollars to *The
Lens*, a news website with an almost entirely white staff. Although the site depicted itself as upholding civic responsibility,
in practice it often attacked Black community leaders or elected officials. The Open Society Foundation, funded by George
Soros, gave $750,000. Why did progressive money flow to a
website whose editor used to work for a far-right wing think
tank (Louisiana's *Pelican Institute*)? Because of the myth that
journalism is always neutral and good.

Journalists often follow a cult of false objectivity. In this dogma, the principles of patriotism, nationalism, hetero-patriarchy, and white supremacy stand unchallenged—and that is seen as "serious," nonbiased reporting. But a reporter bringing a different set of values is condemned as an activist. Glenn Greenwald, in his work with Edward Snowden, is one of those accused of crossing the arbitrary line into activism. "It is not a matter of being an activist or a journalist; it's a false dichotomy," Greenwald said in response to the accusations. "It is a matter of being honest or dishonest. All activists are not journalists, but all real journalists are activists. Journalism has a value, a purpose—to serve as a check on power. . . . I have seen all sorts of so-called objective journalists who have all kinds of assumptions in every sentence they write. . . . Rather than serve as an adversary of government, they want to bolster the credibility of those in power. That is a classic case of a certain kind of activism."[11]

During the 2016 presidential campaign, media outlets effectively created the Donald Trump phenomenon by *giving* him the equivalent of nearly $2 billion in paid advertising. This was far more than the combined presidential advertising budgets of any other election ever, nearly three times the coverage given to Hillary Clinton, over five times the coverage given to Bernie Sanders, and nearly more than the combined total of free coverage for all candidates combined.[12]

Throughout this excessive media coverage, the press abdicated their basic responsibility to the truth. As data cruncher Nate Silver pointed out, "Trump has frequently invoked misogyny and racism; he has frequently lied, and he has repeatedly encouraged violence against political pro-testers. . . . These are matters of fact and not opinion and to describe them otherwise would make our reporting less ob-jective. Other news outlets will bend over backward to avoid describing them in those terms, however."[13] As an example, Silver pointed to a *New York Times* article that said "Over the years, Donald Trump has said things about women that *his critics* have called offensive" [emphasis added].

Journalists often like to imagine themselves as a check on the powerful, like Woodward and Bernstein, the *Washington Post* reporters who helped bring about the fall of President Nixon. But too often these self-described heroes are either members of the ruling class or servants to it, jockeying for the chance to attend the parties at which the wealthy dance and mingle. Sadly, this is the path both Woodward and Bernstein ended up taking in their post-Watergate careers. "I think of the mainstream media as having not so much a rightwing or leftwing bias but a status-quo bias," writes Rebecca Solnit. "A tendency to believe people in authority, to trust institutions and corporations and the rich and powerful and pretty much any self-satisfied white man in a suit, to let people who have been proven to tell lies tell more lies that get reported without questioning, to move forward on cultural assumptions that are readily disproven, and to devalue nearly all outsiders, whether they're discredited or mocked or just ignored."[14]

A better model for journalists to follow would be Ida B. Wells, who, beginning in the late nineteenth century, spread the word about the epidemic of lynching throughout the South. Wells was more than a journalist. She was an activist who personally felt the weight of the importance of the stories she was covering. In 1875, years before Homer Plessy or Rosa Parks committed similar acts, she was arrested for refusing to give up her seat on a white train car, an act of civil resistance as racist state and non-state forces were forcing an end to the racial progress of the Reconstruction era. She summed up her driving passion by saying, "One had better die fighting against injustice than die like a dog or a rat in a trap."

Judy Richardson, an activist with Student Nonviolent Coordinating Committee and later a producer of the *Eyes on The Prize* documentary series, was part of a team that documented racist violence in Mississippi from 1961 to 1964. In the 1980s she compiled a similar document on racist violence in New York City. "The purpose of both chronologies was the same," writes Richardson. "To clearly show that these incidents weren't happening because some *individual* police officer just hadn't had enough sensitivity training. It wasn't happening because a certain group of white folks was displaying errant behavior. No, it was about *systemic white supremacy.*" "I didn't learn this in someone's J-School," she adds. "I learned it in SNCC."[15]

Unfortunately, these journalism stories are rarely told, and there are few resources available for those today who would follow in the footsteps of Wells or Richardson. The media were mostly silent when Ramsey Orta, who filmed the 2014 murder of Eric Garner by the New York City police, was put in jail as retribution for his act.

While Ramsey Orta remains unknown, *New York Times* columnist Nicholas Kristof has built a reputation as a journalist-activist. In fact, he is neither. Or the worst of both worlds. If saviorism as journalism can be personified, it is Kristof. On nearly every major topic mentioned in this book—Teach for America, sex work, KONY 2012, Occupy, Black Lives Matter—he has come out on the wrong side.

Kristof never met a savior he didn't like. "My protagonist will be some American," he says. "Who's off in the middle of nowhere. The reason is that it's an awful lot easier to get readers to read about a New Yorker who is off in Haiti than a Haitian who's doing good work in Haiti."[16] While it's an effective journalistic technique to give your readers a protagonist they can relate to, Kristof has a long track record of cheering "heroes" who eventually fall from grace as their full stories come out. Kristof rebuffed my attempts to interview him for this book and give him a chance to respond directly to these complaints, but in his writing and public speaking he seems to respond to charges against him by doubling down on his original errors.

Kristof was an early acolyte of Greg Mortenson, the mountain climber who claimed to be building girls' schools in Afghanistan and Pakistan. Kristof wrote in 2008 that "a lone Montanan staying at the cheapest guest houses has done more to advance U.S. interests in the region than the entire military and foreign policy apparatus of the Bush administration." Investigative journalist Jon Krakauer later showed Mortenson to have been a serial liar.[17] Kristof doubled down in his defense of Mortenson, writing, "As we sift the truth of these allegations, let's not allow this uproar to obscure that larger message of the possibility of change."[18]

Kristof had a similar defense of KONY 2012 after the backlash to that project. "There's no doubt that it is kind of cool for young Americans to worry about problems halfway around the world and sometimes to worry more about problems in Malawi than in Newark," he told NPR. "On the other hand, I think it is really commendable that a lot of young Americans find that their empathy doesn't stop at the border, and I don't think they should apologize for the fact that they have compassion for families who are being killed and raped and mutilated in the Central African Republic."[19] He also declared, "If I were a Congolese villager, I would welcome these uncertain efforts over the sneering scorn of do-nothing armchair cynics."[20]

"For the most part, critics of the campaign were not 'armchair' anything," responded Kate Crawford and Amanda Taub, in the *Atlantic*. "Rather, they were Ugandans, aid workers, journalists, survivors of LRA [Lord's Resistance Army] atrocities, and researchers who had lived in the region and are experts on the LRA."

> Dismissing these critics' concerns as "sneering scorn" reveals a belief that only certain opinions are worth listening to. . . . Kristof and his pals seem to believe that expertise come[s] not from knowledge or practical experience, of which the critics have plenty, but from emotional engagement and personal risk-taking. . . . It seems that the difference between an armchair critic and a person of moral authority is that the latter possesses a personal narrative that includes an eye-opening discovery of suffering in distant lands, followed by the decision to forgo the comforts of the developed world and risk life and limb to help. If that story sounds familiar, it's because we've been hearing it, in one form or

another, since Rudyard Kipling wrote his 1899 poem urging readers to "take up the White Man's Burden."[21]

Empathy should not stop at the border—on this I agree with Kristof. But who are his protagonists? Is he really building empathy for the people of Malawi and the Central African Republic, or is he encouraging more brave Americans to rush in to save them, like liberal Rambos, armed with charitable gifts instead of guns? Kristof's lionization of heroes keeps his audience from seeing how change actually happens: as a collective effort that they can be part of but do not need to lead.

In 2011 Kristof joined a police raid in Cambodia aimed at "rescuing" sex trafficking victims. While even Kristof admits that at least one of the women he "rescued" made a decision to go back to sex work, he sees that as her own failure, not his. The rescue of sex trafficking victims became a major focus for Kristof, turned into a book, movie, and organization, all branded *Half the Sky*. Another of the heroes he championed is Somaly Mam and her acolyte Long Pross, two Cambodian women who claimed to be sex trafficking survivors. Mam ran an NGO dedicated to rescuing girls and women from trafficking and became an international celebrity, at least partly because of Kristof's endorsement.

When a reporter found inconsistencies and fabrications in the life stories of Mam and Pross, Kristof was again unapologetic. "Let's remember that this is about more than one woman." He's right—it is about more than one woman. So, putting aside the truth or lies of her narrative, what about her life's work? Do anti-trafficking non-profits work to help those forced into the sex trade?

As far back as 2010, Human Rights Watch issued a deeply critical report on police harassment of sex workers under the guise of fighting trafficking. The report found that Cambodia's 2008 anti-trafficking law was in fact being used to "criminalize advocacy and outreach activities by sex worker groups and those who support them."[22] (The 2008 law, by the way, was sponsored by the U.S. Agency for International Development—USAID).[23]

Journalist Anne Elizabeth Moore, writing in *Salon*, said the problem was that the day-to-day work that Mam was praised for was more about pushing women into the "right" kind of exploitative jobs. "I spent seven years researching and doing work in Cambodia, made concerted efforts to learn the language, developed a strong stomach and reliable sources, and honed my skills in investigative reporting before I could even understand what, really, anti-human trafficking NGOs do," she wrote. "What they do is normalize existent labor opportunities for women, however low the pay, dangerous the conditions, or abusive an environment they may be. And they shame women who reject such jobs."[24]

Moore says that anti–trafficking NGO's that focus on the sex trade are a particularly attractive cause for corporate backers. "Garment workers know an entire international trade system relies on their willing participation, which was how they built such a strong showing in the last elections," she writes. "The big brands know it too, which is why the Nike Foundation funds Half the Sky—as do other multinationals that both enforce, and rely on, women's desperate poverty around the world."[25]

The work of these rescuers is to funnel women sex workers into a different form of exploitation. "What anti-trafficking NGOs are saving women from, in other words, is a life outside the international garment trade, which, according to folks who sell us our clothes, is no kind of life at all," she writes. Somaly Mam is "saving girls" by "installing them firmly within a system of entrenched, gender-based poverty. This matters to all of us who would like to see that system's demise."[26]

Elena Shih investigated former sex workers in Thailand and China working with jewelry makers who themselves work for nonprofits that publicize them as being rescued. She found that the women were horrified to learn that people in the United States were being told that they had been forced into sex work. Elizabeth Bernstein writes that Shih found "adult women who had previously chosen sex work as their highest paying option, but who, after accumulating some savings, (elected) to engage in evangelical Christian 'prayer work' and jewelry-making instead."[27]

Here too many women found this "rescue" to be worse than the lives they had left. Bernstein writes, "After signing on to the jewelry-making projects, they soon discover that their lives will henceforth be micromanaged by their missionary employers, that they will no longer be free to visit family and friends in the red-light districts, and that their pay will be docked for missing daily prayer sessions, for being minutes late to work, or for minor behavioral infractions."[28]

Shih found that the women were proud of the decisions they had made, both to enter sex work and eventually to leave. "The mere suggestion that they are victims of gender discrimination, or duped because of limited education, makes them feel betrayed by their employers," she writes. "Similarly in Thailand, the alleged 'victims' consumers are instructed to pity, are boastful that sex work helped them put children through university and paid for aging parents medical bills."[29]

Journalists like Kristof do more than enable the lies of Somaly Mam and supply more low-wage workers to the garment industry. NGOs know that donors and journalists want a certain kind of hero and a certain kind of victim, and they shape their narratives to deliver to people like Kristof the protagonists they want. Without Kristof, there would be no Mam. "Donors were getting an interest, and were sending their people with crews of journalists to take pictures," said Pierre Fallavier, an advisor to Mam's organization. "I used to tell Somaly to send them away, that all they wanted were exotic stories of violence and sex with the picture of a beautiful hero saving children so they could sell their papers. But they came with the funders."[30]

Mam's ex-husband agreed. "She used the system, and she has been used by the system," he told a reporter. "I've worked with a lot of organizations, and you confronted the same issue when you wanted money. If you have no story, you don't have money."[31]

In all of his focus on international trafficking, Kristof missed the bigger and more interesting story: the global movement of sex workers organizing themselves. He could have started with the Asia Pacific Network of Sex Workers (APNSW), which made a music video, "Bad Rehab" (set to the tune of Lady Gaga's "Bad Romance" and starring Barbie dolls), that critiqued Somaly Mam's much praised rehab. Or Kristof could have spoken with the Women's Network for Unity, an organization of sixty-five hundred sex workers in Cambodia. In India he could have profiled the Durbar Mahila Samanwaya Committee, an organization of men, women, and transgender sex workers in West Bengal that has sixty-five thousand members. Or the seven thousand members of the Kenya Sex Workers Alliance. Empower, in Thailand, works with twenty thousand sex workers—including two hundred workers who collaborated on one study, which concluded, "There are more women in the Thai sex industry being abused by anti-trafficking practices than there are women exploited by traffickers."[32]

In 2014 Kristof decided to scold activists from the Black Lives Matter movement that they had picked the wrong murder victim to complain about. In a tweet, Kristof advised activists they should have ignored the death of Mike Brown and focused on the police killing of twelve-year-old Tamir Rice in Cleveland. Melissa Harris Perry offered a passionate response on her MSNBC show. "Unlike you, Nick—these activists were not searching for perfect martyrs to tell a neat story," she said. "They were responding to the realities of loss and experiences of injustice as they happened. These activists—who you felt the authority to counsel on Friday afternoon—didn't wait for Rice because they were dodging tear gas in Ferguson and stopping traffic in New York and disrupting shopping in Minnesota because they did not want another unarmed man, woman, or child to be killed."[33]

Kristof's criticism of Black Lives Matter shows the many levels on which he does not understand how change works. He doesn't understand the decentralized nature of Black Lives Matter (that activists can focus many on places). He also doesn't understand the central idea behind Black Lives Matter. He can't see that the movement by definition must demand justice for Mike Brown in addition to Tamir Rice and all the other lives cut short by racism. Choosing the "perfect victim," as Kristof chooses his perfect saviors, is exactly the opposite of the movement's underlying principles.

Kristof's critique of the Ferguson protesters was not the end of his lecturing to Black communities about what they should do. Just a few months later he decided throw his support behind the old conservative complaint about the "breakdown of the African-American family." Kristof wrote a column defending Daniel Patrick Moynihan's legendary 1965 report (*The Negro Family: The Case for National Action*). He then went further, supporting former vice president Dan Quayle's much-mocked 1992 attack on cultural depictions of single mothers (including television's fictional single mom *Murphy Brown*). Kristof approvingly quoted Moynihan's report, "A father's absence increases antisocial behavior, such as aggression, rule-breaking, delinquency and illegal drug use."[34] This report laid the foundations for the racist attacks on the Black community that still exist today. It places the blame on individuals and ignores the systemic racism that destroys both individuals and communities.

As usual with Kristof, he refuses to see the systemic issues at play. He doesn't see housing discrimination, underfunded schools, redlining, or police violence. Kristof "does not connect the dots or see the patterns of power behind the isolated 'disasters,'" writes Teju Cole. "All he sees are hungry mouths, and he, in his own advocacy-by-journalism way, is putting food in those mouths as fast as he can. All he sees is need, and he sees no need to reason out the need for the need." Cole adds, "There is much more to doing good work than 'making a difference.' There is the principle of first do no harm. There is the idea that those who are being helped ought to be consulted over the matters that concern them."[35]

Kristof responded to his critics, saying he's "become more sympathetic to Band-Aids over the years." Kristof does not believe in fighting for systemic change. He is impatient. The need is too desperate to wait. If he's being honest, he might admit that a straight white male *New York Times* columnist may not want systemic change. If anyone has something to lose in a fairer society, it's him.

A book could be written on the harmful adventurism of Nicholas Kristof. Anthropologist Laura Agustín calls him attention-seeking and disingenuous. Writer Sayantani DasGupta calls him a tool of racism and neoliberalism. The blog *Africa Is a Country* calls him the "white savior extraordinaire," and scholar Laura Seay has critiqued his writing, research methods, goals, and nearly every other aspect of his work. But his popularity among elites is just one symptom of a greater problem. Much of our media reflect and re-create the savior. If we want to build a different world, we need new media, media not afraid to challenge the powerful, and we need to promote and support voices reporting on their own communities.

Chapter Six
Is Teach for America Saving Our Children?

Sophie Lucido Johnson was an English major in her senior year at Whitman College in Washington State who had little interest in teaching when she was contacted by a Teach for America (TFA) recruiter in 2008. The recruiter sat with Johnson in a one-on-one conversation and stroked Johnson's ego, telling her very seriously, "These kids need you."[1]

"We especially want to place teachers here," said the recruiter, pointing to New Orleans on a map. "I know the storm was horrible for a lot of people, and I would never say it was *good*, but in some ways, it was the best thing that could have happened to New Orleans, because the education system there was completely broken before the storm hit. Now, America is really *looking* at New Orleans. We have the opportunity to rebuild this system *the right way*, from the ground up."[2]

This language was not an anomaly. A few months after Hurricane Katrina devastated the city, neoliberal economist Milton Friedman wrote, "This is a tragedy. It is also an opportunity."[3] Education secretary Arne Duncan later told a reporter that Katrina was, "The best thing that happened to the education system in New Orleans." Paul Vallas, superintendent of the Recovery School District in Louisiana and Paul Pastorek, Louisiana superintendent of education, both agreed with Duncan.[4]

This was the view of many people who had not suffered through this disaster but instead came later to profit from it. It was a "blank slate," a status that saviors love for the power and control it brings them. The storm offered an opportunity to remake the school system without any need for messy democratic oversight that might slow them down or raise too many questions. The views of parents, students, and teachers had become silenced, and the saviors and "reformers" could now experiment without having to be accountable to those their schemes would affect.

Johnson didn't know any of this as she was sent to a short training session in Phoenix and then dropped into New Orleans, one of hundreds of young white idealistic recruits who had little knowledge or background and insufficient training to deal with the situation they had been placed into. She found herself pitted against veteran teachers that she would rather have had as mentors.

Johnson didn't know it at the time, but she was following a well-worn path of activism, idealism, and revolutionary fervor redirected into voluntarism. Today Teach for America has become perhaps the most well known project for funneling youthful energy away from systemic change, but it follows a model of national service made popular by programs like the Peace Corps and Americorps.

President Kennedy started the Peace Corps in 1961, and President Johnson followed it up with VISTA (Volunteers in Service to America) in 1964. VISTA was the first federally sponsored national volunteer program, and it recruited mostly white, college-educated young people to provide social services in southern Black communities. Simultaneously, the Student Nonviolent Coordinating Committee (SNCC) was recruiting a demographically similar volunteer population through their Freedom Summer program. One key difference between VISTA and SNCC was that the white and privileged volunteers of SNCC were under the direction of local Black leaders, a situation almost unheard of at that time (and still rare today). Without the radical leadership of SNCC, VISTA activists had little analysis to help them see the structural causes behind the issues they were working to solve. Many of them were inclined to prejudices about the communities they were supposed to be helping. "While they never quite blamed the poor for their plight, they did locate the causes of poverty within a cluster of social and psychological inadequacies," according to one study of the volunteers. "The poor, it seemed, 'believed in nothing and [had] little faith in their own capacities.' Such views provided both emotional distance from hardship and assurance that the Volunteers could 'fix' the people they encountered. 'All we had to do was clean up this one generation,' a former Volunteer recalled many years later, 'educate these people and lift them up, and it would be over with. We really believed that.'"[5]

Despite the lack of critical analysis, the 1960s and 1970s student volunteers in VISTA often rebelled against their directives. "Nationally, VISTA volunteers in the 1960s and 70s came into conflict with local political leaders in communities where they worked. Some recruits openly questioned Jim Crow laws, and some allied with civil rights resistance," writes researcher Emily Danielson. "In response, President Nixon placed restrictions on all VISTA participants, confining their activities to politically neutral service provision. As a result of the new regulations, increasing numbers of VISTA volunteers grew so frustrated with the restrictions on their work that they chose not to complete their service year."[6]

In the following decades, a lack of systemic analysis was locked into the architecture of VISTA, which under the Bill Clinton presidency was combined with a newer program called AmeriCorps. In 1996 the general counsel for the Corporation for National and Community Service, the agency that oversees AmeriCorps, wrote: "National service has to be nonpartisan. What's more, it should be about bringing communities together by getting things done. Strikes, demonstrations, and political activities can have the opposite effect. They polarize and divide."

As AmeriCorps evolved, it took on more of the social safety net roles that should be performed by government, playing a role in helping cut government responsibility for the poor. In New Orleans after Hurricane Katrina, the organization funded a lot of young white people from out of town to come and take jobs in the recovery, while Black New Orleanians were still being kept out.

AmeriCorps and VISTA helped inspire Teach for America, which has also diverted students away from more radical and accountable opportunities to pursue change. Born in 1989 as the senior project of Princeton undergraduate student Wendy Kopp, the first corps went out in 1990, as President Bush's "thousand points of light" was in vogue.

Initially TFA focused on school districts that had teacher shortages. Gary Rubinstein, one of those first recruits, was assigned to Houston, Texas. "At the time, there were massive teacher shortages in high need areas," he says. "We knew that we weren't going to be great teachers. It was unrealistic to believe otherwise. But we also knew that the jobs we were taking were jobs that nobody else wanted." Principals were desperate, says Rubinstein. "If not for us, our students, most likely, would be taught by a different substitute each day. . . . The motto for TFA back then could have been 'Hey, we're better than nothing.'"[7]

Teaching children is one of society's most important jobs, and good teachers deserve praise and support. For this reason, despite their best intentions and the good work many of its teachers do, Teach for America represents an unhealthy trend in education reform. It focuses on pitting "bad teachers" versus "good teachers" while ignoring systemic inequality and other forces. It also treats teachers as cogs that can be easily replaced. It undermines the importance of training and dismisses the idea that it matters if they are from the culture or community of their students. TFA corps generally earn the same salaries as entry-level teachers—a savings over the pay of veteran teachers and also a good way to undercut teachers' unions.

Over the years, TFA began shifting from districts with teacher shortages to expand into as many cities as possible. This shift conveniently lent cover to a rise in demonization of teachers and their unions. *No Child Left Behind*, signed by

President Bush in 2002, required more standardized tests, and tied teacher evaluations to the tests.

After the 2008 economic crash, TFA increased its ranks as teachers were being fired across the United States. In 2009, Reverend Al Sharpton and Newt Gingrich took a nationwide tour together to support (mostly non-union) charter schools and other parts of the neoliberal education agenda. The strategy of blaming teachers reached a new height in 2010, as *Newsweek* ran a cover story titled "Why We Must Fire Bad Teachers." That same year, the film *Waiting for Superman* made a similar argument. TFA became the hero of these stories—inexpensive teachers with no unions or contracts, undermining the idea that training or experience matters in creating good teachers. From 2008 to 2013, 324,000 teachers' jobs in local school districts were eliminated, and TFA corps filled many of those formerly unionized jobs. They sent hundreds of corps members into Chicago, Philadelphia, and Detroit after mass teacher layoffs in those cities. In Seattle in 2011, TFA corps members took jobs in a city where 13,800 experienced teachers had applied for just 352 full- and part-time positions.[8]

This coincided with attacks from politicians like Governors Scott Walker in Wisconsin, Chris Christie in New Jersey, and Andrew Cuomo in New York, as both Republicans and Democrats took aim at teacher salaries, tenure, vacations, benefits, and unions. Right wing media dismissed the extra time that teachers took to prepare for class and described the workday of a teacher as short and easy. This climate gave Governor Walker cover for his plan to dismantle public sector unions in Wisconsin.

TFA administrators remain remarkably silent on the deeper issues affecting our education system. They are silent about the school-to-prison pipeline—in fact, they often work with charter schools that encourage a "zero tolerance" discipline policy that feeds into it. They are silent about unequal funding for schools with mostly minority populations—in fact, by focusing on teachers, they steer the conversation away from funding. They are silent about the fact that many school districts are as segregated now as they were at the time of *Brown v. Board of Education*.

TFA tells us we don't need to address poverty, homelessness, gentrification, or criminalization. Just give kids a teacher from an Ivy League school, taking a break for two years before working at a hedge fund, and they'll be fine. And if they don't succeed, it's probably the kids' own fault. Or the fault of their parents.

Less than 1 percent of U.S. teachers are part of the current Teach For America corps.[9] But the organization has an outsized influence on our education system. TFA describes itself as a "movement" and announces that it will "help our nation deliver on the promise of equal opportunity for all kids." Columnist Nicholas Kristof is a fan, of course. He calls TFA "the most thrilling program for young people" today and says of CEO and co-founder Wendy Kopp, "It would be hard to find a secretary of education who influenced education more."[10]

There's a lot of money at stake in education, especially as charter schools open the doors to privatization. TFA itself is a financial force to be reckoned with, holding net assets in 2014 of $419 million and annual revenues topping $300 million, including a $50 million innovation grant awarded by the Obama administration. Kopp herself earns at least $400,000 a year. The organization spends nearly $1 million a year on lobbying and about $3.5 million on advertising and promotion.[11] Google, PricewaterhouseCoopers, Ernst and Young, General Electric, Bain & Company, JPMorgan Chase, and McKinsey & Company are among TFA's top employer deferrals (meaning they will hire a recent college graduate and allow them to defer their start date until after they finish two years with TFA). Deloitte, Pearson, Target, Morningstar, Parthenon Group, and Capital Group are among TFA's top recruiters of alumni.[12] The organization has also expanded internationally, through the Teach for All network, which has implemented versions of TFA in forty countries.[13]

In response to complaints that many TFA recruits did not stay in teaching long enough to learn the skills to do their job well, Kopp is nonplussed. "We spend some time around here asking ourselves if enough of our people are leaving [teaching]. Are enough of them going into policy . . . are enough of them going into business?"[14]

Sarah Matsui's interviews with TFA corps members in Philadelphia, *Learning from Counternarratives in Teach for America*, reported that participants were recruited with the message that they do not need to stay in teaching. One interviewee named Elliott told her, "Main message from TFA: We don't give a crap about how good of a job you are doing in your classroom. Fulfill your commitment, don't make too much noise, and do big things after two years."[15]

As TFA moved into cities where they were displacing teachers rather than filling empty slots, the organization was also rebranding. "We're a leadership development organization, not a teaching organization," Kopp said in one interview.[16] As of 2014, more than seventy TFA alumni were in public office, and the organization had initiated a $750,000 fellowship to train alumni for posts as state cabinet secretaries or school superintendents. Among the most notable alumni was Michelle Rhee, who took over the Washington, D.C., school system in 2007 and quickly closed twenty-three schools, fired thirty-four principals, offered buyouts to seven hundred teachers (while pressuring hundreds more to leave), and fired ninety-eight employees from the school district's central office. The next mayoral election became a referendum on her "reforms," and, despite support from the *Washington Post* and much of the city's elites, the mayor who appointed her, Adrian Fenty, was solidly defeated.

The rise of TFA coincided with the rise of charter schools, publicly funded schools that are not controlled by local school boards. In 1991, a year after the first TFA corps went into schools, Minnesota became the first state to pass a law opening up their public school systems to charters. California authorized charter schools the next year, and soon the majority of states had passed similar laws. In the ideal cases, parents and community members controlled these new charters. But charter laws also opened the door to privatization of the public school system.

The idea of charter schools was first proposed by neoliberal economist Milton Friedman in 1955.[17] It was no coincidence that this was one year after *Brown v. Board of Education* called for an end to official segregation in public schools, and white parents began to pull their kids out of the integrated systems and enroll them in private schools. But Friedman's vision of the state subsidizing private corporations' profit in education did not come true for nearly forty years. Even today, while it's estimated that privatization of the education system could mean a $1 trillion corporate profit gold rush, education activists have succeeded in passing laws in half a dozen states banning for-profits from running schools.[18] Nationally about 13 percent of charters are run by for-profit corporations.[19]

Neoliberal reformers took the opportunity of Hurricane Katrina to push through education policies, like charters, that did not have popular support. The local school board went from controlling 124 out of 128 schools to overseeing five, as the rest were taken over by the state to be turned over to charter operators. In this new system, nearly seventy-five hundred teachers and other school system employees found themselves not only without homes but also without jobs. Teachers who wished to come back to their old jobs had to reapply. And even when rehired they lost the job protection that had formerly come with their seniority and union contract.

TFA, which had been a presence in the city since 1990, rushed to fill in the gap, making New Orleans one of their main sites, sending about four hundred new teachers per year to fill the jobs of displaced teachers. Only four other cities in the United States—like New York City, with more than twenty times more students—receive more TFA recruits. At the same time, other programs, like Teach NOLA, followed the TFA model of recruiting from out of state. Thousands of young, idealistic, and mostly white recent college graduates flooded into New Orleans to teach at the city's public schools.

Students were traumatized. They had seen their city underwater and abandoned by the government, their homes and possessions lost, their neighborhoods demolished, and their health-care system taken apart, and they were living under the rule of arguably the most violent and corrupt police force in the United States.[20] Now they were being taught by young, privileged white people from out of town, who were also quickly gentrifying the students' former neighborhoods. What could go wrong?

While charter advocates claimed to have improved the city's broken education system, parents and teachers replied that the newer, more complicated system may have offered improved schools for some kids but has made conditions worse for the kids who have the least resources. They say charters are less likely to be able to accommodate special needs kids (despite a state law that says they must) and that "zero tolerance" charters have led to more student expulsions and even arrests for minor offenses.

In New Orleans alone, at least thirty-two TFA alumni have gone on to lead schools and many more are designing curricula, driving city and state policy, and working in advocacy. Among those alumni are John White, the head of the Recovery School District, and Kira Orange Jones, a twice-elected member of the state school board who won her elections with an influx of nearly half a million dollars from out of state. That money included donations from billionaires like Eli Broad of education reform institution the Broad Foundation, Reed Hastings of Netflix, Houston energy hedge fund profiteer John Arnold, Wal-Mart heiress Carrie Walton Penner, and New York City's billionaire former mayor Michael Bloomberg.[21]

New Orleans's pre-Katrina population was about 67 percent African American, but its public school system was over 90 percent African American (and just 3 percent white). Most white students in the system were (and still are) clustered at a handful of schools, and other ethnicities only make up small portions of the system, so the majority of schools remain almost entirely Black. Before Hurricane Katrina, the majority of teachers were Black women, mostly from New Orleans and often living in the neighborhood of the schools they worked in. Overall 72 percent of teachers in the city were African American, compared to an average of just 15 percent in large cities in the rest of the country.[22] Of that pre-Katrina workforce, 37 percent had twenty or more years in the classroom.

Before the storm, new hires coming to New Orleans had a large pool of veteran teachers, based in their communities, to mentor them. The early TFA corps, of which only 5 percent were African American, were trained by these veteran teachers. Now only 15 percent of New Orleans teachers have twenty years experience or more.[23]

Identity is not the only meaningful factor in a teacher, of course, but it is important. "White teachers aren't required to have any analysis of systems of white supremacy or anti-Blackness, *and their own complicity in both*, before they enter classrooms to teach Black children, some of whom will be introduced to those realities *by the behavior of these white teachers*," writes Mia McKenzie (emphasis in original). "Having done little or none of the necessary work required to examine their complicity, what gives these teachers the right to teach our children? How have they earned the privilege of being such an influential figure in a Black child's life? Why do we grant them access to the minds of our vulnerable youth, who will already have to face so much racism in the world?"[24]

In the years after Katrina, nearly 70 percent of new teachers hired were white. By 2014, the percentage of Black teachers had dropped by 30 percent.[25] In New Orleans, this dynamic of white teachers and principals overseeing a Black student body is one of many racial shifts that left Black residents feeling unwelcome. In the brief training they were given before taking responsibility for educating New Orleans's next generation, TFA corps members like Sophie Johnson were told they were heroes and would be rescuing children in crisis. But in the context of post-Katrina Black displacement, they were more likely to be seen as invaders than greeted as liberators.

As thousands of experienced teachers tried to get their jobs back, TFA recruits were being used as scabs to break a union rather than as volunteers helping in a shortage. The case of the fired teachers worked its way through the Louisiana court system for years. Teachers won a massive judgment at trial that was affirmed in a state court of appeals but reversed by the state supreme court. Even if the teachers had won, the school district (as with the city) had already become a very different place from the one the teachers had been dismissed from. And many of the teachers, displaced by Katrina and then fired, were never able to return to their homes.

Amid these changes made without the consent of anyone affected, high school students were among the loudest voices of dissent. Their protests began in spring 2006, soon after the school system had opened back up.

Students at John McDonogh High School staged demonstrations and press conferences, protesting that their school had more security guards on staff than teachers. They formed a group called Fyre Youth Squad and even took their complaints to the state school board in Baton Rouge. The tensions in the school system continued as more students returned to the city, and the tension broke into mass protest again in October 2012, when students at Walter L. Cohen High School marched out in protest of the firing of veteran teachers and the announced shutting down of the school. Among their demands: "In the future, if a faculty member is to be dismissed, written documentation and a plan must be created and followed."

Jonshell Johnson was a student at Sarah T. Reed High School at the time. She helped organize protests at Cohen as well as at her own school, through a youth-led activist group called United Students of New Orleans. "Most teachers that were being fired, we had built strong relationships with, they knew our parents," she says. "We asked them what's wrong. They said they were being pushed out. We said, 'if they're hurting you, they're hurting us.'"

Jonshell, then just fourteen years old, says the students called the veteran teachers "dinosaurs," a term of affection. "A dinosaur would be more active about my life. She can directly see to my face and understand me in that moment."

Jonshell says that many students looked to teachers for help and guidance. "There is a lot of distrust of social workers, so many students turn to teachers," she says. But when students went to the new teachers for help, they seemed unresponsive. "It's more like they're reading from a rulebook. They would send you somewhere if you came to them with problems."

Jonshell remembers one particular "dinosaur" as being "really interactive and passionate. We never stayed doing the same thing for more than three days." But this teacher was replaced with a twenty-four-year-old who students found difficult to relate to. "Students couldn't understand her vernacular," says Jonshell. "She talked like she was still in college."

Jonshell also found that the new, younger teachers seemed to be overly caught up in the partying culture of New Orleans, taking extra days off during Mardi Gras season and other festive holidays. "Younger teachers tend to not have a sense of urgency," says Jonshell. "When a teacher misses three or four days a week, what example does that make?"

The students at Cohen won some victories, including a delay in the scheduled closing of the school. But tensions were rising in other parts of the city as well. In November 2013, dozens of students at Clark High School, where the principal was a white former Teach for America recruit, protested after a Black veteran teacher was fired. Among their demands were for teachers they could relate to and respect for the school's "Black history."

Days later, over one hundred students walked out of two other schools, George Washington Carver Collegiate Academy and George Washington Carver Preparatory Academy. (A charter operator named Collegiate Academy runs both schools, along with another called Sci Academy.) The Carver students also released a statement on the issues that caused them to walk out. "The teachers don't connect with us or where we come from," wrote the students. "There are no Black teachers. The only Black role models we have at the school are janitors, cafeteria workers, secretaries, security guards, and coaches. Some of the teachers are racially insensitive. None of the teachers are from New Orleans. They can't relate to us, our neighborhoods, or our community. They have no respect for our customs and culture, and simply want to make us more like them without understanding us and our background."

I spoke to "Sara," a twenty-four-year-old white school-teacher who requested anonymity because of a confidentiality agreement she had signed with a charter operator named KIPP that runs eleven schools in the city. Sara was recruited from New York by Teach NOLA, a local organization modeled on TFA. At KIPP, she was part of an overwhelmingly white group of teachers: over 90 percent white, by her estimate.

Sara told me she regretted who she was just a year before, when she was a fresh graduate and believed the hype that she was going to make a difference. Her disillusionment came quickly, as from the beginning of her time at KIPP she was disturbed by the atmosphere at the school. As part of her new teacher training, she and other teachers were told to role-play as students acting out. "There was this whole room of young white people pretending to be young Black children cursing each other out," Sara says. The performance made her un-comfortable. When the school year started, it got worse. The school has some of the harshest rules in the city, including no speaking allowed during lunchtime and mandatory security guards escorts for students going to the bathroom. Discipline policies like those found at KIPP and Collegiate form what Brittney Cooper calls "the unholy marriage of carcerality with education."[26] Zero-tolerance schools and zero-tolerance po-licing policies combine in school systems with rules that the rich—including education reform funders like Bill Gates—would never put their kids through.

For Sara, placing white people in the role of disciplinar-ians to Black children made her feel like an "overseer" rather than a teacher. "It felt like I was in a bad cartoon," she says. "Everyone is smiling all the time, but the things we're doing are extremely torturous or offensive."

Rebecca Radding, another young white teacher recruited by TFA, says that when she taught at a KIPP school, she was told that her pre-kindergarten students didn't "deserve" the amount of recess time recommended under state law. "I was told that if they were better resourced and had families that supported them at home then they could play. But that they don't have time to play at school because this is their only time to be exposed to teachers like me."

Jonshell Johnson's brother was a student at Carver, and she gives me the view from the other side of the dynamic described by these teachers. Jonshell says the school's strict discipline was depressing and dehumanizing. "It was 'lonely,' that was his word," she says. "He said they were treated like property, not people."

Kenyatta Collins, another New Orleans student, described a link between the way students were treated in New Orleans charter schools and the Indian boarding schools of the nineteenth century:

> Most of the administrators working in the schools I have attended are white and not from Louisiana. This makes me think back to the beginning of the United States, when the Native Americans were being 'Americanized' by white Europeans. The white people made the Native Americans convert to their religion, stop speaking their native language, stop wearing their traditional clothing, and change their names to "American" and "Christian" ones. They even had to start wearing their hair like the white people wore theirs. I see a similar process happening in schools with all of these stringent rules, which leads me to the question: Are we being trained for the professional world or for the white world?[27]

On April 15, 2014, lawyers filed a complaint on behalf of parents and students at the Collegiate schools. Among the fifteen grievances listed were suspensions for trivial reasons (68.85 percent of students at Carver Collegiate were suspended over the course of one year, and suspended students were often sent home without their parents being informed), bullying and harassment of children with special needs by teachers and administrators, male teachers walking in on female students in the bathrooms, school administrators withholding meals from students as punishment, and intimidation and retaliation against students who have spoken up about these abuses—including those who led the protests.

Across the United States, TFA recruits have been placed in situations they are unequipped to handle. Sarah Matsui's research documents near-epidemic levels of alcoholism, mental health issues, and panic attacks among TFA corps members she interviewed. "A lot of people came into this thinking they were going to be a great white knight on a shining horse," one TFA teacher told her. "Those were the first people to get their asses kicked. In fairness to them, they had spent their lives achieving at a certain level, and they thought this was going to be the same thing. . . . I don't think TFA really prepares its cohorts for that. At TFA, it's all sunshine and rainbows."

Sophie Johnson was one of those lost souls. But change came through her friends Hannah Sadtler and Derek Roguski, TFA corps from her year who had similar stories of disappointment after a recruitment that fed into their idealism and desire to create change. At Sadtler's first placement there were only four veteran teachers. The rest were new arrivals, and almost all were white. Now looking back at her first months as a teacher, she feels shame at who she was and what she did. She thinks that what appeared to be altruism now feels self-centered. "I knew so little about my students' communities or culture," she says. "The way I was being taught to teach had really nothing to do with actually getting to know people or seeing children as individuals or taking time to connect with their families. It was all about what I was saying, and not at all about listening."

Sadtler and Roguski began speaking to former teachers, mostly Black women, and found they were learning much more about teaching from these veteran teachers and community members than they did from their TFA training. Katrena

Ndang was one of the veteran teachers displaced and fired after the storm, after seventeen years in the school system. Like most of her coworkers, she found out through watching the news, while evacuated after Hurricane Katrina, that she'd been fired. "Even though we had given them forwarding addresses, they never sent us notice," she says. Ndang was unable to find a job in the new system, which she says was hostile to the veteran teachers. The pre-Katrina system was plagued with problems, and many reformers saw veteran teachers as part of the problem. "Many of the new school leaders came in with the attitude that they were coming in to change the culture," she says. "So [in their eyes] whatever was there before, including the old teachers, you don't want it to be there."

Ndang helped start a project, supported by the teachers' union, called the Racial Healing Circle. This regular, informal gathering has brought together veteran teachers—mostly African American—with new ones. "The new teachers were able to come and tell us that 'things are not working, we don't have anyone in our schools [to whom] we can go to for advice,'" says Ndang. "Some of the veteran teachers started mentoring new teachers. Many of the teachers were angry, but there were those who were willing to help. And they would say, 'In exchange for our help, get the word out. Let people around the country know about what is not working here.'"

Sadtler and Roguski were among the new teachers that benefited from participation in the Healing Circle. Through teachers and civil rights movement veterans, Sadtler and Roguski also learned about a method of organizing in New Orleans called *story circles*. Started by activists with the Free Southern Theater, the theater arm of the civil rights movement, story circles are a method of finding common ground and building trust by sharing stories. Through this process, and through reaching out to their fellow teachers and engaging them in conversation, Sadtler and Roguski, along with Rebecca Radding and others, built an organization called the New Teachers' Roundtable. In addition to story circles, the Roundtable has social functions and reading groups, and they have spent time individually to train other teachers to have the same conversations they have had, reaching out to new recruits and challenging the savior narrative that TFA tells the teachers about themselves. As students of civil rights history, they hoped their work would be a response to the call from Black civil rights leaders for white activists to organize in their own communities.

"We've been part of creating an atmosphere where its been okay to question the dominant narrative of education reform," says Sadtler. "And we've been a place where people can find community with others who have dissenting opinions."

In founding the Roundtable, Sadtler, Radding, Roguski and their peers found they were not alone in their experiences and concerns. They estimate that nearly four hundred teachers have now been reached by the Roundtable, and more than a hundred have been more involved. Dozens of young teachers have told Sadtler that the organization has changed the way they teach and their relationships with their students, the student's families and veteran teachers, and they've told her the organization has been a source of support in challenging oppressive policies at their schools.

Sadtler hopes that she can help others avoid her mistakes. "I feel incredibly sorry for how disrespected my students and their families must have felt by me," she says. "The posturing, playing teacher when I wasn't one. I think the only way that I was able to buy into that, to maintain that position and stand in front of those kids, was because of internalized messages of superiority that I bought into it."

Organizations similar to the New Teachers' Roundtable have sprung up in other cities, and a movement has grown to combat the abuses of TFA. At a conference in Chicago in 2013, Sadtler and other Roundtable members joined TFA veterans speaking out against the organization and helped form a national network of veteran teachers, TFA alumni, and community members fighting back against TFA. The next year United Students Against Sweatshops launched a national "Teach for America Truth Tour" across college campuses, with the goal of discouraging college students from joining TFA, rebranding it as a project that hurts teachers and schools. Some progressive college professors announced that they would no longer write recommendations for students seeking to apply for TFA.[28] In fall of 2014, the school board of Durham, North Carolina, voted six to one to end its relationship with Teach for America. One board member said, "It feels like despite the best intention and the efforts, [bringing in TFA teachers] has potential to do harm to some of our neediest students."[29]

By 2014, Sadtler and Roguski had begun to transition out of their roles in the New Teachers' Roundtable. They empowered others who came after them to take on more responsibility, seeing the movement as bigger than them and seeing new leadership as a sign of a healthy and dynamic group.

As dissent continues to grow, it becomes clear that helping students requires more than just showing up and having good intentions. Many TFA teachers who arrived at their positions seeing themselves as saviors now have learned from students like Jonshell Johnson and teachers like Ndang. This transformation happened because organizers built a movement accountable to their community, and didn't abandon the TFA volunteers as lost causes. This model of change seeks to bring the misguided in, not push them out. "What we did was pretty simple," says Sadtler. "We just tried to do what we felt people of color organizers were asking us to do and create a space where new teachers could feel comfortable admitting what they didn't know and find support. They changed and grew on their own because they already had the desire to."

Jonshell says the activism she has been involved in has made a difference in changing the system. They were able to change the dialogue about changes in the school system and build accountability to the students, who are those most affected by the changes in the system, moving the center of gravity away from the newly arrived teachers and administrators who hold power in the new system. "A lot of administrators are aware of us," she says. "Now they ask us. We are kind of like a requirement. I don't want to say we're a threat, but we have influence." At the same time, the coalitions built between new and veteran teachers has led to a resurgence of the teachers' union, United Teachers of New Orleans, which has won recent union elections at two schools and has active campaigns at several more.

This growing alliance of students, veteran teachers, and parents, with new arrivals coming as allies and doing more listening than talking, points to an alternate history of post-Katrina recovery, to what could have been. Instead of salivating over the lack of accountability represented by a blank slate, so-called reformers could have allied with those who knew the school system the best. The wisdom required to build a great school system already existed in New Orleans. What was missing was not idealistic young white people but funding. Veteran teachers were not obstacles to change but vital sources of knowledge and experience. Students were not empty vessels to be filled with knowledge but the people with the most at stake in the system, the ones who most knew what was needed.

The attention brought by TFA veterans speaking out critically has also had an effect on the organization. In 2015 its number of applications went way down. Internally, efforts at diversity have increased. In New Orleans the percentage of African American TFA recruits has tripled, to 15 percent of the overall cohort, with 31 percent overall teachers of color now, and the numbers across the United States have seen similar increases. TFA also now requires more training for corps members. It remains to be seen if this is the beginning of substantive change in the organization or window-dressing to assuage critics.

The work of Sophie Johnson, Rebecca Radding, Hannah Sadtler, and Derek Roguski is a powerful demonstration of one way to challenge the savior dynamic. When they came to New Orleans and realized the project they had joined was not what they thought it was, they could have stayed silent. They could have walked away and been the "cool" white people, denouncing who they once were and pronouncing themselves better than their former colleagues. They could have quit in despair and left social justice, as many people do.

Instead they proceeded with humility and a real desire to change the system. They listened to people of color who were being affected by TFA and followed their lead. They took action and used their place of privilege to engage with the people inside the system, the idealistic young people who were being told they were on the side of justice.

What I saw and experienced living in New Orleans in the years before and after Katrina inspired both positive and negative examples in this book. Tens of thousands of idealistic young people came to the city wanting to save it and ended up acting like a colonizing army. Many of them, like the New Teachers' Roundtable members, realized their mistake, changed their behavior, and developed to become an important part of the local resistance to the neoliberal agenda for the city. The national movement against Teach for America gives me hope that these changes are happening across the country and that this idealistic energy will no longer be sapped away in support of so-called reform that ends up displacing veteran teachers and using students of color as experimental test subjects.

Chapter Seven
The World's Oldest Excuse for Male Violence

Whether or not it's true that sex work is the world's oldest profession, rescuing women is probably the world's oldest justification for male violence. It's a classic Hollywood story, in films like *Taken* (where Liam Neeson rescues his daughter from sex slavery) and TV shows like *Law & Order: SVU*. A young girl (usually white and privileged) is kidnapped and forced into prostitution (often by men with darker skin). She is the pure and innocent victim, waiting for Liam Neeson or Nicholas Kristof to come in and rescue her. But in the real world, the identity of these so-called traffickers is more complicated, and these "rescues" usually end with the woman put into prison "for her own good." In the words of author and journalist Melissa Gira Grant, "We permit some violence against women to be committed in order to protect the social and sexual value of other women."[1]

Of course, men sell sex too, but they are rarely seen as needing rescue. This view of women, especially sex workers, as needing salvation and rescue is fundamentally tied to patriarchal views of women as unable to make their own decisions, especially about sexuality. "Rescue is for kittens," notes activist and writer Emi Koyama.[2]

The war on sex work has recruited media, politicians, and idealistic young people of all political stripes under the banner of a war on trafficking. The appeal is clear: no one should ever be forced to have sex or into any type of labor. But what do we mean when we talk about rescuing women in this context? What is the difference between sex work and trafficking, and why is "sex trafficking" separated from other forms of labor trafficking?[3]

According to sociologist Laura Agustín, the category of prostitute is a relatively recent invention. Until the mid-nineteenth century, English words like "whore" and "prostitute" referred to any "loose" woman. "Literally every woman who yields to her passions and loses her virtue is a prostitute," wrote one author in 1851. "But many draw a distinction between those who live by promiscuous intercourse, and those who confine themselves to one man."[4] Agustín adds, "The sole fact of standing on a notorious street corner, going bare-headed, wearing 'garish' dress, talking in a loud voice or engaging in 'rowdy' behavior were enough to incriminate women of any class or education."[5] As we see in the next chapter, the crimes of being in the wrong place and wearing the wrong clothes can still get you arrested today.

It was not just men given the task of rescuing. For middle- and upper-class women of the 1800s and early 1900s, the professions associated with helping to rescue "fallen" women represented an important expansion of the amount of "decent" paid jobs available to women. Wealthier women were expanding their career options off the backs of the poor. Agustín writes that in Aberdeen, Scotland, "with a population of less than 70,000 in the 1840s, rescue organisations included . . . the British Ladies' Society for Promoting the Reformation of Female Prisoners and the Association for the Promotion of Social Purity, as well as the Aberdeen Association for Reclaiming Fallen Females and the Aberdeenshire Association of Ladies for the Rescue of Fallen Women." As rescuers, these women worked in concert with police and judges to control the lives of poor women. "Reformers, who believed they knew best because of their class and gender, considered their efforts to be intrinsically different and better than the policeman's or the judge's," writes Agustín. "But like the work of the policeman and the judge, theirs depended on defining others as mistaken, misled or deviant, and not listening to poorer women's own versions of their lives assured that helpers would always have the upper hand."[6]

These reformers began as protecting poorer women from themselves, forcing away their "improper" desires. But the 1800s also saw a rise in language about protecting the "virtues" of white women from other, external threats. Keeping white women safe from predatory Black men was the justification given for the lynching of Black men throughout the nineteenth and twentieth centuries. It was a public rationale for the founding of the Klan. You could say that the 1915 white supremacist film *Birth of a Nation*, in which the Klan rescues women from predatory and animalistic Black men, was the prototype for *Taken*.

The phrase *white slavery* entered popular use in the late nineteenth century, combining the sexual morality and white supremacy that went hand in hand throughout the Victorian era. Author Karen Abbott sources the term to a story about an 1887 lumber camp. "Authorities raided a Michigan lumber camp, finding nine women working as prostitutes. Eight accepted their prison sentences, but the ninth woman protested that she [had been] tortured and forced into sex slavery."[7] The resulting public furor, including demonizing of the immigrant owners of the lumber camp, led to the woman being released. "As a result of the scandal," writes Abbott, "Michigan lawmakers passed a bill that increased fines for owning a brothel," and reformers began adding more anti-immigration language to their missions. "People reviled prostitutes," Abbott writes, "but pitied white slaves."[8] During this time, anti-prostitution evangelical groups revised their platforms, adding the fight against white slavery to their mission.[9] Scholar Marlene Beckman writes, "The energetic outburst against white slave traffic grew out of the Progressive Era view that women were naturally chaste and virtuous, and that no woman became a whore unless she had first been raped, seduced, drugged, or deserted."[10]

The moral panic about white slavery was encoded into international law in 1904, when the League of Nations (precursor to the United Nations) signed the International Agreement for the Suppression of the White Slave Traffic. In 1910, Congress passed the White-Slave Traffic Act, also known as the Mann Act. The law criminalized the passage of women across state lines for "immoral purposes," and its enforcement was the first task given to the FBI, founded in 1908.[11]

Little has changed since the era when both the FBI and Klan proclaimed their mission as protecting the virtue of white women. The Klan morphed into the more polite racism of today's Republican Party, Fox News, and local police. And while the FBI expanded its purview exponentially, policing sex is still a core part of their mission. It's also still true that nothing captures the attention of politicians and journalists like a story of sex slavery, and the strong arm of patriarchal rescue is any easy solution to offer.

The Mann Act codified the male obsession with controlling women's bodies and stemmed from men's fantasies about pure women needing rescue from sex. Since white slavery was hard to find outside of these racist and patriarchal fantasies, the law was quickly used to lock up women for a wider range of activities. This is a pattern that continues to shape practices today. Those who seek to control women or to make their careers from rescuing women are still trying to expand the definition of trafficking to cover all sexual behavior they don't approve of.

From the beginning, more women needing "rescue" led to more women being put in jail. In 1927 the first federal prison exclusively for women prisoners was opened in Alderson, West Virginia. Marlene Beckman has examined the records of 156 women sentenced under the Mann Act and committed to Alderson. She divided the women into four groups, based on their charges. The list reveals what these women were being "rescued" from. It wasn't slavery. Twenty-three percent of the women had been arrested because they were "traveling with their boyfriends across state lines and either one or both of them was married to someone else. One predominant pattern involved a single woman traveling with a man she loved and intended to marry, and who turned out to be married; both the woman and the man were arrested as coconspirators when the man's wife turned them in." In 16 percent of cases, prostitution was "incidental" to the interstate travels, for example, "a woman who, at her boyfriend's insistence, engaged in isolated instances of prostitution to earn enough money so that they could complete their journey." Fifteen percent were women engaged in commercial prostitution to support themselves. For example, "a woman worked in a brothel and was arrested when she solicited at a hotel across the state line." The largest group, 46 percent, comprised "women who, themselves often prostitutes, were arrested for aiding or securing transportation for another woman to cross state lines for prostitution." This group included a range of activities, from one madam who ran a brothel and recruited new workers to a "woman who wrote a letter to a friend back home suggesting that the friend would do well to come North and join her in her illegal activity" and another woman who "was sentenced to eighteen months because she gave a friend's name to her boyfriend for this purpose."[12]

Only one woman of all those surveyed by the author met the profile of the women the act sought to rescue. She was from Mexico, spoke no English, and had been forced into prostitution by a boyfriend. But far from being rescued by the Mann Act, this woman was imprisoned and later deported. Little has changed today, as sex workers who are deported are still regularly counted as having been "rescued" by law enforcement.

Using the language and imagery of fighting slavery to support more police and prisons is deceptive, hypocritical, and all too common. In the second half of the twentieth century, President Nixon used this language to demonize and lock up people of color, in this case in his War on Drugs. "The men and women who operate the global heroin trade... are literally the slave traders of our time," declared Nixon. "They are traffickers in living death. They must be hunted to the end of the earth."[13]

Writer Elizabeth Nolan Brown is one of many observers who have compared today's war against sex work to the War on Drugs. Brown notes that references to "trafficking" (like Nixon's references to slavery) were used to support the drug war and now are used to describe sex work. And, like in the War on Drugs, "mission creep" leads to mass arrests of people on the fringes of society, while headlines speak of gang leaders and kingpins captured and victims rescued.

Comparing sex work to slavery helped bring a larger constituency into alliance with conservative law and order forces. In the late 1970s, radical feminists fighting rape culture found common cause with conservative Christians who also railed against pornography and sex work. During the Reagan administration, feminists like Andrea Dworkin and Catherine MacKinnon joined with the right wing on Attorney General Edwin Meese's anti-pornography crusade.

In recent years the framing of sex work as "modern slavery" has seen a resurgence, what American University law professor Janie Chuang has called "slavery creep." Slavery creep places the leadership of the mostly white anti–sex work movement as not only spokespeople for sex workers but experts on the subject of slavery. Robyn Maynard, a Black feminist writer and harm reduction worker, critiqued this modern co-opting of the word *slavery*:

> (In) an era where police killings of Black men, women, and children are institutionalized and enshrined in law in the same way that slavery once was, the question must be asked: how legitimate can a "new" anti-slavery movement be when the legacy of the transatlantic slave-trade is a living, breathing horror for anyone living with Black skin in the Americas? And what does this say about the value placed on Black lives that fighting "slavery" is only popular when it is whitewashed of any Black-led struggles for justice?

> For anti-prostitution campaigns pushing for the criminalization of the sex industry, "slavery" has been

decontextualized from Black struggle and repurposed
to describe the multiplicity of workplaces where sexual
services are exchanged consensually and for remunera-
tion, such as strip clubs, brothels and massage parlours
and on the street. As a Black woman with experience
in the sex industry and as a long-time outreach worker
with both street-based and indoor sex workers in Montreal, this rhetoric has always troubled me. . . . By hijack-
ing the terminology of slavery, even widely referring to
themselves as "abolitionists," anti–sex work campaigners have not only (successfully) campaigned for funding
and legal reform; but they do so without any tangible
connections to historical or current Black political
movements against state violence.[14]

Maynard also sees the "new" anti-slavery movement as
taking energy away from the movement to abolish the prison
industrial complex, a more legitimate descendant of slavery
abolition. "In their push for criminalization, anti-prostitution
advocates under the borrowed term of 'abolitionists' are taking
the space that rightfully belongs to grassroots Black-led/allied
abolitionist movements against the prison industrial complex
and the ongoing lived effects of slavery. And they do so while
promoting practices that harm Black communities and Black
organizing efforts against law enforcement."[15]

The term *sex trafficking* entered popular use around 1984,
pioneered by anti–sex work feminists but also used widely by
their new allies in the Christian right. At least 80 percent of
labor trafficking is related not to sex work but to other forms of
labor, like farm work or restaurant work.[16] But many so-called
"anti-trafficking" organizations spend very little time talking
about these forms of labor exploitation, perhaps because when
we talk about them we indict ourselves directly, in the food
we eat and the clothes we wear. As religion scholar Benjamin
Corey has written, "The vast majority of modern slaves are in
chains not for sex, but so that you and I can save a few bucks
at the store."[17] Human trafficking operates in the shadows, so

reliable figures are hard to come by, but some organizations and politicians, in order to raise support on the issue, have taken advantage of this gray area to simply make up statistics.[18] For example, one politician called "child sex trafficking in the United States" a $9.8 billion industry, a figure the Washington Post called, "A fantasy, unconnected to any real data."[19]

In the 1990s, under Clinton's "New Democrats," liberal and feminist organizations like NOW joined the conservative (and racist) "law and order" agenda, pushing for police and prisons as a solution to the problem of domestic violence. This alliance helped to pass the Violence Against Women Act (VAWA) in 1994 as part of the Violent Crime Control and Law Enforcement Act, the largest crime bill—and largest expansion of the prison industrial complex on the federal level—in U.S. history. The $30 billion legislation provided funding for one hundred thousand new police officers and $9.7 billion for prisons. Then-senator Joe Biden, a major champion of the bill, said at the time, "The liberal wing of the Democratic Party is now for 60 new death penalties . . . the liberal wing of the Democratic Party is for 100,000 cops. The liberal wing of the Democratic Party is for 125,000 new state prison cells."[20]

Among other provisions, the law called for mandatory arrests when police are called into domestic violence situations. The predictable result of this was that VAWA actually led to more women being arrested on domestic violence calls. Once again it turned out that the only way police know how to rescue someone is to arrest them. Barnard professor Elizabeth Bernstein named this trend of turning to police to solve problems of women *carceral feminism*, describing it as a commitment to "heteronormative family values, crime control, and the putative rescue and restoration of victims. (Or what Janet Jakobsen has alliteratively glossed as 'marriage, militarism and markets')."[21]

Carceral feminism represents "a vision of social justice as criminal justice, and of punitive systems of control as the best motivational deterrents for men's bad behavior," says Bernstein. "The evidence indeed suggests that U.S. antitrafficking campaigns have been far more successful at criminalizing marginalized populations, enforcing border control, and measuring other countries' compliance with human rights standards based on the curtailment of prostitution than they have been at issuing any concrete benefits to victims. . . . This is not just a question of 'unintended consequences' but rather has transpired as a result of feminists directly joining forces with a neoliberal project of social control." Bernstein says this human rights activism is attractive to young evangelical women "who imagine themselves more ethical and free than their 'sisters' in the developing world. The embrace of the third-world trafficking victim as a modern cause thus offers these young evangelical women a means to engage directly in a sex-saturated culture without becoming 'contaminated' by it; it provides an opportunity to commune with third-world 'bad girls' while remaining first-world 'good girls.'"[22]

Author and organizer Victoria Law added to the critique of carceral feminism, writing, "Casting policing and prisons as the solution to domestic violence both justifies increases to police and prison budgets and diverts attention from the cuts to programs that enable survivors to escape, such as shelters, public housing, and welfare. And finally, positioning police and prisons as the principal antidote discourages seeking other responses, including community interventions and long-term organizing."[23]

Laura Lederer is an instructive example of a feminist leader whose anti-sex work politics brought her into alignment with right-wing forces in a war against women's sexual agency. In 1977 Lederer was a founder and national coordinator of Women Against Violence in Pornography and Media. In 1978 she collaborated with San Francisco supervisor Dianne Feinstein on an anti-pornography zoning ordinance targeting sex-related businesses. In 1980 she edited a book titled *Take Back the Night* that helped launch the marches against sexual violence on college campuses that continue to this day.

By the 1990s Lederer had shifted entirely to fighting sex work and worked to bring liberal and progressive organizations like Equality Now into alliance with conservative religious groups like the Salvation Army and National Association of Evangelicals. At a 1999 press conference with progressive senator Paul Wellstone she linked the War on Drugs to a war on sex work, saying, "Unlike drugs . . . human beings can be sold over and over again."[24]

In 2001 Lederer's work with the right wing led her to join the Bush administration, working with the Office to Monitor and Combat Trafficking in Persons at the Department of State. In 2008 she gave an interview to *Today's Christian Woman* magazine, saying that her work against trafficking had led her to convert to Christianity and its good-versus-evil framework. She described having been recruited by a Christian friend at the Justice Department. "I began to go to church with him, and attended weekend retreats," she said. "I came to the Lord as a result of my work. After I became a Christian, I realized God had been right there by my side all along, even in the darkest of days, and after that I didn't experience the same fear or pessimism; I know I'm not facing this evil alone."[25]

Feminists, especially feminists of color, immediately and consistently spoke out against carceral feminism. From at least the 1970s, intersectional feminists rejected the hypocrisy of feminists working with the state. In 2001, INCITE! Women of Color Against Violence, working with the prison abolitionists of Critical Resistance, issued a call to action to "develop responses to gender violence that do not depend on a sexist, racist, classist, and homophobic criminal justice system" and to "make connections between interpersonal violence, the violence inflicted by domestic state institutions (such as prisons, detention centers, mental hospitals, and child protective services), and international violence (such as war, military base prostitution, and nuclear testing)." Among the concrete solutions INCITE! put forth:

> **Center stories of state violence committed against women of color in our organizing efforts.**

Oppose legislative change that promotes prison expansion, criminalization of poor communities and communities of color and thus state violence against women of color, even if these changes also incorporate measures to support victims of interpersonal gender violence.

Promote holistic political education at the everyday level within our communities, specifically how sexual violence helps reproduce the colonial, racist, capitalist, heterosexist, and patriarchal society we live in as well as how state violence produces interpersonal violence within communities.[26]

Under carceral, anti–sex work feminism, all sex workers are seen as trafficked. Not much has changed since the nineteenth century, when all women in the sex trades were seen as fallen victims in need of rescue. This may seem to be a step up from seeing them all as criminals, but the result is the same—arrest and prison. The only difference between criminalization and rescue is that the arrest and prison are always portrayed as for the women's own good. This framing helped bring bipartisan support for increased federal funding to "fight sex trafficking" and ignited young activists on college campuses to raise awareness of the "new slavery."

The liberal feminism that sees a need for police and state violence is most attractive to those who already have more privilege. It's no surprise to see it embraced by Hollywood actors. In 2015, as Amnesty International (AI) was considering a policy of support for decriminalizing sex work, a star-studded lineup of Hollywood feminists signed a letter demanding that AI reject the new guidelines. Meryl Streep, Kate Winslet, Anne Hathaway, Angela Bassett, Kevin Kline, Emma Thompson, Emily Blunt, Eve Ensler, Henry Louis Gates Jr., Chris Cooper, Lisa Kudrow, Carey Mulligan, Anna Quindlen, Lena Dunham, Allison Williams, Kyra Sedgwick, Debra Winger, Marcia Gay Harden, and Jonathan Demme joined author Robin

Morgan and feminist former CIA employee Gloria Steinem in signing the letter.[27]

Using the term "prostituted individuals," the letter asserted that "should Amnesty vote to support the decriminalization of pimping, brothel owning and sex buying, it will in effect support a system of *gender apartheid*." Rachel Vorona Cote, in the blog *Jezebel*, remarked snarkily, "Here's the thing, guys: Amnesty International has probably not contemplated this issue with the careful discernment of, say, Lena Dunham or Kate Winslet. We need them to guide us as we come to our own conclusions."[28]

"Everybody thinks they're helping us. They never stop to talk to us," complained Kristen DiAngelo, the executive director of Sex Workers Outreach Project (SWOP)-Sacramento, in response to the letter.[29] As one sex worker told the *Daily Beast*, "If Kate Winslet and Lena Dunham are trading sex in a criminalized environment, then they should speak out. [But] the role of an advocate and an ally is to step back and let these people speak. . . . The fact that celebrities who have no stake in this and will not be impacted by it are getting the largest voice is frustrating and, frankly, dehumanizing."[30]

A supposedly kinder and gentler policing tactic supported by anti–sex work campaigners is the capitalism-friendly term *end demand*. This is also known as the Nordic model, because in 1999 Sweden passed laws making prostitution legal but "discouraged," supposedly through criminalizing clients, followed soon after by Norway and Iceland. However, it's just criminalization under another name. No matter how often you declare that your targets are "johns," the police will arrest those who are easy to arrest. In Chicago, under a major campaign to "end demand," 97 percent of prostitution-related felony convictions were of sex workers.[31]

Fortunately Amnesty did not listen to Hollywood and instead in 2016 not only supported decriminalization but also released a powerful report that took sharp aim at the Nordic model, describing an atmosphere of fear and intimidation for sex workers. Under the Nordic model of rescue, the Oslo police

launched Operation Homeless, a campaign that involved pressuring the landlords of sex workers into evicting the women,
making them homeless, often with as little as an hour notice.
Most of these women were immigrants from Thailand or Nigeria. In fact, an Oslo police representative told Amnesty International, "The initiative 'focused exclusively on foreign prostitutes'
and that the police 'didn't want to stigmatize normal Norwegian
prostitution.'" In addition, migrant women who went to the police to report sexual assault were deported. "A representative of
Oslo police district acknowledged that: 'We deport trafficking
victims. Many of them don't know that they are victims, but they
are according to the law.'" The report also found that Oslo police
regularly discuss their plans to "choke" or "crush" prostitution.[32]

"The scale and forms of punitive intervention in the commercial sex market that the Norwegian government and legal
framework now support are compromising the safety of many
people who sell sex and are directly contributing to violations
of their human rights," concluded Amnesty.[33]

These anti-sex work campaigners rarely see the possibility of women having agency. In 2014 a group of current and
former sex workers with the Red Umbrella Project traveled
to an anti-trafficking conference in Toledo, Ohio, to bring
sex workers' voices to a conversation that usually is *about* sex
workers but not including them. Attendees they spoke to were
confused by the idea of sex workers advocating for themselves.
One well-meaning woman asked, "But if your organization is
made up of current and former sex workers, how do you keep
the current ones from recruiting the former ones?"[34]

Kate Mogulescu is founder and director of the Legal Aid
Society's Trafficking Victims Advocacy Project in New York
City, the first anti-trafficking project run out of a public defender office. Her team sees close to two thousand clients each
year charged with prostitution, many of whom have experienced trafficking. She told me that not much has changed
since the passage of the Mann Act.

"There is a real interest in trafficking right now in this
country," Mogulescu told me. "It's the focus of countless

articles. And I think at times that we are doing a disservice, particularly to the people that we purport to want to help, by making it such a huge media issue focusing on these sensationalist stories of rescue."

In her experience with victims, women who have been forced to trade sex are unlikely to be helped by police intervention. "One of the things that we spend a lot of our time doing is trying to reverse or undo the harm that the criminal justice system has caused our clients who have been trafficked," she says. "There's this notion that the more people you come in contact with through the criminal justice system, the more you're going to get at the issue of trafficking. That somehow, when the smoke clears and the dust settles, you're going to be able to figure out who's a trafficker, who's a victim, and justice will be done. And what we've seen repeatedly is that that's not the case."

Kate D'Adamo of the Sex Workers Project in New York City agrees with Mogulescu that the underlying economic issues have been ignored in this drive to rescue through arrests. "New York City funds roughly 200 beds for a population of 4,000 unaccompanied, homeless youth," D'Adamo says. "When all the beds are full, it is street economies like the sex trade which they turn to in order to provide basic needs. If we want to identify the most vulnerable, all we have to do is provide support when someone stands up and says 'I need a place to sleep tonight.'"[35]

Despite the century-old image of women sex slaves rescued from dangerous pimps by heroic officers empowered by ever stronger anti-trafficking laws, people's real lives are always more complicated. Researcher Emi Koyama says we need to change our view of both traffickers and victims. "Media often depict people as 'pimps' when they are arrested or charged with crimes of facilitating or promoting prostitution," she writes. "But most of these people are not actually what most of us think of as pimps. They are often friends, partners, mentors, family members, photographers, drivers, bodyguards, and others who do not control the person trading sex in any way. When a youth 'trafficking victim' is 'rescued' from a 'pimp,' the person they arrest as the 'trafficker/pimp' is often another youth, such as a boyfriend of the 'victim.'"[36] One study found that 56% of cisgendered men who were "pimps," and 100% of cisgendered women in the same category, had previously traded sex for money.[37]

Koyama says that even in the cases of abuse, often the situation resembles domestic violence more than kidnapping.

> Another problem with the equation of "pimps" as "exploiters" who use force, fraud or coercion to exploit youth and adults is that this is simply not true in many people's lives, even if we were to limit the discussion to the 'real' pimps (as opposed to partners, friends, etc. who are labeled as such by the police). I do not question the assertion (backed by my own experiences as well as others I've seen) that many pimps are violent or abusive, but that should not be confused with sexual enslavement of people who have abusive pimps. Let me explain . . . .
>
> Most of the times, victims receive something from the relationship, whether it is financial security for themselves and their children, affection (when the abuse is in remission), or something else....
>
> That many victims of relationship abuse choose to stay with their abusers should not be treated as consenting to the abuse: they consent to the relationship, not the abuse. But it would also be wrong to suggest that these victims are held captive by the violence; they are not staying because of the violence, but in spite of it.[38]

Koyama adds that there is "a huge policy implication to recognizing agency and resilience among people who stay with their pimps instead of treating them as passive, powerless victims or 'sex slaves.'"[39] In other words, even in the most abusive cases of so-called pimps, the best way to help the woman is in finding them support and resources, not arresting their abuser.

A study led by sex workers found that violence and harassment by police was the biggest danger reported by those in the business. Thirty-two percent of respondents reported violence or harassment from police, including sexual assault, while only 4 percent reported violence from pimps. The report, from the Young Women's Empowerment Project in Chicago, concluded that the biggest threat was not the work itself but the atmosphere created by making it illegal.[40]

A New York City survey by the Sex Workers Project found similar results. Thirty percent of outdoor sex workers reported threats of violence from police, 14 percent of indoor workers reported that police had been violent with them, and 16 percent reported that police had initiated sexual interactions with them.[41]

A 2002 study from the Center for Impact Research found an epidemic of violence from police. "Twenty-four percent of women on the streets who said they were raped stated a police officer was the perpetrator, while about one-fifth of other acts of sexual violence against women on the streets was attributed to the police."[42]

On the National Blacklist, a website with 140,000 entries written by sex workers to warn each other about violent clients, thieves, and other threats, at least 12 percent of the listings are about police.[43]

The story is the same internationally. In West Bengal, a survey of twenty-one thousand women by the Durbar Mahila Samanwaya Committee, a sex worker collective, found forty-eight thousand reports of abuse or violence by police and four thousand reports of violence by customers.[44]

In 2013 Melissa Gira Grant wrote of an FBI sting that arrested sex workers who agents found on an online message board set up to share information about dangerous customers. "Speech meant for women's own protection had been flagged as a potential threat."[45] Twenty-two sex workers were arrested, all adults, none of whom had been forced into their work. The FBI press release headed "Human Trafficking in Colorado" stated, "We are working hard to stop human trafficking—not only because of the personal and psychological toll it takes on society, but also because it facilitates the illegal movement of immigrants across borders and provides a ready source of income for organized crime groups and even terrorists."[46] Women seeking to help and protect one another had been rebranded as engaging in trafficking, and even cynically linked to terrorism.

A 2015 investigation by the Associated Press reported that at a gathering of more than seventy police chiefs, nearly all reported that they had dealt with an officer accused of sex crimes. A researcher in Ohio found that sex-related cases were the third-most-common cause of arrest of officers, behind violent crimes and profit-motivated crimes. The Cato Institute found that sexual misconduct is the number two complaint against officers, behind excessive force.[47]

While noting that not only are the vast majority of rapes not reported, and that victims are especially fearful to report rapes by police officers, the AP report found an epidemic of sexual assault by officers. Even with many states either not tracking sexual assaults by officers or refusing to release figures, the numbers are terrifying. The report found that 550 officers were decertified for sexual assault from 2009 to 2014, including rape and sodomy. During the same period, "some 440 officers lost their badges for other sex offenses, such as possessing child pornography, or for sexual misconduct that included being a peeping Tom, sexting juveniles or having on-duty intercourse."

"I didn't know what to do," testified one minor who was raped by Daniel Holtzclaw, a cop in Oklahoma City who raped at least thirteen women, most of them Black sex workers. "Like, what am I going to do? Call the cops? He was a cop."[48]

Police, prosecutors, and judges have continually shown they do not value the lives or rights of sex workers. In 2007 Philadelphia judge Teresa Carr Deni, ruling in the case of a woman who had been gang-raped at gunpoint, reduced charges to "theft of services" because the victim was a sex worker. The judge said that calling this violent gang rape a crime "minimizes true rape cases and demeans women who are really raped."[49] In 2013 a jury acquitted Ezekiel Gilbert of shooting and killing a sex worker because she refused to have sex with him. His defense was that, because Texas law allowed him to use force to retrieve stolen property, it was his right to kill a sex worker who didn't have sex with him.[50]

Through a century of calls to save victimized women, every new reform still leads to abuse, arrest, and prison for the women most in need. In part this is because no matter what anti–sex work activists say about concern for women, they ultimately are okay with some "fallen" women spending time behind bars.

"Forcing others into sex or any sort of labor is abhorrent, and it deserves to be treated like the serious violation it is," writes Elizabeth Nolan Brown. "But the activity now targeted under anti-trafficking efforts includes everything from offering or soliciting paid sex, to living with a sex worker, to running a classified advertising website." Brown reports that in 2012 federal agents arrested at least 579 minors—supposedly "rescued" from trafficking—for prostitution and commercialized vice. "Prosecutors say they need this as a 'bargaining chip' to make the victims testify against their perpetrators," says Brown. "'We're just using state violence and the threat of incarceration against children in order to save them!'"[51]

Brown lists many others charged under trafficking laws for behavior she says may be "unsavory" but should not warrant federal attention and massive prison sentences. "Since when is what adults—or even teenagers—willingly do with their genitalia a matter of homeland security?" asks Brown. Listing some of the examples from arrest records, Brown cites "Julie Haner, a nineteen-year-old Oregon sex worker who was charged with trafficking after taking her seventeen-year-old friend with her to meet clients . . . Aimee Hart, forty-two, who served seven months in prison and faces fifteen years on the sex-offender registry for driving her adult friend to a prostitution job . . . Hortencia Medeles-Arguello, a seventy-one-year-old Houston bar owner arrested as the leader of a 'sex trafficking conspiracy' because she allowed prostitution upstairs . . . and Alfonso Kee Peterson, twenty-eight, arrested . . . for telling a seventeen-year-old on Facebook that he could help her earn a lot of money from prostitution. The 'teen' turned out to be a police decoy."[52]

Like the war on drugs, we are told that the war on sex work involves rescuing victims and imprisoning perpetrators. But that's not how wars work. In reality, this war just meant more tools for police, which means more people on the margins going to prison. "In TV broadcasts, campus panels, and congressional hearings, the most lurid and sensational stories are held up as representative. Legislators assure us that their intent is noble and pure," says Brown.

> But remember: Tough-on-drugs legislation was never crafted or advertised as a means to send poor people to prison for life over a few grams of weed. It was a way to crack down on drug kingpins, violent gang leaders, evil crack fiends, and all those who would lure innocent children into addiction, doom, and death. Yet in mandating more police attention for drug crimes, giving law enforcement new technological tools and military gear with which to fight it, and adding ever-stricter prison sentences and punishments for drug offenders, we unleashed a corrupt, authoritarian, biased, and fiscally untenable mess on American cities without any success in decreasing drug rates or the violence and danger surrounding an activity that human beings stubbornly refuse to give up.[53]

Kate Mogulescu says the answer to the problem of trafficking has to come from addressing the root causes. "Anyone who wants to do anti-trafficking work needs to really roll up their sleeves and start doing anti-poverty work," she tells me. "Because what we're talking about here is a group that's disproportionately affected by poverty, by gender-based violence, by racism, by xenophobia. But we don't want to talk about that stuff because that stuff is actually kind of hard to fix. But if we write a big piece about trafficking and sex slaves and the police are going to solve this problem, we feel good about that."

Saviors seek the quick fix and convince themselves that whatever lives are damaged along the way deserve what they get. In Phoenix, Arizona, I saw firsthand some of the lives damaged in this war to save women.

Chapter Eight
Monica Jones versus Dr. Dominique

Dr. Dominique Roe-Sepowitz, an associate professor at Arizona State University's School of Social Work, is a white cisgendered feminist who built her career fighting sex work. She founded Project ROSE (Reaching Out on Sexual Exploitation), a collaboration between police, prosecutors, and her academic department. In 2013 she invited me to spend a weekend observing her rescues firsthand.

"Once you've prostituted, you can never not have prostituted," Roe-Sepowitz told me. "You are always identified, even by yourself that way. Having that many body parts in your body parts, having that many body fluids near you and doing things that are freaky and weird really messes up your ideas of what a relationship looks like, and intimacy."

Following in a two-hundred-year tradition of blurring the line between sex work and trafficking, Roe-Sepowitz told me that everyone she sees selling sex has someone forcing them into the work. "I have yet to meet someone who'd never had someone who controlled them or never took their money," she says. "We call them pimps. We call them traffickers. They might call them boyfriends."

And even when the women do take home a good income, Roe-Sepowitz says it's not worth it. "It's big money, and it's dirty money and it's painful money," she says. "That money never goes into their bank account. They never have anything to show for it. It's not a life that people really get to build on. ... It's a life you get stuck in, and your body starts failing you. And your customers stop wanting you because you get old and tired, and you get diseases and you get hurt, and you get sexually assaulted and bad things happen to you. ... It's a life that beats you up and kills you."

"No child at ten years old says, ... 'I don't wanna be a princess. I wanna be a prostitute,'" she added. It's a line I've heard frequently from anti–sex work campaigners.

In 2006 Monica Jones was twenty-one years old and shopping at a bookstore when a man she found attractive asked her on a date. She was already going to say yes, and then he offered her three hundred dollars. Her first thought was, "You can get paid for sex? Awesome."

Despite her uncomplicated feelings about sex work, she was worried about being arrested. As a proud Black transgender woman, she already stood out in a crowd, and often faced harassment from police just for walking down the street.

In Phoenix prostitution law facilitates this harassment. Officers do not need to have heard someone offer to have sex for money, they can just witness behavior that they think looks like how a prostitute might act. Evidence can include what they are wearing, what neighborhood they are in, and even asking someone if they are a police officer or attempting to "engage passerby in conversation."[1] John Tutelman, the charging bureau chief of the Maricopa County Attorney's Office, described to me other behaviors that might qualify: "Standing on a corner waving at cars that just have single men in them. Approaching cars that are stopped at traffic lights and leaning in and engaging in the kind of banter [that a prostitute might make]."

Referencing racial profiling and "driving while Black," Jones refers to "walking while trans." "If you're a police officer and you're trans-phobic and you have bias, you just use that law," she says.

The City of Phoenix has had a diversion program since 1997. On their first prostitution conviction, people are offered the choice to take classes through a several-month-long program offered by Catholic Charities instead of jail. If they complete the program, they will not have a conviction on their record. Not long after she began doing sex work, Jones was arrested and placed in that program, and described it as, "basically, you're wrong for doing this and you need help and we're going to save you." Jones was outspoken throughout, refusing to go along with the program's view that prostitution was unambiguously bad, and was "released early."

Project ROSE, started by Roe-Sepowitz in 2011, brought an innovation: for two weekends per year, those arrested are brought straight to a donated space in a church rather than taken to jail or seeing a judge. Once there, they meet with representatives from the police and prosecutors, and if they agree to stay, they meet with social service agencies and are asked to take the diversion program offered by Catholic Charities. If for any reason they do not complete the program, they still face prison.

Jones' experience with the diversion program led her to join a Spring, 2013 protest against Project ROSE led by the Phoenix branch of Sex Worker Outreach Project (SWOP), a national network of sex workers and their allies who fight against the criminalization of sex workers. At that protest, Jones met another student and former sex worker. Jaclyn Moskal-Dairman is three years older than Jones. She has the privilege of a cisgender young white woman who lives in a pretty house in a nice neighborhood and is a straight-A student, quick with facts and ideas. But Moskal-Dairman grew up working class, raised by a single mother with four kids by four different fathers and "a lot of abusive boyfriends." At thirteen she was homeless, addicted to heroin, trading sex, and desperate for stability and a way out. Instead, the state sent her to juvenile detention seven times. "I actually begged them to put me into long-term housing, like somewhere where I could stay so I didn't have to go back home to my mother because she would end up kicking me out. Somewhere I could be taken care of." But all she got was another sentence to juvenile prison.

She was pregnant by seventeen, and two months after she became pregnant the father was sent to prison for five years for his involvement in a drive-by shooting. The stability and relative safety she has now came through a long struggle. Both Moskal-Dairman and Jones know that they could easily have gone to prison instead of college.

Arizona is one of a handful of states that dictates mandatory minimums and felony upgrades for sex work. Those convicted for the first time serve fifteen days in jail with no possibility of probation or parole. The fourth conviction rises to the level of an automatic felony and a minimum of 180 days. Having a criminal record is more likely to keep people doing sex work and make other jobs—and career paths, such as Jones's toward social work—impossible. "If you decide to leave sex work for any reason, then you have a charge on your record forever," Jones told me. "Trying to get a job, trying to get to school, trying to get a degree, even travel. It's pretty hard."

"I've worked on these issues for more than twenty years," Dr. Penelope Saunders, an advocate for reform of policies related to sex work and director of Best Practices Policy Project, told me. "I've been a harm reductionist, I've been a service provider, I've been a researcher, and even I was not aware of the degree to which people are being incarcerated here in Arizona for prostitution-related offenses."

The harm-reduction approach that Dr. Saunders advocates for is seen globally as a best practice, but U.S. government policy has been to support what's generally called the prohibition approach. When someone engages in behavior that is illegal or carries health risks, such as taking injection drugs or selling sex, the prohibition approach is to arrest them to get them to stop. The harm-reduction approach is to recognize that people will do risky things and to offer them things that they need—like clean needles or a safe place to live—that will make their behavior safer.

As an alternative to incarceration, many cities and states offer diversion programs to those arrested for drug possession. More recently, some cities like Phoenix have offered this to sex workers as well. While this is sometimes described as a harm-reduction approach, and at least it may keep some people out of jail, it is in most cases only a small improvement. It still involves arrest and often ends in imprisonment.

I sensed a moral panic driving the Project ROSE team. Melissa Morrison, a graduate student volunteer at Project ROSE, typified the judgmental attitude I saw. "At the last Project ROSE, I met a woman with a man's name tattooed across her chest," she wrote to her colleagues. "This young woman may have legally met the definition of adulthood, but it is profoundly ignorant to assume she branded herself of her own free will, and likewise, that she prostituted herself of her own free will."[2]

Roe-Sepowitz never had Monica Jones as a student, but she did once invite Moskal-Dairman to speak to her class about the criminalization of sex workers. Roe-Sepowitz said she could only speak to her class if she shared the time with a police officer. Moskal-Dairman did not feel safe with that option.

Moskal-Dairman, and other activists in Phoenix saw Project ROSE as just more violence against women on the margins—mostly desperate, dragged in wearing handcuffs, and terrified—and the new chapter of SWOP decided to fight back. Through their contacts at Arizona State, SWOP members heard that Project ROSE was scheduled for a May weekend in 2013. They went to the streets, speaking to women they found there, as well as online, and warned sex workers of the upcoming arrests. Then, on the day of the sweeps, they organized a protest outside the church where the women were brought after arrest. It was at this protest where Moskal-Dairman met Jones, who was the loudest person at the protest, leading chants like "Jesus's best friend was a prostitute!"

The next day Jones was walking down the street on her way to a gay bar, and she was arrested. Although she had not offered sex, she was charged with manifesting intent to prostitute. Talking to an undercover cop was enough. She was taken to Project ROSE, the same site she'd protested the day before. When Jones told officers she was innocent and asked to see a lawyer, she says she was told that the only lawyer she could talk to was the prosecutor.

I asked prosecutor John Tutelman why defense attorneys were not allowed to be present at Project ROSE. "We have considered that," he told me. "But this is not a legal process. You are entitled to an attorney to defend you when it's a legal process." Tutelman said, "The women are not under arrest. They go in and they talk to police officers in the police room here. And they give them a lot of information. And it's not because they are under arrest or they are in any way compelled to do it at that juncture, just like we're not compelling them as prosecutors."

Tutelman's stance that the women were not under arrest did not seem to match the reality I saw around me, women in handcuffs, led in by police officers. I asked him about what happens when police put these women in a car and tell them they are coming to Project ROSE. If the woman asks if she is under arrest, what will police officers say? "They are under arrest," admitted Tutelman. "But when a police officer arrests someone, they don't have to book them into jail. And basically, that's what they're doing." Anyone who has seen how the justice system works in the real world would have reason to question whether those arrested and denied attorney are really not "compelled" to speak with officers and prosecutors.

Project ROSE offered a range of services: drug treatment, housing assistance, free clothing. The idea was that women would come through the program site, see the options available to them, and realize they could leave the life they were trapped in. But there is reason to be concerned about the involvement of these organizations. When people see nonprofits cooperating closely with police, it makes them less likely to trust those agencies or seek help.

In a 2009 report researched and written by a team that included young women in the sex trade, the Young Women's Empowerment Project wrote, "We were surprised how many stories we heard from girls, including transgender girls, and young women, including trans women, about their violent experiences at nonprofits and with service providers. This was upsetting because adults and social workers often tell us that seeking services will improve our lives. Yet when we do the systems set up to help us actually can make things worse."[3]

The service agencies collaborating with Project ROSE do not have such mixed feelings about cooperation with police. "There has too long been a divide between social work and law enforcement," wrote Holly Williamson of the Phoenix chapter of the National Council on Alcoholism and Drug Dependence, one of the Project ROSE partners. "*Consent is entirely absent from the process* . . . sex trafficking is an act that *exploits vulnerable people* on multiple levels who have little to no skills or resources to exit such *coerced* lives [italics in original]."[4]

An editorial in a social work journal questioned the ethics of social workers collaborating with police. "Social workers should be deeply troubled by social work interventions that target individuals for arrest as a means of providing services," wrote Dr. Stéphanie Wahab and Meg Panichelli. "We believe that targeting people for arrest under the guise of helping them violates numerous ethical standards as well as the humanity of people engaged in the sex industry."[5]

"Project ROSE seems to be blurring the lines between linking people to social services and arresting them," agrees Dr. Saunders. "There's a justification to say even if we help only one person, or ten people, the rights violations of all the other people are worth it. And I would say that that's a false dichotomy." In other words, you can provide aid without also partnering with police.

Monica Jones says social workers should follow a different code. "You go out into the community that you're trying to serve and you spend time with them," she says. "You ask them questions like, 'What kind of service do you guys need?' They will tell you, then you build upon that."

"They're forcing their morals on you," Jones adds. "It doesn't help the women that are single mothers and trying to make money. It doesn't help a runaway teen. It doesn't help a person out there making money for themself."

Project ROSE brought in one hundred officers or more for two days of mass arrests. For Roe-Sepowitz the large number of officers involved is part of the appeal; more officers means more women rescued. "These are people who are gonna get arrested anyway. It's against the law to sell and trade sex for money or drugs or things. We're just trying to work within the system that we have, within the context of our laws to be as helpful as possible." On the first day of Project ROSE, she was fretting that more officers weren't involved, because some had been reassigned to a drug operation.

About 10 percent of those arrested and brought to Project ROSE do not qualify for any assistance—generally because they have an outstanding warrant or too many convictions. I watched as these women were led out in handcuffs and taken to jail. Of those who remain and take the diversion program, about 30 percent complete it, and overall about 10 percent are rearrested within the first year. If they don't complete the program, they are given a court date and will almost certainly go to jail. These percentages of completion and rearrest are nearly the same as without Project ROSE.

For those women that fail the Project ROSE program, their arrest could become a death sentence. Marcia Powell was a forty-eight-year-old indigent woman with mental health issues who had been convicted multiple times for drug possession and prostitution. In 2008, an officer's claim that she offered him oral sex for twenty dollars got her a twenty-seven-month felony sentence at Perryville prison, just outside Phoenix, where a series of small infractions got her status changed to maximum custody, then placed on suicide watch. But instead of keeping an eye on her, corrections officers placed her in a cage in the blazing sun for nearly four hours on a 107-degree day. Powell died in that cage.

A report from the Arizona Department of Corrections recommended negligent homicide charges against at least seven of the officers, but the district attorney declined to pursue charges. While sixteen corrections employees faced some sort of discipline or suspension, no one was held fully accountable for her death. "If one person faced what Marcia Powell faced, then many, many other people who are incarcerated in Arizona are also at risk," Saunders told me.

Saunders, who also made a film, *No Human Involved*, about the Powell case, points out that Powell is one of many women most in need who would not have qualified for the help offered at Project ROSE. "Prison is not a safe place for women. Your health will get worse while you're in prison. You are not kept safe. Violence can be perpetuated against you. You can lose your life. Marcia Powell was sentenced to twenty-seven months in Perryville Prison for prostitution. But really it was a death sentence."

In the fall of 2013, I drove the streets of Phoenix with Jaclyn Moskal-Dairman as she tried to warn sex workers the day before arrests planned for Project ROSE. She brought safe sex and drug use supplies that she handed out to them. "By viewing all sex workers as victims and then going out and revictimizing them through using police force, which is violent and traumatic, it just seems very counterintuitive," Moskal-Dairman told me. "The way they're going about it completely lacks a nuanced analysis of these women's lives. For example, if I was working and taken off the street and told I couldn't work, then I wouldn't be able to afford basics or I wouldn't be able to go to school, or take care of my children, or have child care."

There is a disconnect between the way Roe-Sepowitz and her colleagues describe the women they were serving, and the actual women who I saw brought in. The founders of Project ROSE talked about women forced to sleep with dozens of men in a day. In their view, every woman was working against her will and needed rescue. But the women I spoke with did not see their lives that way. They certainly did not think that they had been rescued.

In two days at Project ROSE I watched dozens of hand-cuffed women led in by police. It was clearly a traumatic experience. "This is hostile. I'm the one being kidnapped," said one woman during her intake. Despite their claim that this was an arrest alternative, I saw women with previous arrests on their record led out in handcuffs. And that doesn't count the ones not led out in handcuffs that day but who went to jail later under these charges.

Despite the trauma I saw, Roe-Sepowitz insisted that the arrest was a positive experience for the women. "They do get handcuffed when they come," she says. "That is prevention-based. That's saying, 'We're not kidding. This isn't just free food and free clothes and some services. This is a real issue and you're gonna get in trouble if this continues.'"

Lieutenant Jim Gallagher is Roe-Sepowitz's friend and partner in Project ROSE and falls into another kind of savior stereotype. An eighteen-year veteran of the Phoenix police department, he presents himself as a liberal. But his role as savior of women still leads him to the belief that if women don't stop sex work when given the chance, they need to go to jail. "I think there has to be some degree of penalty. You could offer all the help in the world, but there does come that point when our victims can transition to victimizer.... There has to be that penalty for those people."

Like many supporters of criminalization of sex work, Gallagher sees every sex worker as both a victim of trafficking as well as a potential trafficker. His definition of trafficking is so broad that it's no wonder he sees all sex work under this umbrella. "What we have found through our investigations, through interviews and our contacts with the victims of this problem, is that everybody's trafficked by something," he says. "Most often they're trafficked by a pimp. Other times they're trafficked by an economic need or, you know, a need for so-cialization, or they've got a kid that they have to feed." In this case, it sounds like a sex worker's child could be arrested as a trafficker. It's not an outrageous idea. The way trafficking laws are written, anyone who receives money earned by sex work could be arrested for trafficking.

"I never met anybody that willingly wanted to do this," Gallagher told me, referring to sex work. It didn't seem to oc-cur to him that no one wants to be doing what they're doing at the moment they're being arrested.

I wanted to understand how Gallagher, Tutelman, and Roe-Sepowitz see these women as simultaneously victims and criminals, needing both arrest and rescue. In the case of Project ROSE, literally *arrest and rescue at the same time*. I asked Tutelman, from the DA's office, how he reconciled these two views. "That's why we have legislators," Tutelman told me. "I am not the person who made prostitution illegal. What I can say is based on my experience that these women that I have seen are very vulnerable, were very vulnerable, and are being exploited. And just like child labor laws, it's not something that we want to encourage, or support, or even allow." Tutelman expanded on the labor law comparison, comparing the arrests to guidelines from the federal Occupational Safety and Health Administration. "And we have all kinds of OSHA-regulated professions where we have said, 'Society is not gonna let people work under certain conditions.'"

I pointed out that under OSHA and child labor laws the workers were not subject to arrest. Tutelman changed direction. "In some ways, it's supply and demand. It's a lot easier to identify the people who are selling than it is the people who are buying and a lot easier to arrest them. But there's also another side to it. And that is that there is a community here. And the community doesn't like to see certain types of criminal activity."

Tutelman told me an anecdote about the prosecutors he works with. When they go to court, they bring pens for defendants to use, so demonizing defendants that they don't want to touch things the defendants have touched. "Maybe it's hygiene," he said. "Maybe it's just a stigma." He meant this as an inspiring story, because when his coworkers come down to Project ROSE, he says that they don't bring "defendant pens." To me this story reveals how deep the well of hate is within prosecutorial system, the extent to which prosecutors don't see defendants as human.

Another moment in our interview revealed how far Tutelman was from understanding the plight of the people he sends to prison every day. "There are all these people who complain that there are no good jobs in the world today, that all the new jobs are what they call McJobs," he said. "But you know what? If you go to work at one of those McJobs, you may be cooking French fries. And then you can become a shift leader. And you become a manager. And maybe you can move out of a fast food restaurant to a dinner house. And there is a career path there. Prostitution and the sex trade has a reverse career path." Hearing this white male lawyer-savior talk about how many options there really are for poor women of color, how much advancement is possible from working in fast food, made me angry and sick.

In our interview, Gallagher also told a story that I found revealing and sad, though not for the reasons I think he hoped. The story was about a woman he had arrested nine times—his record for a single person. "I got to know her really well; got to know her mom," he said. "Knew that she had kids." The most recent time he had arrested her, she had been "super-unhappy—she was crying, screaming, asked me to give her a break." Gallagher says he "took her to a 7-Eleven, called her mom. I said, 'Hey, this is what's going on. You know, she's gotta go in. She's got a warrant and we arrested her.' She talked to her kids. You know, said some nice things to her kids, made 'em feel better. And then I bought her, like, a hot dog and a soda. Took her handcuffs off, let her wipe off her face, you know, blow her nose, that kind of thing."

But Gallagher's sympathy only went so far. After that he took her to jail. "So we go to trial and, you know, we say hi to each other, 'cause we actually had a pretty decent relationship. And judge calls the case and—she's like, 'Oh, I'm guilty. There's no question about that.' She said, 'I just wanna come into court and just say for the record that Officer Gallagher is one of the good ones. He always treated me nicely and treated me like a person. He never really, you know, treated me badly.'"

Gallagher clearly was proud of his relationship with this woman he repeatedly sent to prison. "Over the course of my career I've run into her a couple of times," he adds. "And, you know, I always get a smile, and she always tells me, you know,

'Hey, thanks for helpin' me out and, you know, treating me nicely.' You know, that's what it's really all about."

For me this story gets at the essence of what is wrong with this form of salvation. It still involves these women going to prison. They just are sent with a smile and are expected to be grateful to their savior cop. I wished I could find this woman, and hear her side of this story, ask how her kids felt about Gallagher's help.

At Project ROSE I met a twenty-six year old Black woman named Cacee who had just been arrested for the third time that year. She invited the Al Jazeera America news crew of which I was a part to her house to talk more, and when we arrived she was making us food. She was open and generous, even hours after her arrest.

The youngest of three daughters, Cacee was raised in Oklahoma City by her parents to work hard and be independent. She was a popular girl in school, friends with "the preppies and the gangsters." She still sings in a choir in church every Sunday. Her mother is now a police officer in Texas, and her father lives in Australia, and both know that Cacee is involved in sex work.

Cacee got married while still in high school and soon after her husband was locked up in jail. She was working various jobs and doing well until she had a daughter at the age of twenty and started struggling for money. At that point, sex work seemed to be the only way she could get by. "If someone offers you two hundred bucks and says 'let's go have some sex,' you're just like, 'oh wow,' she said. "What you can do in ten, fifteen minutes to bust a nut with somebody, you can get two hundred bucks. It's like, 'wow—I've been doing it all my life for free.' It's so easy to make somebody come. Somebody can look at your breasts and just come."

Cacee has tried other jobs and was good at them. "I was the assistant manager [at] Denny's for all the servers, and I was the trainer for all the servers," she says. "I even worked at McDonald's. I did CNA work. I just never wanted to struggle, ever."

Despite the claims of Project ROSE leadership, most women I spoke with did not have a "pimp," and Cacee was no different. For her first few years, Cacee was doing well from sex work, making about sixty thousand dollars a year, running her own business, self-sufficient. Most of her work came via Craigslist, and when that site stopped taking escort ads in 2010, she had a lot more trouble finding clients. Things also got less safe, and her first arrests came soon after, three in one year from 2012 to 2013.

On one of those arrests, in the spring of 2013, she was offered the diversion program through Project ROSE. She successfully completed the program but went right back to sex work—she needed the money. "When I was going through the Project ROSE, I was getting kicked out, evicted from a lot of places," Cacee explained. "I didn't have money for rent because I was doing so much to, you know, trying to be good and have a job and stay out."

Cacee's arrest during Project ROSE in fall of 2013 meant jail time. She was resigned to it. Another strong, smart, kind, single mother going to jail because of the limited choices available, and the actions of her so-called rescuers.

My experience reporting on Cacee, Monica Jones, and others in Phoenix for Al Jazeera America taught me a difficult lesson. Progressive media like Al Jazeera indulge in tropes common to media coverage of sex work. Stories seem always to feature the same clichés: lascivious views of women walking the street or working in strip clubs or hyperbolic tales of victims sold into sex slavery. Frequently repeated myths, like the story of a rise in trafficking at sporting events[6] or the disproven claim that most sex workers start work at age thirteen or younger,[7] were repeated in stories on our network.

The news piece I delivered was filled with voices rarely heard in the debate on sex work—the women themselves. All of my previous reports aired after a few days of editing, but approval of this story dragged on for weeks. During this time, I saw my reporting distorted into something that I thought no longer represented reality. Monica Jones was edited out. "I can't understand what she's saying," I was told by a senior producer. "She speaks unaccented, jargon- and slang-free English,"

I responded, frustrated. I had always believed that people of privilege have problems hearing voices of those without privilege, but I'd never seen it demonstrated so literally. Senior producers also demanded I remove the most judgmental language used by Roe-Sepowitz.

As I was fighting for my story to get out, the arrests in Phoenix continued. In 2014 Phoenix was one of the cities participating in Operation Cross Country, a national FBI sweep of arrests of sex workers, aimed at "rescuing" them from traffickers. According to an FBI press release, the operation was a success. But the stories I heard later show the reality behind the press releases. "One twenty-year-old 'victim' had her arm broken by the cops when she tried to flee. A sixteen-year-old victim was booked on prostitution charges when she refused to let officers contact her parents. After failing to secure emergency shelter for two adult victims who had no money and no identification, police returned them to the motel where they'd been apprehended 'so they could try and arrange funds to get back [home].'"[8]

The opposition I faced at Al Jazeera in reporting the Project ROSE story made me want to continue to explore this kind of rescue. There is no doubt that there are some who really do experience forced labor in the sex trade. Their stories are incredibly painful to hear. And they do want—and should receive—help. But what kind of help?

My research led me to an anti–trafficking law passed in Alaska in 2012 and to survivors of trafficking working together to overturn it.

Tara Burns is a brilliant and thorough organizer, writer and researcher with a master's degree in social justice. She lives deep in the wilderness of Alaska—you can't reach her home by any roads. She chops wood and butchers animals to eat. And she is a trafficking survivor who organizes against the laws said to be for her.

When she was a child, Burns's father took her to work in a brothel. A cop who was a former neighbor tried to help her once and even spent a long time developing a pretty solid case against her father. But, according to Burns, "The DA ultimately decided not to prosecute because juries don't find teen prostitutes to be compelling victims."

Later Burns stayed in a youth shelter. When her caseworker had her kicked out, she had to do sex work for a place to stay. This time it wasn't her father forcing her but the state. "My caseworker called all my friends who I'd previously stayed with and told them that to let me stay with them anymore would mean a felony charge of harboring a runaway," Burns says.

"I think that the biggest sex trafficker, what induces the most people into prostitution, is the state," she adds. "As a homeless teenager, my case worker would come and take my money from me. She would be like, 'Well, you're just going to use this to buy drugs.' The system essentially removed my entire safety net and then kicked me out into the cold Alaskan winter. The only choice I had was . . . prostitution or sleeping in a snow bank. I literally did dig holes into the snow bank. But, you know, at sixty below, you'll freeze to death . . . so you've gotta turn a trick."

For her master's degree, Burns surveyed forty-eight Alaskan sex workers and found that she was not the only one who had been victimized by the state. Of the women who reported being coerced, manipulated, or forced (in other words, meeting some of the federal definitions of trafficking), half had sought state shelter at some point as Tara had, and all had been turned down. Eighty percent had tried to report being a victim or witness of a crime. The police took reports in one-fifth of cases, and the rest were either arrested or threatened with arrest.

In addition, three-quarters of those who meet the federal definition of a trafficking victim reported having been assaulted by police before ever becoming involved in sex work. Overall, 26 percent of those she surveyed had been sexually assaulted by an officer, while 9 percent had been robbed or beaten by an officer.[9]

A new Alaska law redefined many activities associated with prostitution under the banner of *sex trafficking*. "Promoting

prostitution," advertising sexual services, co-managing or owning a location where prostitution takes place—all these became trafficking.

The first people charged under the new law were adult
women engaged in activity that would previously have been defined as misdemeanor prostitution. None of them were accused
of the behavior that most people think of when they hear *trafficking*, such as using force or activity involving minors. But these
women were labeled under the law, and in news reports, as "sex
traffickers." Some of them were charged with being their own
trafficker, both victim and perpetrator against themselves.[10]

Collaborating with a sex work activist named Maxine
Doogan, Burns cofounded Community United for Safety and Protection (CUSP), an organization of Alaska's sex
workers and their allies, to work to overturn the law. In January 2013, a few months after it was passed, police went to
a massage parlor in Kenai, a town south of Anchorage with
a population of about seven thousand. They arrested a forty-
nine-year-old woman and a nineteen-year-old and a twenty-
year-old. All three were charged with prostitution. But the
forty-nine-year-old was also charged with first-, second-, and
third-degree sex trafficking, apparently because she was accused of owning the business.

A few months later, a twenty-four-year-old woman who
had allegedly advertised on Craigslist was caught by police
in an online sting. It appears that police did not have enough
evidence to support a prostitution charge, though. According to police reports, the woman would not "guarantee sexual
contact" in person, so she was charged with "promoting prostitution," a misdemeanor. Because of the new law, she was initially charged with sex trafficking, apparently because she was
accused of advertising sexual services online, even if she didn't
offer them in person.

The next year, police in Anchorage arrested Amber Batts
for allegedly running a sex trafficking ring. Batts appeared
to have run a model sex business. It featured safety screen-
ings of clients, was a safe place to work (with other people

around), and provided advertising, independent contractor agreements, and help with processing credit card charges. Police and press reports labeled all of this *sex trafficking*. An article described a section on her website that recommended etiquette for clients seeing a sex worker as "advice for patrons of the sex trafficking ring."

Batts, thirty-nine, was charged with eight different counts of sex trafficking, including running a sex trafficking enterprise, running a place of prostitution, procuring customers, inducing a person under the age of twenty into prostitution, accepting proceeds from prostitution, and facilitating prostitution. Batts was also allegedly having sex for money. Therefore, as someone charged with trafficking everyone on site, she is her own trafficker.

"The police are turning around and telling the reporters, and the reporters are turning around and telling the public, that somebody is being rescued for being a sex traffic victim," says Doogan, who describes anti-trafficking campaigns as a "weapon of mass destruction to the prostitute nation."

I watched as Doogan and Burns and other members of CUSP testified against anti-trafficking initiatives in front of Alaska state legislators, and I saw them visit local organizations to gather support for reform. "The state coerces people into prostitution by denying them access to shelter, SSDI, and foster care," Burns says. "We had women freeze to death because they couldn't get into the shelter. When the state makes survival harder, they force people to make desperate choices. But then when those same people turn to prostitution to survive, they are labeled as sex traffickers."

"I think any time that a woman is selling her body for sex, it should be illegal. It's very degrading and exploitive," says Sergeant Kathy Lacey, who started and runs the vice division of the Anchorage Police Department. She sees herself as rescuing women trapped in desperate situations. Even Lacey admits that "arrest is not the best answer," but she says it's the only tool she has. "We don't want to punish them. We want to remove them from that situation, and the tools that we have to remove them from that situation are to arrest them and to remove them from that trafficker."

Like the Project ROSE leadership, Lacey also uses the terms *trafficker*, *pimp*, and *boyfriend* interchangeably. "It's not like she goes out on a date and she makes four hundred dollars, and she gives two hundred to him and she keeps two hundred. In most cases she gives everything to him," says Lacey, echoing the language used by Project ROSE and other rescuers. However, as in Arizona, the sex workers I met in Alaska mostly worked independently. And when they did work with someone, like the women who worked with Amber, it was not the story we've been told of the evil exploitative pimp, it was a woman who also was a sex worker, who helped them work safely.

Today Burns is engaged in some of the most important research in the United States around sex work. She is obtaining documents from every charge of prostitution, sex trafficking, and promoting prostitution in every state and also researching more about the cases behind the charges. Among the early results: "Some district attorneys never charge anyone with prostitution without also charging them with something crazy like sex trafficking [of] themselves or sexually assaulting the undercover officer who hired them for sex (by touching his penis). Some states never charge someone with sex trafficking without also charging them with prostitution of themselves in the same case, and some states consistently charge women with felony pimping of themselves."[11]

Burns has also written about her views and experience as a survivor of trafficking. One article she wrote brought criticism from Katha Pollitt, who wrote in *The Nation* that she assumed Burns was "a highly educated woman who has other options and prefers this one." In response, Burns wrote that Pollitt, "Doesn't care about my victim credentials, unless I present as a good, sobbing, opinionless victim she can use as trauma porn to promote her own ideas."[12]

The lesson I learned from those whose lives are on the line—from Monica Jones, Jaclyn Moskal-Dairman, Tara Burns,

Cacee, and many others—is that helping sex workers does not mean rushing in to save them or sending police in to save them. Support means using whatever privilege and access you have to influence the systems that have power over the lives of sex workers. "Your feelings about sex work do not make much difference to the vice police working tonight," writes Melissa Gira Grant. "If you must have your feelings, take them to people who will listen: neighborhood associations, health clinics, labor unions, domestic violence shelters, queer and women's organizations— your own people, whoever they are. Rather than narrow in on sex workers' behaviors, turn your questions outward. What are these people doing that might harm sex workers? Why not help them, rather than sex workers, change their behavior?"[13]

The tide has begun to turn in public perceptions of sex work, led by sex workers themselves. In the global south, mass protests by hundreds or even thousands of sex workers are not uncommon. Durbar Mahila Samanwaya Committee, the sex workers' collective in West Bengal, does more than protest. They formed a consumer cooperative and microcredit program with more than five thousand members putting in their small savings. In just 2007 the program had dispersed more than $310,000 in loans to members and had a turnover of $1.5 million. The organization also runs two hostels, has a cultural wing, and owns a football team and seventeen schools, both for children of members.[14] The organization is also cofounder of the National Network of Sex Workers, which includes organizations across India, like Veshya Anyay Mukti Parishad (VAMP) a collective in Southwest India with a membership of five thousand sex workers.[15]

As long as there have been sex workers, they have fought to tell their own stories, and they do that today through books, magazines, zines, and blogs. In the United States, *Spread Magazine*, a publication by and about sex workers, was published from 2005 to 2010. The final issue was written and edited entirely by sex workers of color.

One of today's most popular blogs run by sex workers is *Tits and Sass*, which features important reporting and personal stories, but there are many more. From the grass-roots, people with experience of sex work, or even those who know sex workers, have moved into the corporate media, and sympathetic stories have now come from MSNBC, the *New York Times*, and *Vice*. In 2015, when Homeland Security raided the offices of Rentboy, a website popular among sex workers, the *New York Times* came out against the arrests. "Gay men in the United States turn to sex work for a variety of reasons," the editors wrote. "In New York, where homeless shelters for gay and transgender youths have lengthy waiting lists, sex work can mean the difference between sleeping on a bed and sleeping on the street. For others, it is a way to afford a degree.... Federal authorities should consider whether continuing to spend time and money turning the website's operators into felons is worthwhile."[16]

Activists noted a double standard. The *Times* was silent when the FBI went on a similar raid against MyRedbook, a site used mostly by female sex workers, the previous year. Still, the language used by the *Times* editorial board was a step forward, and I believe it happened in part because of sex workers telling their own stories elsewhere.

In the early days of 2014, a conversation between sex workers on Twitter, including N'Jaila Rhee and Molli Desi (with support from Melissa Gira Grant and activist Suey Park), evolved into the hashtag #notyourrescue. It was a group expression of the frustration at criminalization under the guise of rescue. The hashtag quickly caught fire, and the messages came from all over:

> Because you fight for laws that will kill people like me and I have unresolved issues around that.

> Because I don't exist so you can feel warm & fuzzy about "rescuing" me. Rescue a stray dog instead.

> Laws that seek to control my sexual behavior create the opportunities to exploit and abuse me.

Because sex workers who work from home are then evicted and rendered homeless. How is this rescue?

Because your idea of rescue looks a lot like reckless endangerment.

Cuz anti-trafficking should be about lowering barriers to migration, improving working conditions, not arrest and hype.

Because sex workers should not have to worry about their parents/kids/partners being accused of pimping.[17]

While it is more online than in the streets, #notyourrescue marked another turning point in the conversation and a way for affected communities to come together and speak out.

Organizing led by sex workers continues to shift the debate. In March 2015, Monica Jones traveled from Phoenix to Geneva, Switzerland, to testify on behalf of sex workers' rights before the UN Human Rights Council as part of the UN Universal Periodic Review (UPR) process, through which countries' human rights records are submitted to scrutiny every four years. She also traveled as far as Australia, sharing her story and linking with activists internationally. In 2016 she graduated from Arizona State University.

In 2015 the A&E network premiered a "reality" show called *8 Minutes* that followed a pastor as he "saved" sex workers. The outcry from sex worker activists led to the show quickly being canceled, and all episodes were taken down from the A&E website. When several of the women who had been featured on the show came forward to talk about how they had been abused and lied to by the show instead of "saved," it was other sex workers—including Tara Burns—who stepped in with concrete support, finding them money and offering counsel.

As one sex worker activist noted, "*8 Minutes* is a perfect allegory for the rescue industry."[18] While it claimed to rescue the women, it actually made things worse. It was up to women who had been demonized and threatened with arrest to support each other. The actual rescue was the mutual aid happening far from the attention of TV cameras. The supposed victims were helping each other, fighting to undo the trauma brought by the saviors.

Sex workers have a range of experiences. Some love their job, and some hate it. Some have huge incomes, while some are trading sex for food or drugs or a place to sleep. Some have people in their life who are exploiting them or forcing them into the work, and others are entirely independent. The vast majority are somewhere in the middle of these extremes or travel between these statuses, living complicated lives like the rest of us. In this exploitative, racist, patriarchal, capitalist system, most of us have our choices constrained. This is especially true for those on the bottom of our country's race, class, and gender hierarchies. If you want to make a difference, the first step is to listen to those you want to help. Support them in what they say they need, not what you think they need. Confront and challenge your own privilege. And if you want to help those who are the most exploited, work to overthrow the unjust systems we all live under.

Chapter Nine
Demanding the Impossible

Although the savior mentality sometimes seems to be embedded in our national DNA, movements of recent years have filled me with hope that we can move beyond this trap and build a more responsive and accountable movement. I have seen activists at the grassroots in cities across the United States and around the world who are very clear about the systemic roots of our problems and are fighting to build a new world, not just tinker at the edges of this one. Looking at both the successes and failings of recent movements like Occupy Wall Street and the Movement for Black Lives, there are concrete lessons for anyone seeking to move beyond the savior mentality.

The 2008 financial crisis helped spur a global movement that challenged entrenched power and inequality. Mass popular struggles were rising up, based not on charismatic saviors but on grassroots outrage. It was a moment in which people at the grassroots were saving themselves.

This global movement changed Nelini Stamp's life. Fiery and confident beyond her years, Nelini was raised in Brooklyn by a working-class Black, Puerto Rican, lesbian mom. At the age of five, Nelini was a child actor. At the age of seventeen, she volunteered to help register people to vote in the 2004 elections and felt like voting was an important part of making change. A year later, as the economic crisis was beginning, she and her mother were evicted from their Brooklyn home, and Stamp felt she had no choice but to drop out of high school.

Soon after, she began organizing with the Working Families Party, a progressive New York State organization focused on electoral politics. She was canvassing for them on a New York state senate race in 2008, when Barack Obama was elected president. "I thought everybody was going to get health care," she says. "I had such hope. That day I said, 'Wow, we're going to get a lot. This is the hope and change we wanted. We're actually going to see this country change.'"[1]

That hope did not last long. By summer of 2009 she saw that the community organization ACORN was being attacked instead of banks, and at that point she knew that there would not be universal health care and that change was not going to come from within the system.

The worldwide economic crash of 2008–2009 had led to widespread discontent. The election of Obama was a reflection of this ferment. But when he did little to address the fundamental inequality, corporate profiteering, and corrupt financing that had caused the crisis, people began to lose faith in change within the system. Meanwhile, around the world, the rich were using the global crisis to grab more wealth, and the rest of us were getting restless.

Four thousand miles away from Stamp, in Sidi Bouzid, Tunisia, a twenty-six-year-old man named Mohammed Bouazizi had been the main earner for his family since he was ten years old, including putting his two sisters through school.[2] Every morning he would go to the supermarket and load his cart with fruits and vegetables and then walk the cart several miles to the *souk* (open-air market), where he would spend the day reselling them at a small markup. Nearly every day the police would harass him, sometimes confiscating his scales, sometimes with arbitrary fines. In June 2010 they fined him for the equivalent of two months' work. After six more months of harassment, one day he fought back against officers when they came to harass him. He was badly beaten. He tried to complain to municipal government, but no one would talk with him.

Desperate, humiliated, and helpless, Bouazizi set himself on fire outside of the municipal offices on December 17, 2010. It turns out he was not as alone as he thought. His drastic and tragic act crystallized the feelings of a nation of people sick of being cut out of a chance in life.

Protests began in Sidi Bouzid that same day and quickly spread across the country. The movement was based in public squares, as people gathered by the tens and hundreds of thousands in city centers and refused to leave until the government was gone.

Bouazizi died in a hospital on January 5, 2011. By January 14 the government had fallen and the corrupt president, Zine El Abidine Ben Ali, had fled the country. Eleven days later, masses had taken to the streets in Egypt, and eighteen days later Hosni Mubarak, a brutal dictator who had been one of the biggest regional allies to U.S. empire, was gone.

Activists in Egypt dismissed the widely repeated story that the Arab Spring was a "Twitter revolution." Rabab El-Mahdi, an associate professor of political science at the American University in Cairo, said that she saw so-called "soccer hooligans" as playing a more key role than Twitter. They had a skill for quickly identifying spies and provocateurs and could "light a car on fire in three seconds." She also noted the important role of unions, which called for strikes and other mass actions at key moments during the revolutionary upheaval. Radical journalist and blogger Hossam el-Hamalawy added that most of the twelve million people who took to the streets had no Internet access. Local newspapers, with circulations of millions of people, would report something posted on Facebook, and although most people read about it in the paper, it was still credited as if social media had been the actual medium that had reached millions.[3]

Four days after the fall of Mubarak, similar anger, pain, and passion for change erupted in the United States, as tens of thousands of protesters took to the capitol of Wisconsin to stand against Governor Walker's right-wing agenda, including a bill that would practically destroy public sector unions in the state.

Max Rameau, a Haitian-American organizer based in Miami, was also seeing changes. Rameau, living in a city that had become known as the capital of the housing foreclosure crisis, had founded an organization called Take Back the Land. It made national headlines with a simple strategy: move people without homes into homes without people. "We were intentionally breaking the laws that we think are immoral," Rameau explained. "The laws that defend the right of corporations to maintain hundreds of thousands of vacant homes when there are hundreds of thousands of human beings that need homes sleeping out on the street."

When Take Back the Land started, Rameau was surprised to not only find supportive neighbors when they took over abandoned homes, but also to find that even the corporate press was sympathetic. "Five or ten years prior, we would have been kicked out of the neighborhood by the neighbors," he said. Now he was seeing support from all over, including a profile of his work in the *New York Times*. Starting in late 2010 and early 2011, organizations started contacting Take Back the Land and asking how they could do similar actions. "We said, 'Something different is happening right now. Something feels different. Something is different. We feel like we're about to reach a critical mass of organizations who want to do something that they were not willing to do a year ago.'"

In Europe, people were also taking the public squares to protest austerity. On May 15, 2011, the *Indignados* movement took squares in cities across Spain, including fifty thousand people in Madrid. Tens of thousands camped out. The next month, on June 23, protesters in Senegal announced that the African Spring had begun. After President Abdoulaye Wade had proposed constitutional changes that many said would consolidate his power, protesters took to the streets. They won immediate concessions, including Wade's withdrawal of the proposed changes.

Reading the news, Nelini Stamp thought, "It's got to happen here. It's happening all over the world. It's brewing, it's brewing. It's got to come here."

On June 14, the movement to retake the commons moved to New York City, as over a hundred protesters began camping outside of New York City Hall, in an encampment called Bloombergville (a name that recalled Hoovervilles, shantytowns that were built during the Great Depression both as places to live and to protest the Herbert Hoover administration's economic policies that had led to mass unemployment).

Bloombergville lasted for nearly a month, until July 5. Within a couple weeks, activists in New York began planning for a new occupation, this time on Wall Street. Activist and PhD student Manissa McCleave Maharawal came to a meeting on August 2, as activists sat on the ground near the infamous Wall Street statue of a bull and talked about occupying Wall Street. "I thought, 'that's never gonna happen.'"

The occupation of Wall Street was called, somewhat arbitrarily, for September 17, 2011. The date had come from a widely circulated but vague call put out by *Adbusters*, a design-oriented anticapitalist magazine that had a relatively wide activist reach. "We were handed a date," says author and professor David Graeber, who was among those at the initial planning meetings. "Ninety thousand people on the Internet thought something was going to happen on the seventeenth."

The organizers of that September 17 protest had a few potential public and near-public sites near Wall Street they had scouted. Although they had planned for an occupation, they were unsure if people would really stay the night. At their most optimistic, some hoped the protest might last two to three days. Amin Husain, a former Wall Street lawyer who had left his lucrative career to become an activist, was one of those organizing before September 17. For him, it was always deeply connected to the international struggles. "This is not only a democracy or neoliberal issue, but a decolonizing issue," he says. "Those regimes were placed by the colonizer. Then the ruler looked like the colonized. Then they instituted neoliberalism in the framework of a police state. Who made that possible?"

Husain, a Palestinian, was connected with activists from Spain and from Egypt who were also living in New York and involved in the organizing for September 17. "A different alignment was taking place since 2011," he says. "And it was between the oppressed across national boundaries, retaining specificities of struggle, moving towards a shared horizon of liberation, reclaiming our cities."

The day of the protest, more people came out than expected—about one thousand people. Police had blocked all access to Wall Street itself. Seeing their planned route cut off, organizers moved to Plan B—a nearby semi-public square called Zuccotti Park. The group had a *general assembly*, and dozens decided to spend the night.

Stamp found the first general assembly, on September 17, to be chaotic at first. "This is cool," she thought. "But also weird. There's a lot of white people here." When the assembled crowd decided to break into working groups, she began to get hooked. "I'm so used to these structured kind of things, then all of the sudden they said, 'Break up in to groups.' What groups? 'Groups that you think we need to get more people here, groups that you think we need.'"

Stamp remembers thinking, "Wow, this is really organized for what folks are calling an unorganized group of people." She decided she had to stay and see what was going to happen. "Then and there I said, 'This has a really big potential to kick everyone in their butts [and] get them to move a little bit.' And it totally did. That night I said, 'I have to stay here. There's no way I'm going to go home.'" She knew that if she left, she'd be wondering, "Did it go down? What happened?'"

Police blocked activists from setting up tents that first night, but people snuggled up for the night in blankets and sleeping bags. Amin Hussain immediately saw the potential. "To me it was like, *How do you keep people there?*" he explains. "Because the moment that you can keep people there is the moment that they begin believing."

The following Wednesday, the State of Georgia executed Troy Davis. Davis was the thirty-fifth person executed by lethal injection in the United States that year, but his case galvanized public support because of the strong evidence of his

innocence. People from around the world, including Arch-
bishop Desmond Tutu, former president Jimmy Carter, and
Pope Benedict, called for his life to be spared. Demonstrations
were held around the world. A dozen Howard University
students and one professor were arrested outside the White
House. For some, the execution was a further demonstration
of the fundamental racism and unfairness of the government.
It helped many people to visualize the links between systems of
capitalism, police, prisons, and race.

The Wall Street occupation might have died out. It was
ignored by most of the media. I was working for Al Jazeera
English at the time, and despite the channel's reputation for
more grassroots coverage (the channel's slogan is "Voices of the
voiceless"), I saw no interest from anyone in the news division.
But independent media knew that this was an important story.
Democracy Now was covering it every day (it also had live coverage from outside the prison where Troy Davis was executed),
and media activists were using the then-new technology of live
streaming to reach viewers directly, without the filter of the
corporate media.

On September 24, two young white women who were part
of an Occupy Wall Street demonstration were pepper-sprayed
by police. Although police violence much worse than this happens every day, especially in Black communities, their gender
and race, as well as media-savvy activists who captured it on
video, helped their screams of pain amplify around the world.
Police repression brought more media attention to the protests, and more people kept showing up. One week later protesters tried to march across the Brooklyn Bridge in the largest
protest yet, leading to seven hundred arrests. The size of the
protest and the number arrested brought more attention. Millions of people had been waiting for someone to speak out on
these issues and to put their bodies on the line.

Boots Riley is a singer in the Coup, a rap group from Oakland that gained critical respect and sold-out crowds across
the world with their brand of revolutionary party music.
He raps humorously about killing CEOs and landlords and

raising feminist daughters. Riley was one of those inspired to join Occupy in his city. Despite having a busy music career, he let Occupy consume his life, spending a lot of time at Occupy Oakland. Riley saw the police violence against protesters as important but had no illusions regarding why it grabbed attention. "If it hadn't been caught on video, and if it was someone Black, you wouldn't have even known about it. I'd be trying to tell people about it, and they'd only halfway believe me," he said. "The media has most of white America looking at people of color as deficient, savage, and when they see something happen to them by police they believe that it was somehow their fault. So, when this happens to a white person it's something new exposed to them."

Soon there were hundreds of Occupy encampments starting in cities and towns across the United States. The idea of occupying public space and not just demanding change but building a small alternative world within that space caught fire everywhere. The media coverage helped Occupy grow rapidly, but it also created problems. For Amin Husain, the media coverage exacerbated the issues of representation. "The truth is, people of color were made invisible by the media," he says, adding that there was a strong international presence that was also ignored. "People of color were engines in the movement. It was because we knew fighting here was fighting for over there."

With each week, more people were building a community in Zuccotti Park. Most who camped at Occupy found a beautiful, life-changing experience forging deep connections with other activists. They weren't just protesting but also practicing another vision of what democracy could look like. It was *prefigurative politics*: building the world we want to see through living and organizing as if it already exists. Every aspect, from the consensus decision-making process to reclaiming public space, was about challenging not just existing institutions but also the way we are told that change happens. "When [we are] engaging in direct action, rather than engaging with authorities, we're acting as if they don't exist," said David Graeber, who had been at the first organizing meetings. "Occupation comes from this. What we're saying is, well, this is a public space; we are the public. The public should not have to ask permission to occupy [our] own space."

Manissa Maharawal found the consensus decision-making process used at Occupy helped pull people deeper into involvement. "When you're doing something where you can say 'I can just make a working group' or 'I can make a decision where I can enter a group and what I have to say about what's happening, no matter who I am it will matter,' that feeling, that sort of feeling of power almost, over decisions that affect people has been really inspirational for people who want to get involved."

"What I saw was beautiful," added Amin Hussain, who had become one of the main organizers. "There's hope in people [wanting] to sit on the ground rather than in a chair, that people could follow a process where they actually spent more time hearing than speaking, that people want to facilitate but that they facilitate out of wanting to hear the conversation rather than being empowered to have someone speak and someone not speak. Those to me were the critical components that just moved me, and I thought that it was just the foundation upon which something organic [could] rise."

The name *Occupy* was not without problems, given that the entire country is an occupation of Native lands. As some Indigenous activists said, "The belief that settlers have an inherent right to a future on stolen land has got to go."[4] There were also sexual assaults in some camps. Activists wanted to build a new world, but building safety and accountability while also organizing against police violence and disruption is a difficult task, and many Occupy activists were not up to it. "I think there were some [Occupy camps] that allowed homophobia and sexism to thrive in a really significant way," says Rameau. "I think homophobia and sexism in society exist everywhere but were allowed to thrive in some of these areas."

"There was a lot of racial tension," adds Stamp. "There were a lot of young people who were like, 'The American dream is supposed to be mine,' and they didn't realize the American dream never belonged to a lot of us."

"I love the discourse of the 99 percent," said PhD student Manissa Maharawal. "I think it's great. I think it's been really unifying. But I would like it to go along with saying something like, 'We are the 99 percent, but the way that we experience the 99 percent can be very different.'"

Alicia Garza, at that time the thirty-year-old executive director of a Bay Area organization called POWER (People Organized to Win Employment Rights), was also relatively ambivalent about Occupy. "It was actually a couple different percents," she says, noting divisions of race and class that she observed at Occupy Oakland. "The people at the bottom of that 99 percent were not included." Garza later went on to coin the phrase Black Lives Matter, helping the rise of a movement that specifically centered race and gender along with the class analysis so present at Occupy.

"We have to recognize that the 99 percent is hierarchically developed by itself," says scholar and activist Dr. Angela Davis, who adds that she saw in Occupy a continuation of the history of organizing in prisons. "I see the precedents for the Occupy movement as having been established by Attica," she said, referring to the legendary 1971 prison uprising. "Many people don't talk about the role that prisoners have played in attempting to build democratic communities, the fact that the brothers at Attica took over and occupied the prison for four days and produced all of these incredible demands."

The marches and mass arrests had brought the initial press attention, but soon the media started paying attention to the space that was being held, even if they still didn't understand it. There was a lot of criticism of Occupy for not having demands. But for many, the lack of demands was freeing and important. "I think there is a danger in figuring out what the demands are too early," noted Max Rameau. "Because we don't know what this historic time could represent."

Rameau described an important lesson about demands from his study of the civil right movement. In December 1955, when Rosa Parks's direct action helped start the Montgomery Bus Boycott, the protesters did not initially demand integration. "The primary demand was that Black people could sit in the back of the bus and work their way up to the front and that white people, then, couldn't sit behind Black people and force us to move to the back," he explains. "The Montgomery Bus Boycott, as it started, was not an integration movement, it was a segregation with respect movement."

The lesson, adds Rameau, is to not declare your demands before you know what is possible. "If this is a time where we could only win a little bit, then it doesn't make sense to push to fundamentally transform society," he says. "And conversely, if this is a time we could fundamentally transform society, it makes no sense whatsoever to only ask for a little bit."

> When Rosa Parks sat there and refused to get out of her seat, we couldn't imagine at that time we could win the end of all laws that distinguish between Blacks and whites. We couldn't imagine that was even possible, and so we made demands at that time which seemed like they were possible. And so, in retrospect, it looks kind of silly that none of the demands were even integration. So we can't make the same mistake today of making some demands which in five years, ten years, twenty years will seem silly and seem like we sold ourselves short.

Maharawal agrees. "When we don't have a set list of demands, then we aren't sort of constrained by that. Instead we can be as wide open to radical change as we want to be." For Husain, no demands means you're more of a threat. "You're always more dangerous when the thing that you're asking for is impossible, because it's inclusive."

Nicholas Kristof wrote about Occupy several times in the fall of 2011. He was not opposed—I would describe him as condescendingly supportive. He called the movement "pretty silly" and made a reference to "half-naked anarchists manning the barricades," but he also conceded that the protesters had a point and admitted that their ideas made more sense than the philosophy of greed spouted in the corridors of power on Wall Street. In

one column, he suggested his own list of demands for the movement, a list of modest reforms like closing tax loopholes. Reading his columns on Occupy, it's clear that Kristof fundamentally
did not understand what was happening and does not believe
that change can come from a movement in the streets.

Brandon Darby visited too, working with right-wing
media outlet Breitbart. Ironically, Darby was now presenting
himself as a defender of women. In the tradition of Thomas Jefferson speaking about civilizing Native women, Darby
wrote that police should "rescue" the women of Occupy from
the threat of sexual assault by other activists. "Far from 'em-
powering' women, the Occupy movement's anarchist and socialist principles and policies are exposing female activists to
greater danger," wrote Darby. "They cannot maintain order
because they are in the midst of rebelling against it."

That November, on the night before her birthday, Stamp
was there as police came to evict Occupy from Zuccotti Park,
and she was almost immediately pepper-sprayed. When she
saw the overwhelming force and violence from the police, she
thought, "They want us gone. They want any presence gone.
They want to smash not just the movement but the people.
They want to smash our hopes and smash everything." She
was arrested later in the evening while just walking on the
sidewalk. "That night they had their targets," she says. "They
arrested people for just standing there." She spent her birthday
behind bars, released thirty-two hours later. Stamp has relatives who are officers, and while she had long been aware of
the prison industrial complex, she was always quick to clarify
that there are good cops. But the violence she saw that night
was formative for her. "That night my entire narrative about
the cops changed."

Similar evictions were happening across the United States,
many within days of the New York City eviction. The evictions
changed Occupy, but the movement was not over. Direct actions continued and in some ways escalated.

As someone who had seen her family evicted when she
was teenager, Stamp gravitated to Occupy Homes, a group

that sought to replicate the eviction defense work of the 1930s, when neighborhood groups were formed during the Great Depression to physically stand in the way of evictions. They were influenced by the home takeover actions that had been started by Max Rameau and Take Back the Land. On December 6, 2011, activists in several cities moved homeless people into empty homes or undertook similar actions that drew attention to the fundamental injustice at the heart of the housing crisis. In Brooklyn's East New York neighborhood, Stamp was among those who moved Alfredo Carrasquillo, Tasha Glasgow, and their two children into an empty house and stayed to help them hold onto it.

Occupy changed the national dialogue around the economic injustice of this country. For months before Occupy started, media and politicians were talking about federal negotiations on raising the national debt ceiling. Within weeks the conversation became about inequality, and the 99 percent versus the 1 percent. The media coverage of Occupy brought national awareness to the militarization of our nation's police. And while the Occupy encampments were all gone after a few months, the people who Occupy brought in to the movement got a taste of the power of the people, together, fighting for liberation. It was a new moment, and it was not about saving people but about building something together.

Months after Occupy had been evicted from Zuccotti Park, the chance came for Occupy activists to express their vision for a better world in a different way. Hurricane Sandy, the widest Atlantic hurricane on record, took people in the northeastern United States by surprise, doing over $50 billion in damage, leaving thousands temporarily homeless, millions without power, and killing seventy-two.[5]

In the aftermath of Sandy, the relief and recovery efforts by government and large charities like the Red Cross were again shown to be inadequate. While there was not the large loss of life and property of Hurricane Katrina, the same pattern of unequal response and corporate opportunism presented itself.

By the time of Hurricane Sandy, awareness of the failures of the Red Cross had become widespread. Jay-Z, talking about the aftermath of Katrina, wrote, "I got together with Puffy [rapper Sean Combs] and we donated a million dollars to the relief effort, but we donated it to the Red Cross, which is barely different from donating to the government itself, the same government that failed those people the first time. Who knows how much of that money actually made it to people on the ground?"[6]

Marsha Evans, the president of the Red Cross, was forced out months after Hurricane Katrina because of the disastrous failures of relief efforts led by her organization. But little had changed within Red Cross since then.

In the midst of homelessness created by Hurricane Sandy, the *Wall Street Journal* reported that the Red Cross was paying $310 a night for workers to stay in the Soho Grand Hotel, for a total cost of $181,000.[7] Meanwhile, the organization still seemed to be both incompetent and overly focused on PR. "In another diversion, an emergency response vehicle was dispatched to an early December photo-op with supermodel Heidi Klum to tour affected areas with Red Cross supplies," reported *ProPublica*. "Did you know it takes a Victoria's Secret model five hours to unload one box off a truck?" recalled a senior Red Cross official.

Into this breach came Occupy. Widespread disgust with official responses made even people politically opposed to Occupy open to the movement's efforts. The wide networks of support the organization had built up during the previous year made for a fund-raising boon. Occupy Sandy quickly brought in $1.4 million, far more than Occupy Wall Street had ever raised. Near its height the organization had an estimated "2,500 volunteers, 15,000 meals and 120 carloads of supplies sent to recovery sites."[8]

Like Common Ground in the aftermath of Hurricane Katrina, Occupy Sandy sent an important message about the problems with the government/corporate relief structure by building a bottom-up alternative based on the anarchist principle of mutual aid, meaning a nonhierarchical approach based on an assumption of radical equality and exchange. This was the prefigurative politics of Occupy, showing that people could organize outside of traditional power structures and still be effective. Many Occupy Sandy volunteers had volunteered in New Orleans after Hurricane Katrina and tried to combat the tendency toward disaster masculinity seen then.

But in bringing together a broad political front under a message of rebuilding without systemic demands, they also may have unwittingly undermined the greater structural analysis of Occupy. "Unbeknownst to them and surely unintentionally, I think they're kind of reinforcing a right-wing message that government isn't the answer," Joel Berg, executive director of the New York City Coalition Against Hunger, told Al Jazeera America.[9] They also repeated many of the same mistakes of Common Ground, like a tyranny of structurelessness that allowed people of more privilege to rise to the top. And they had lost much of Occupy's willingness to directly challenge the state.

For all the flaws of Occupy, it was a mass movement that was not afraid to call out systemic problems. Many individuals, especially those of more privilege, may have entered as saviors, but the common denominator was people recognizing that the system was not working (or working exactly as intended, intended to make the rich richer and the poorer). To see a mass movement grappling with these issues and connecting with international uprisings was inspiring and exciting. And the movement's work still continues in projects like Strike Debt, a network that formed as part of Occupy Wall Street, aimed at eliminating most forms of debt.

As Occupy Sandy was coming together, a new movement was also being born in Canadian Indigenous communities. On November 12, 2012, four women from Saskatchewan, Canada, organized a teach-in that they called Idle No More to raise awareness about federal legislation that would threaten First Nations sovereignty. A month later, the women called for a national day of action, leading to protests in at least a dozen locations across Canada, including a hunger strike by northern Ontario Attawapiskat Chief Theresa Spence, calling the Canadian government to "initiate immediate discussions and the development of action plans to address treaty issues with First Nations across Canada."[10] The movement soon expanded to the rest of the continent (called Turtle Island in some Native traditions) and embraced direct actions, highway blockades, flash mobs, and more, inspiring solidarity demonstrations across the Americas and from New Zealand to Palestine.

"This is a continuation of the five-hundred-year-long Indigenous resistance," explained Indian Country Today Media Network contributor Gyasi Ross. "It's much bigger than one piece of legislation. . . . It's about this continual resistance that we've got to a consumeristic, non-Indigenous, non-sustainable way of life."[11]

"Idle No More ain't Occupy," wrote Canadian activist and author Harsha Walia. "It's all those voices rising up that many in the Occupy movement resisted when they/we called on Occupy to decolonize, learn anti-oppression, and understand the systemic differences of inequality amongst the '99%.'"[12]

As Idle No More spread, another movement was growing in the United States that would address more directly the issues of race and gender that Occupy only confronted when it was at its best (and too often tried to ignore).

Chapter Ten
Black Lives Matter

The popular uprisings that became known as the Movement for Black Lives blazed another path away from the savior mentality. The modern phase of the movement dates to the murder of Trayvon Martin by George Zimmerman in February 2012, although it could just as easily have started in any other year, with any other young Black man killed by police or vigilantes. Black people in the United States have always lived under the threat of white supremacist violence and have always found ways to resist that violence. You could say the 1831 uprising against slavery led by Nat Turner was an early Black Lives Matter protest, or that Harriet Tubman and Ida B. Wells are early Black Lives Matter leaders.

There is a direct line from the system Nat Turner fought against to today's prison industrial complex. The modern police force is an institutional descendant of slave catchers, and today's prisons are a continuation of the system of slavery.

The first step in ending the prison industrial complex is in breaking our imagination free from the limited options presented by our current system. Even some progressives say, when talking about someone convicted of a horrible crime, something like, "I hope he rots in prison" or "I hope he's raped in prison." I can relate—there are people I wish horrible fates upon. But this desire for punishment cedes power to a brutal state and accepts the principle of systematizing revenge. It says that some people should be raped or tortured or locked away—the only argument is over who "deserves" the punishment, not over the morality of torture and prison. We must create a world where no life is thrown away as worthless and where prisons are a distant memory, a rumor, an incomprehensible myth told to future generations as a warning. Poet Alexis Pauline Gumbs captures this vision in her poem *an archeology of freedom*:

prison
an obscure word
footnoted in
dictionaries scholars
say
it was how the ancients
wrote "we are not yet
ready"
on their wrists every morning[1]

Scholar and prison abolitionist Ruth Wilson Gilmore has explained that to overturn this awful system we need to stop talking about "nonviolent offenders" or the "wrongfully convicted." We have over seven million people in prison, jail, probation or parole, by far the largest prison population on the planet. Twenty-five percent of all prisoners in the world are in U.S. prisons. This will not change by a piecemeal approach of reducing charges. Gilmore says we must follow the example of Harriet Tubman, who escaped slavery and went back to free as many others as she could. "Harriet Tubman didn't say, I'm only going to bring to the land of freedom the nonviolent, non-serious, non–sexual offenders," says Gilmore. "She said I'm bringing everyone to freedom."

Modern-day slavery demands modern-day abolition. "Abolition demands that everything changes so that the people who are locked up can come back," says Gilmore. "But more importantly, abolition also demands that we change how we do things so it is less likely that people commit harmful things, that people are desperate and commit property violations, that people get caught up in the criminal justice system." Finally, we need to "change the political logic that defines this country. And that logic is: 'The way we solve a problem is by killing it.' Our logic has to be: 'The way we solve a problem is by loving it.'"[2]

Norris Henderson spent twenty-seven years in prison for a crime he did not commit. While in prison, his son was murdered. Norris shared that he wanted revenge on the man who killed his son. But, he added, "In a fair and just society, you can't create laws based on how you feel at the worst moment of your life." Whatever personal desire for revenge we might have, no society should be built on vengeance.

There are many organizations creating this more just world. *The Revolution Starts at Home*, edited by Ching-In Chen, Jai Dulani, and Leah Lakshmi Piepzna-Samarasinha, lays out solutions for justice outside of the prison industrial complex, ways that people can find safety in community rather than the state, highlighting organizations like the Audre Lorde Project (ALP) in New York City. The Safe OUTside the System Collective, started by ALP in 1997, created a tool kit for ways to create community safety without policing. Among the strategies is a program that allows businesses to declare themselves safe spaces for people walking late at night. As *The Revolution Starts at Home* points out, because of the historically racist and violent practices of police, many communities have been forced to find ways to be safe without relying on the state. To varying degrees, many working-class communities in the United States and around the world still have to do this.

For all of U.S. history, popular uprisings, especially in communities of color, have been met with armed state violence. The U.S. military has been used to fight slave rebellions, strikes, and civil rights protests. The SWAT (Special Weapons And Tactics) team was born in response to the protests and uprisings of the 1960s, like the Watts riots of 1965.[3] The first use of the Los Angeles SWAT team was in 1969, in an operation against the Black Panther Party.

This trend continued in the 1980s and 1990s with the massive expansion of policing under the so-called War on Drugs and ramped up even more with the so-called War on Terror. "By the mid-2000s, 80 percent of law-enforcement agencies in towns with populations of 25,000 to 50,000 had a military-style unit, compared with just 20 percent in the mid-1980s," reports the *New York Times Magazine*. "One Pentagon program has sent at least $5.6 billion in equipment to police departments, including 625 armored tactical vehicles, more than 200 grenade launchers and around 80,000 assault rifles."[4]

It is in this context of war against communities of color that on February 26, 2012, seventeen-year-old Trayvon Martin was killed by George Zimmerman, a violent and paranoid local neighborhood watch volunteer. Police did not immediately press charges, and most media initially ignored the case. It took weeks of pressure initiated by Martin's family members before the killing became a national story and the state finally pressed charges.

A few months after Trayvon Martin was killed, the case of Marissa Alexander, a Black woman who faced charges brought by the same prosecutor that Zimmerman would face, showed a double standard at play. After firing a warning shot against her abusive husband, she was charged with aggravated assault. Prosecutor Angela Corey launched an aggressive prosecution, and Marissa was found guilty and sentenced to twenty years in prison.

In June 2013, Zimmerman went on trial for the killing of Trayvon Martin. This time it was clear that the state was not as committed to securing a conviction. After a lackluster prosecution, on July 13 the jury returned a verdict of not guilty, and Florida attorney general Corey seemed to almost celebrate the verdict. "We are so proud to stand before you," said Corey after the verdict, as she wore what one reporter called, "the weird smile of an event planner."[5]

Across the United States there was pain and outrage. Bay Area organizer Alicia Garza expressed her pain on Facebook. "Stop saying we are not surprised. That's a damn shame in itself.

I continue to be surprised at how little Black lives matter. And I will continue that. Stop giving up on Black life. Black people, I will NEVER give up on us. NEVER."[6]

Minutes later Garza's friend Patrisse Cullors responded by adding a hashtag to Garza's phrase: #blacklivesmatter.

Cullors is an organizer in Los Angeles. She and Garza are so close they call each other Twin. Like Garza, Cullors felt a personal pain with each incidence of police violence. Her earliest memory was of a battering ram crashing through her door and police physically tearing her home apart. "By the time I was thirteen, I had seen my entire community decimated by law enforcement." By the age of sixteen, her brother had been arrested and brutally beaten by police. "We knew the local police department, we knew the local police officer that would harass my siblings." Cullors grew up in the shadow of state violence but also found conflict from her family, who did not accept her because of her sexuality. She later found a political home in a radical grassroots organization called the Labor Community Strategy Center, where, she says, "I was trained to believe in an international fight against U.S. imperialism."[7]

Garza's activism started in middle school, advocating for sex education and peer counseling. Her activism continued through college, but it was not until after she graduated that she came to a full leftist analysis, through studying with SOUL, the Oakland-based School of Unity and Liberation. SOUL is a revolutionary organization and helped give her an "analysis around capitalism and imperialism and white supremacy and patriarchy and heteronormativity." Through SOUL she began working with a grassroots organization called Just Cause and eventually with another base-building group, POWER (People Organized to Win Employment Rights), that became her political home for nearly a decade.

Cullors and Garza, along with millions of others, expressed their pain on Twitter and Facebook and in spontaneous protests in the streets. Cullors messaged Garza: "Twin, #blacklivesmatter campaign? Can we discuss this? I have ideas.

I am thinking we can do a whole social media/all out in the streets organizing effort. Let me know."

That night Garza couldn't sleep. She woke up at 4:30 a.m. "crying and howling with grief and rage," and thinking about her younger brother and other young Black men in her life. "I just wanna be with my baby brother right now. I wanna hold him so tight and just pray," she wrote on Facebook. "I want Black people to be free." She thought about the words of civil rights movement leader Ella Baker: "Until the killing of Black men, Black mothers' sons, is as important as the killing of white men, white mothers' sons, we who believe in freedom cannot rest."[8]

The next morning Garza went to Sole Space, a store and community center in downtown Oakland that had made itself a space for activists and grieving community members. She and others made signs for a demonstration that day, using the slogan Black Lives Matter.

Another friend, Opal Tometi, joined later that week. She encouraged Garza and Cullors to grow from a hashtag to an organization. The child of Nigerian immigrants, Tometi had been organizing in support of immigrants in Arizona and had recently moved to New York. Her work centered around building bridges between African Americans and immigrant communities.

Cullors announced on Facebook: "#blacklivesmatter is a movement attempting to visiblize what it means to be Black in this country. Provide hope and inspiration for collective action to build collective power to achieve collective transformation. Rooted in grief and rage but pointed towards vision and dreams."

Garza added the next day. "#blacklivesmatter is a collective affirmation and embracing of the resistance and resilience of Black people. It is a rallying cry. It is a prayer. The impact of embracing and defending the value of Black life in particular has the potential to lift us all."

From the beginning, Tometi, Garza and Cullors saw Black Lives Matter as part of an existing liberation movement. "We knew that this movement wasn't started by us," says Cullors. "Its roots lie in the Black organizers of centuries ago, our ancestors who, in the face of violence like chattel slavery, lynching, whipping, rape, theft and separation of our families fought for freedom from the state."[9] Garza also sees roots of the movement in the mass displacement of African-Americans after Hurricane Katrina. "Had Black folks not been forced to once again take care of ourselves and each other," she said, reflecting on post-Katrina organizing, "Had none of this happened, there would be no Black Lives Matter."

Very quickly things moved from a Facebook group to a website, organizing meetings, protests, and a board. Black Lives Matter developed into a key force in what would later be called the Movement for Black Lives, which was made up of many different organizations fighting the systems of white supremacist violence against Black people and communities. For many, the phrase *Black lives matter* beautifully encapsulated a statement of resistance, a movement demand, and a cry of anguish against negation. If our system recognized that Black lives matter, Trayvon would be alive. Troy Davis would be alive. Oscar Grant would be alive. Marissa Alexander and CeCe McDonald would not have gone to jail for defending themselves.

While Garza was mourning and organizing in California, another gathering of movement activists was coming together in Chicago. Charlene Carruthers, a queer Black feminist organizer, was part of a gathering of one hundred Black millennials committed to social justice. When the verdict was announced during their gathering, it was what Carruthers calls "a moment of collective trauma, but also a moment of collective clarity." The group later coalesced into a national network called Black Youth Project (BYP) 100, growing to over three hundred members in Chicago, the Bay Area, Detroit, New Orleans, New York City, and Washington, D.C.[10]

Trayvon Martin's death and the acquittal of George Zimmerman was a turning point in other cities as well. For Black communities, the story of police and vigilante violence was nothing new. That April, the Malcolm X Grassroots Movement released a report noting 313 killings of Black men, women, and children in 2012, adding up to one person killed every twenty-eight hours by someone "employed or protected by the U.S. government."[11] But the details of Trayvon's death—the Skittles he had just bought, the hoodie, his youth, the way he was depicted by the media, the lackluster prosecution of Zimmerman—all added up to a clear and traumatic example of the systemic racism faced by Black communities.

There were murders by police and protests in response flaring up everywhere. In Brooklyn, people took to the streets on behalf of Kimani Gray, sixteen, killed by police on March 9, 2013. And there was Jordan Baker, twenty-six, killed in Houston in January 2014. And Victor White III, twenty-two, shot while handcuffed in a police cruiser in rural Louisiana in March 2014. Police claimed Victor shot himself, even though he was in police custody and his hands were cuffed behind his back.

That year Garza left her longtime position at POWER for a new job with the National Domestic Workers Alliance (NDWA), an organization that fights for rights for caregivers. Her new job took her around the country more, but for Garza her work with NDWA was deeply connected to her expanding responsibilities to Black Lives Matter. "Domestic workers, in particular the work I do with Black domestic workers, are mothers who are trying to protect their families from state violence," she explained. "The way that we talk about state violence with Black Lives Matter is that state violence equals structural racism."

In July 2014 an officer was caught on video choking forty-three-year-old Eric Garner to death in New York City. He could be heard to repeatedly plead, "I can't breathe." Less than three weeks later, John Crawford III, twenty-two, was shot while shopping in a Wal-Mart in Ohio. Then, on an August evening in Ferguson, Missouri, officer Darren Wilson killed eighteen-year-old Mike Brown. His body was left in the street, for all to see, for hours. The pain of his death, combined with a particularly brutal justice system in the St. Louis area that basically funded municipal government through the petty harassment of working-class Black people, caused something to snap. Brave young activists from the area, like rapper Tef Poe and fast food workers who had been activists in a campaign for a living wage, came out to protest again and again in the face of brutal police repression. Marches went on into the late night, sometimes traveling miles. Garza went to Ferguson, representing Black Lives Matter and the National Domestic Workers Alliance.

"There are tons and tons of Black workers here in St. Louis who work for poverty wages, who live in communities that have been ravaged by poverty and racism," she said at the time. "If we're only organizing people around class issues, we're missing a huge part of people's experiences. Those young people are making the connection between racism, poverty, police violence, and state violence."[12]

Television cameras and cell phones showed military force deployed against the young people of Ferguson. For those who had not experienced the increasing militarization of policing, it came as a shock to see what looked like U.S. military occupation forces deployed in Missouri suburbs. The repression certainly scared many (and hundreds were locked up on trumped-up charges), but more people kept coming. I've been arrested at protests, but the people on the streets of Ferguson faced major felony charges for simply being on the streets, a risk my privilege has protected me from. Seeing the police react to Black protesters in Ferguson was further dramatic evidence that this country has two racially divided systems of justice.

Grassroots groups from the St Louis area were quick to get involved and lend support, including Organization for Black Struggle (OBS), which was cofounded by Jamala Rogers, a longtime veteran of the Black freedom struggle; and Missourians Organizing for Reform and Empowerment (MORE), which formed out of the ashes of ACORN. But the majority of protesters were local young people who were unaffiliated with any organization. They simply could not take another day of injustice without speaking out.

It was intense. There were protests every day, often lasting for hours, seemingly a perpetual state of unrest. On the night I arrived, two weeks after the protests had begun, I joined a march that started around 10:00 p.m. and lasted until at least 3:00 a.m., chanting, "We're young / We're strong / We're marching all night long." They were not exaggerating.

The protesters I saw were aware of the systemic nature of the problem. While initial demands from Mike Brown's family were not radical, such as calls for the Justice Department to intervene, the people in the street were calling for the whole system to come down and making the connections between police violence and other forms of systemic racism.

They spoke of a municipal court system that profited on the backs of poor, mostly Black residents. In some of the St. Louis suburbs, over 40 percent of the municipal budget came from fines. The town of Pine Lawn was a typical example, issuing 17,155 traffic citations in 2013 despite having only 3,216 residents. As was Country Club Hills, with twelve hundred residents and thirty-three thousand outstanding arrest warrants. Or Florissant and its nearly thirty thousand annual traffic tickets in a town of just fifty-two thousand. Many of these municipalities were mostly white, balancing their budget on the backs of Black people caught driving through their town. The system was obviously rigged—several men who serve as prosecutor in one town serve as the judge in another and a defense attorney in another. For example, Florissant prosecutor Ronald Brockmeyer also served as the chief municipal prosecutor for the towns of Vinita Park and Dellwood and as a judge in both Ferguson and Breckenridge Hills.[13]

Nelini Stamp was among the first activists to arrive from out of state, as part of a group called Dream Defenders she cofounded with thirty students and other young people from across Florida in 2012, after the death of Trayvon Martin. They had already captured national attention as a Black-led group in the Deep South that was unafraid to take direct action and get arrested for the cause of racial justice. The Dream Defenders crew that arrived in Ferguson quickly took a central role in supporting the local organizers. More activists arrived from all over. Patrisse Cullors and a queer Black writer in Brooklyn named Darnell Moore organized over five hundred Black activists from around the country to participate in the Black Life Matters Freedom Ride. Garza said the trip to Ferguson changed and inspired everyone. "People got excited about and really felt passionately about bringing what they had seen and what they had learned back to their communities," she says. "What we saw were people who were inspired by the actions that people were taking on the front lines in Ferguson."

Cullors says the message from the streets was, "We will not compromise for our freedom. We are going to be free no matter what." She was also inspired by "the ways that people were building relationships together, knowing that maybe folks hadn't been connected before, but certainly that they knew that they were going to be connected forever because of what had happened." Activists on the street paid tribute to movement elders like Assata Shakur, a member of the Black Panther Party and Black Liberation Army who was forced to flee to Cuba to escape state repression in the United States. One of the main movement chants was based on a poem written by Shakur while in prison on July 4, 1973:

It is our duty to fight for our freedom
It is our duty to win
We must love and protect one another
We have nothing to lose but our chains.

The movement continued to grow, even reaching an international diaspora. "We saw Afro-Colombian domestic workers sending pictures and photos saying Black lives matter," says Garza. "We saw folks from South Africa, folks from Ireland, folks from all over the world sending messages, not just of solidarity, but lifting up the conditions that Black people are facing in their countries."

Solidarity demonstrations rose up everywhere. In New Orleans I saw over a hundred activists spontaneously take

over a French Quarter police station. In April 2015 protesters in Wisconsin, responding to a police killing in Madison,
demanded an investigation by the United Nations, saying that
the United States could not be trusted to carry out its own
investigations. There was that feeling of anger and hope in the
air that I also felt at Occupy. People who had not protested
before were coming out.

In Missouri, the movement won some reforms, especially
related to municipal charges, despite a Republican legislature
and conservative Democratic governor.[14] More importantly,
like Occupy the movement had shifted the public debate.

It's important that many of the leaders of this movement
have been queer Black women. "Black liberation movements in
this country have created room and space and leadership mostly
for Black heterosexual, cisgender men," says Cullors. "As younger organizers we recognized a need to center the leadership of
women. Among our movement mentors were queer and trans
people whose labor had been erased and replaced with an un-
contested narrative of male leadership."[15] Women and queer
people have been the backbone of movements throughout the
twentieth century, but often their voices and leadership have
been relegated to the background. The Movement for Black
Lives consciously challenged this dynamic.

In contrast to privileged saviors leading from the outside,
this young, Black, female, working-class, queer leadership
shaped the trajectory of this movement. They did not trust
NGOs, the civil rights infrastructure, and older leaders like
Al Sharpton and Jesse Jackson. Growing up Black, they were
intimately aware of the realities of racism. They knew police
disproportionately targeted young Black men—their brothers and cousins and fathers and friends. As Black women they
bore not just the pain of witnessing violence toward their male
relatives but also the knowledge that the murder and abuse
of Black women is even less likely to make the news. Coming
from working-class backgrounds, many knew firsthand about
the lack of opportunities afforded them. For many, queer identity also meant opposition to unjust power. This is an LGBT

politics that remembers that New York's Stonewall riot of 1969 was an uprising against police led by trans women of color. As activists have chanted in Oakland and elsewhere, "Not gay as in happy, queer as in fuck the police."

The Movement for Black Lives is intersectional, non-hierarchical, and led by those most affected by our unjust system. Like Occupy, the Movement for Black Lives has been criticized for not having clear demands, but for Garza the demands are very clear, and systemic. "Nothing different than what Black people have been fighting for, for the last five hundred years," she says.

> We want housing that's quality and affordable. We want free education. We want communities where people can live in dignity. We want to be able to live with our families without fear of being murdered by the people who are supposed to be protecting us. We want full and fair employment for everyone. We want all the things that we have been fighting for since our people were brought here as slaves from Africa. This is not a new set of demands, but it's certainly a new political moment where we have the opportunity to join movements together . . . and really try to advance a new program for liberation in this country. We're just getting started.[16]

Black Lives Matter requires more than ending police violence. "Black lives can't matter under capitalism," says Garza. "We're clear that we're not trying to build Black capitalism; we are trying to transform society."[17] Patrisse Cullors agrees. "I think we can use this moment to look at state violence as a way to look at many other things, such as poverty, such as homelessness," she says.

With a critique of capitalism at its core, the founders are also critical of foundations and nonprofits. "I got love for the people, and the nonprofit industrial complex is not the way we're going to win," says Cullors.[18] This is also a lesson learned from the civil rights movement, which fought co-optation from funders, and every movement since. "I'm very much afraid of this 'foundation complex.' We're getting praise from places that worry me," said civil rights movement leader Ella Baker in 1963.[19]

Garza says that the foundation model has led many organizations to address issues in Black communities as being the fault of those communities. Some organizations based in the Black community "see black folks as deficient, as problems to be solved," says Garza. "They have a mentality that there needs to be some kind of savior to lead us to the Promised Land. We don't think we need that. That kind of model has become less and less relevant to our communities."

Garza adds that Black Lives Matter was built on the principle that "we are the wielder of the tools that can save our own lives. We're not telling people what to do. Our role is to help amplify community-driven solutions and resource the ability of people to get organized and fight back."

Makani Themba, the founding director of social justice training, media, and advocacy organization the Praxis Project, told journalist Dani McClain that she has seen a shift in who have been recognized as Black leaders since the 1960s. During the civil rights movement, says Themba, the leaders were the heads of Black institutions with large membership and constituencies, like Martin Luther King Jr. (Southern Christian Leadership Conference), Malcolm X (Nation of Islam), and Ella Baker (Student Nonviolent Coordinating Committee). By the 1970s and 1980s, the new recognized leaders were "the most deeply penetrated black person[s] in white or mainstream institutions."

"As civil-rights organizations began to depend more on corporate contributions than member donations," summarizes McClain, "and as Reagan-era cuts decimated organizations serving the black poor, black activists who wanted organizing and advocacy jobs turned to the institutions that had the resources to pay and retain them—often unions and economic-justice organizations that operated outside any explicitly black cultural context."[20]

Figures who are popular on Twitter are often lifted up by the media as being spokespeople for the movement, but on the streets it matters to whom you are accountable. "The people who the liberal media and social media have elevated to the position of national leader or spokesperson do not share the values of the movement," says Umi Selah of Dream Defenders. "The ideas that they put forth, the platforms that they put forth, are neoliberal and do not come from a rooting in movement, don't come from a liberation framework, from an abolition framework."[21]

Nelini Stamp, looking back on her organizing during this time, sees herself as having fallen into a savior model in 2014, when she moved to Georgia and within six months cofounded a new racial and economic justice organization, Rise Up Georgia. "If I had the chance to do it again, I probably would have waited another year," she says. "I didn't do the due diligence to build the relationships, talking to people, getting active." Stamp found that even though she was from a working-class background, people in Georgia saw her as being from New York City, one of the richest areas of the country. "One way I addressed that issue was by making sure we had Georgia leaders at the front of the room," she says. "Making sure the organization was led by and accountable to people from Georgia."

Despite being a decentralized uprising, the Movement for Black Lives has real unity of vision. From its founding, the movement was led by and accountable to those most affected, and it has remained focused on the root causes of the problems. From the beginning, leaders have framed it as a struggle against white supremacy, patriarchy, colonialism, and capitalism. It is rooted in a history of radical Black organizing, from slave revolts to the Black Panthers and Black Liberation Army in the 1970s, and from there to the mass civil rights protests in Jena, Louisiana, in 2007.

Pan-Africanist revolutionary movements also inspired the Movement for Black Lives. For Tometi, who had already focused on immigration issues, it was important from the beginning to unite under a name that encompassed more than the

United States. "I had in mind that it was really important that we establish a really broad notion of who is Black America," she says. "My parents are Nigerian immigrants, the communities that I work with are Afro-Latinos and Caribbean, and so on. I wanted to ensure that this platform was big enough that they could also have their voice and their concerns heard."

Like the activists in earlier Black liberation movements that inspire them, Cullors, Garza, and Tometi built connections with activists from around the world. In the first days of 2015, fourteen leaders of the movement traveled to Palestine. They represented the organizations Dream Defenders, Hands Up United, Justice League NYC, Black Youth Project 100, and Black Lives Matter. One of the Dream Defenders, Ahmad Abuznaid, announced, "In the spirit of Malcolm X, Angela Davis, Stokely Carmichael, and many others, we thought the connections between the African American leadership of the movement in the U.S. and those on the ground in Palestine needed to be reestablished and fortified."

"We thought it was important, even though we knew that it might be a huge risk for a lot of us, to show up and let Palestinians know that we are in deep solidarity with them," said Cullors. "And, frankly, we believe that Palestine is the new South Africa."

Jasiri X, a rapper and activist associated with the Nation of Islam, also visited Palestine, as part of a delegation in early 2014. "There's definitely a connection," he told me one night on the streets of Ferguson. "I went to Palestine, and I went through these checkpoints. Dehumanizing things where you [have] to walk through . . . [and] get searched." Gesturing up the road at a National Guard checkpoint in the middle of the street, he added, "There are checkpoints here in Ferguson. The same tear gas they were using in Gaza and Israel they were using on people here—[made] by the same manufacturers." In Ferguson, the smell of tear gas was still in the air from a week of militarized response.

"What I saw in Palestine was: if you're Palestinian, you have to prove that you're not a threat to the system," said Jasiri, who first came to national attention with his 2007 song in support of the Jena Six. "And it's the same with us here in Ferguson. If we're a Black man or a Black woman, we have to prove that you don't have to fear us and you can be safe around us, and if we don't pull back quick enough we can be killed."

From the first days, the solidarity was returned. Palestinian activists from the St. Louis area were among the first on the streets to join protests, and messages of solidarity with the protests came in from occupied Palestine. When Cullors and the other Black Lives Matter activists arrived in the West Bank, they felt an immediate connection.

Although she had been aware of the injustices faced in Palestine, Cullors was still surprised by the extent of the oppression. "Nothing would have prepared me for the level of violence and militarization that the Palestinian people are under. There was also this kindred-ness that we felt with Palestinians as Black people. The constant sort of battering and terrorizing by military, and for us by police, is eerily similar."

Black Lives Matter stands in sharp contrast to the savior model of change. Activists in the movement are critical of the role of foundations and outside funders and instead seek accountability to the communities they seek to serve. Organizers see the systemic roots to the problems they seek to address. They practice principled internationalism, building concrete connections to movements in other countries from a place of shared struggle rather than paternalism. They put their bodies on the line. They prioritize leadership by those who have the most to lose.

It's too early to say where the Movement for Black Lives or other movements of this moment are headed, but it's clear that we live in a polarized time. As the right-wing discourse becomes more violent and hateful, the number of people who see the need for systemic change also grows. Black Lives Matter has grown to include over thirty chapters around the United States, and BYP 100 and others are also expanding. The network was designed to be "adaptive and decentralized with a set of guiding principles," says Cullors. "Our goal is to support the development of new Black leaders as well as create a network where Black people feel empowered to determine our destinies in our communities."[22] In August of 2016, over 50 organizations that make up the heart of the movement released *A Vision for Black Lives: Policy Demands for Black Power, Freedom and Justice*, a detailed and wide-ranging platform of six demands, each broken up into three to ten points, backed up with specific research and resources.

This movement has also invaded mainstream (white) discourse with questions of white supremacy and white privilege. The rise of the Internet and social media has also allowed previously excluded voices to reach larger audiences, whether through blogs, podcasts, Twitter, Instagram, Tumblr, or dozens of other outlets. And new media companies, from Buzzfeed to Al Jazeera, have also made an effort to highlight these previously excluded voices. Those of privilege are becoming aware, however late, that whiteness should not be a central narrative, a lens through which all other experiences are viewed. This has led to mainstream discussions of related issues, such as micro-aggressions: the small but regular insults that people of color face regularly from white people. Hollywood and other mainstream media and entertainment are still celebrating racist work like *Tarzan* and *The Jungle Book*, but this movement has brought a cultural change that is just beginning.

As the movement has grown, it has brought up the question, what is the role for people with privilege who want to challenge the structures of power?

Chapter Eleven
Decentering Privilege

How can a person with privilege challenge systems of injustice without playing into the savior mentality? Across today's movements, I've seen organizers modeling accountable leadership, trying new tactics, and mentoring younger activists.

My first arrest at a mass direct action was in 1995, as I joined a group of City University of New York (CUNY) students blocking the road to the Brooklyn Battery Tunnel in protest of budget cuts being pushed by the Republican mayor and governor, Rudolph Giuliani and George Pataki. When we were arrested and taken to jail, we found out that at the same time as our arrest, dozens of other groups had simultaneously blocked nearly every entrance and exit to Manhattan. There were activists from AIDS Coalition to Unleash Power (ACT-UP) protesting cuts to health care; disability rights activists protesting cuts to services; activists from Committee Against Anti-Asian Violence and the National Congress for Puerto Rican Rights protesting police brutality; and many more. We had all come to protest the issues closest to us, and meeting up in jail we saw the clear demonstration that all of our issues are connected, that we are fighting the same forces. This was not an accident. Leaders from each of these organizations had met together and planned this action as a way to build unity in a sometimes-fractured movement.

Joining in coalition with hundreds of other activists from dozens of organizations helped shape the possibilities that I see today. It was powerful to feel part of a broad coalition. I learned that we can win by uniting our struggles together, despite the divisions imposed on us, and looking at the shared systemic problems at the root.

Later I worked as a union organizer, talking with nursing home workers who were fighting for more rights on the job. In the early days of each campaign, worker's opinions were fluid. They knew there were problems at their workplace, but they weren't sure that things could get better. Maybe 10 percent were excited about a union, and 10 percent were strongly anti-union, and the other 80 percent had very little idea of what a union even was. But in every such campaign there is a moment of polarization. The pro-union workers talk with everyone they can, the company starts its anti-union campaign, and within a couple of days everyone in that 80 percent has chosen a side and most are unlikely to change sides.

Sometimes organizing is about what you do before that polarization. Who can you engage with while they are still listening? How do you make people see that change is possible, when all of politics and media tell them that we are at the end of history and that ordinary people cannot make change? Especially as people with privilege, we need to have those difficult conversations within our communities.

Since I moved to New Orleans I have spent time learning from Curtis Muhammad, a civil rights and Black Power movement veteran from McComb, Mississippi. He taught me that one of the strengths of the civil rights movement was that its activists took the time to get community consensus on issues, and they were led by and accountable to the communities on the front lines of white supremacist violence. He worked with leaders like Ella Baker, who believed that power should come from the bottom and fought for the leadership of young people, poor people, and Black people. Through organizations like SNCC, people at the grassroots built a powerful, broad, rooted movement. And because of grounded clarity, allies from other places, including privileged white activists, could join without taking over. In its best moments, that's what a victorious movement looks like.

Wherever you live, the best way to combat the savior mentality is to act collectively for systemic change in a way that is accountable to the communities affected. The need for revolutionary change is more urgent than ever, and there is a lot of agreement about what is wrong. But many allies do not know how to join the struggle. "We get a lot of folks, especially white folks, who say 'I'm down,'" Alicia Garza of Black Lives Matter tells me. "We say you should be having deep conversations and deep work in your own community, mobilize and galvanize people to make that commitment. Give some direction to other people like you who want to do the right thing. If you're the loudest voice in the room, create space for other voices, literally and figuratively." The people facing the most oppression are already fighting back. They don't need you to tell them what to do.

And, if people from the community you are seeking to support give you negative feedback, if you are a person in a position of privilege and feel "called out," don't act defensively. Don't be fragile. Listen, learn, acknowledge, and use the experience as an opportunity to change your approach.

Over the course of 2015, Showing Up for Racial Justice (SURJ), a national white antiracist coalition, went from twelve chapters to more than one hundred. In several cities, including New Orleans, activists affiliated with SURJ have gone door-to-door in mostly white neighborhoods to have discussions about race and racism. Other solidarity activists have been arrested in the name of supporting Black Lives Matter protests and anti-Trump protests, or they have engaged in other less glamorous support for Black activists, like child care and fund-raising.

Another aspect of this change is approaching people with empathy, understanding where they are coming from. As Che Guevara, another revolutionary child of privilege, once said, "The true revolutionary is guided by great feelings of love." In

2014, the Catalyst Project released an online guide for activists with privilege seeking to shift their culture of organizing and support the Movement for Black Lives. It's a powerful resource for anyone seeking to create change. For example, they describe shifting from "call-out culture" to "build-up culture." To do this, "instead of shaming people for their mistakes and regulating each others' language, appreciate and lift up principled action and leadership where you see it." This transformation also demands moving from individual focus to collective action. Instead of asking, "How can I be the single best white antiracist activist with the sharpest critique, most specialized language, and busiest schedule?" Ask, "How can we find ways to bring more and more people into social justice work, from lots of entry points, to grow vibrant mass movements?"[1] I've seen this kind of *calling in* effort in the work of the New Teachers' Roundtable in New Orleans.

It's easy to criticize other people that share our privilege, but the real challenge is to bring them in and make our movement larger. As a prison abolitionist, I don't believe in giving up on someone who has committed a violent crime. I believe in change and rehabilitation. If we believe we should not lock up for life someone who has committed murder, we should find a way to support change in people who have been involved in KONY 2012 or Teach for America. Part of that is building a vibrant and effective movement, to show in our practice that systemic change is possible. The organizers in the Movement for Black Lives have done this.

We also need to be open and dynamic in our approach to organizing. Being active on Twitter cannot take the place of face-to-face organizing. But hashtags like #notyourrescue and #blacklivesmatter are important, and not just as a social media arm of an on-the-street struggle. They also represent the way in which movements have brought the principles of radical tech activists, like open source programming, to organizing. In the case of Not1More, a popular call to end immigrant detentions and deportations, they call it "open source campaigning." Analyzing their work in Not1More, organizers Marisa Franco, B.

Loewe, and Tania Unzueta see the non-proprietary implications of a hashtag as symbolically crucial. "Instead of building everything in-house and in secret, open source refers to something whose design is public, a central platform that invites modification and improvement through various entry points of collaboration."[2]

Contrasting Not1More with protests where "in some places, you'll see an organization's logo on their sign before the message of their rally," the writers stress openness along with guidelines and accountability. "Open source does not simply mean that the platform or campaign belongs to no one or that anyone is free to do anything. Even an experimental free form jam session has rules. Open source campaigns function best with clear purpose, frame, values that serve as basic parameters."[3]

The attempts by some well-meaning activists (and some not so well-meaning ones) to co-opt #blacklivesmatter to the formation #alllivesmatter is one example of how these rules can be broken. "Changing #blacklivesmatter to #alllivesmatter is not an act of solidarity. What it is, is a demonstration of how we don't actually understand structural racism in this country," says Alicia Garza. "I saw #animallivesmatter one time and I just threw up a little bit in my mouth, actually." Pro-police groups even started using #bluelivesmatter. In all cases these were not additions by allies but hostile attempts to change the subject.

Describing how open source organizing works practically, Franco, Loewe, and Unzueta describe a series of actions against ICE in winter of 2013–14. Families in Phoenix sat vigil outside a local immigration office demanding the release of their own detained children and "issued a call for civil disobedience saying that if the President wouldn't stop deportation, we would stop them ourselves." In Tacoma, Washington, activists responded to the call by forming a human chain, blocking buses that were for deporting detainees. "Those detainees returned to their cells and organized a facility-wide hunger strike that received national media attention. Prisoners in a detention center in Texas saw that news coverage. They later released their own demands in a letter and started their own strike." These actions were not coordinated, they were separate, but "the campaign converged with a month-long fast in front of the White House that became a point of reference when the President answered questions in press briefings."[4] The campaign had become viral. It had taken on a life of its own but kept accountable to the principles it was founded on.

From visiting sites of struggle around the world, I've learned the power and effectiveness that comes from following the leadership of those most affected. I've learned the importance of being suspicious of people like Brandon Darby, who may match the images of a leader that we've been taught to expect by our schools and media. Instead, we can ask who are the people from the community we wish to support that are already doing the work of resistance. Finding these leaders takes more effort, because they are often working without grants or media attention, but this extra work helps build a stronger movement. Organizer N'Tanya Lee, cofounder of West Coast movement strategy organization Left Roots, has said, "If you want a new society, you need to figure out a strategy where the people in leadership are the ones who have the most at stake in changing the society. The ones who are going to be the least satisfied by little victories."[5] People from a position of power are often more drawn towards reform, because we stand to lose some of that privilege in the case of true systemic change. We need to stand with the people with the most to gain from a new world.

This lesson is as old as "The Internationale." The anthem of class struggle, set to music in 1888, declares that the struggle for liberation must be led by the workers themselves. The English adaption, distributed in the songbook of the syndicalist Industrial Workers of the World (IWW), contains the verse:

We want no condescending saviors
To rule us from their judgment hall
We workers ask not for their favors
Let us consult for all.[6]

Our movement also needs radical healing to be inclusive and sustainable. The disability justice movement has taught me this, and I continue to be inspired by their example. One inspiring healing project that came out of the Movement for Black Lives is Harriet's Apothecary, an intergenerational Black-led project committed to "co-creating accessible, affordable, liberatory, all-body loving, all-gender honoring, community healing spaces that recognize, inspire, and deepen the healing genius of people who identify as Black, Indigenous and People of color and the allies that love us." Named for Harriet Tubman, the collaboration is "led by the brilliance and wisdom of Black Cis Women, Queer and Trans healers, artists, health professionals, magicians, activists and ancestors."[7]

We need to learn from and connect to our elders and radical history. I've seen this in practice with Diné youth at Black Mesa, with the New Teachers' Roundtable and its work with more experienced teachers and civil rights movement veterans, and in the Movement for Black Lives and its connection to older radical traditions.

An accountable movement needs media that want to challenge the powerful and lift up alternatives. It's crucial to celebrate and support the media makers who are challenging the powerful, from the legacy of Ida B. Wells to today's heroes like Ramsey Orta.

Visionary art is also necessary, to help us imagine a new world. My inspiration in this is the contributors to *Octavia's Brood*, as well as movement artists, musicians, and cultural workers from Favianna Rodriguez to Boots Riley, Jasiri X, Suheir Hammad, Alexis Pauline Gumbs, and Sunni Patterson. Their art makes our movements more sustainable and brings inspiration and imagination.

In a world where the richest 1 percent—including the funders that decide the priorities of social justice movements—own more than the rest of the world combined, and where we are on the brink (or beyond the brink) of global climate disaster, we need vast structural change.[8] Yes, we need individual improvements along the way to structural change, things that help people survive and improve lives. But the question is, what are the changes that transform our world? The answer is not microloans or the Peace Corps but the principled international alliances seen in the Movement for Black Lives, the Palestine boycott, divestment, and sanctions movement, and the anticolonial work of Idle No More and the Diné resistance at Black Mesa.

In 1970 John D. Rockefeller's Commission on Foundation and Private Philanthropy reported a problem facing the United States. "The spirit of dissent has spread its contagion across our student population and from there to other sectors of American life," the commission wrote. "If they are not to reach their climax in a war of all against all, we are summoned by this turmoil to carefully consider the ways in which we can convert dissent into a force for constructive action and civil peace." In other words, funders sought to encourage safe reforms that would not threaten capitalism, instead channeling energy into arenas that would leave Rockefeller's financial interests and power intact, like Teach For America. "We must evolve more responsive processes through which our young and disenfranchised can secure a fair piece of the social action, whether or not they can acquire a piece of the affluent economic action."[9]

But a "piece of the social action" is not the level of reform that our world needs. As Michelle Alexander has said, "What we have been doing is not working. We must stop pretending to have answers and instead ask some different questions. We are in a reform dance."[10] Ta-Nehisi Coates adds, "A reform that begins with the officer on the beat is not reform at all. It's avoidance."[11]

In 1964 philosopher André Gorz wrote that we should pursue "non-reformist reforms," adding, "a non-reformist reform is determined not in terms of what can be, but what should be."[12] Gorz's position, elaborated today in revolutionaries and prison abolitionists like Ruth Wilson Gilmore and Angela Davis, is that even when we pursue limited reforms, we should be sure that they will not strengthen the system we wish to end. Instead, those who seek change should strengthen entities outside the state. "Structural reform is by definition a reform implemented or controlled by those who demand it," wrote Gorz.

> Be it in agriculture, the university, property relations, the region, the administration, the economy, etc., a structural reform *always* requires the creation of new centers of democratic power.
>
> Whether it be at the level of companies, schools, municipalities, regions or the national Plan, etc, structural reform always requires a *decentralization* of the decision making power, *a restriction on the powers of State or Capital*, an *extension of popular power*, that is to say, a victory of democracy over the dictatorship of profit.[13]

Another view of this is what Russian communist Vladimir Lenin called "dual power," contesting for the power of the state while also building up alternatives to the state. It's a model of change also embraced by popular movements in South America, like the mass movement in Bolivia, which elected Evo Morales as president while also maintaining a presence in the streets, and by anticapitalists going back to French philosopher Pierre-Joseph Proudhon, the first person to call himself an anarchist.

If we believe in abolishing white supremacy, patriarchy, and the prison industrial complex, how do we support reforms that will not strengthen the institution we seek to eliminate? "Progress in prison reform has tended to render the prison more impermeable to change and has resulted in bigger, and what are considered 'better,' prisons," Angela Davis has said. "The most difficult question for advocates of prison abolition is how to establish a balance between reforms that are clearly necessary to safeguard the lives of prisoners and those strategies designed to promote the eventual abolition of prisons as the dominant mode of punishment." For example, "Demands for improved health care, including protection from sexual abuse and challenges to the myriad ways in which prisons violate prisoners' human rights, can be integrated into an abolitionist context that elaborates specific decarceration strategies and helps to develop a popular discourse on the need to shift resources from punishment to education, housing, health care, and other public resources and services."[14]

Another powerful example of this kind of reform in the United States is the *survival programs*, such as free breakfast for children, run by the Black Panther Party (BPP) during the late 1960s and into the 1970s. Although providing food for children seems like a small and simple project, like the soup kitchens discussed earlier in this book, having that project run by a revolutionary group showed the potential of independence from the state and a demonstration of communist principles in action. FBI director J. Edgar Hoover saw the program as "potentially the greatest threat to efforts by authorities to neutralize the BPP and destroy what it stands for."[15] Radical labor movements in the United States have a similar history, building housing for workers, starting cultural programs and newspapers, building alternative structures that reached every aspect of people's lives.

Speaking about the reforms won by the LGBT movement, poverty lawyer and professor Dean Spade has been fiercely critical of goals such as gay marriage and access to the military, writing, "Legal equality goals threaten to provide nothing more than adjustments to the window-dressing of neoliberal violence."[16] In other words, homelessness, police violence, bad schools, and other ways in which poor people experience violence are not addressed by expanding rights to marriage or military service. Even lobbying for progressive laws can be problematic, as "law reform projects often provide rationales and justifications for the expansion of harmful systems." Spade believes we must openly oppose liberal and neoliberal agendas and find "solidarity with other struggles articulated by the forgotten, the inconceivable, the spectacularized, and the unimaginable."[17]

The Rockefeller commission sought to fund nonprofits to prevent a war of "all against all." Today the divide between rich and poor is even deeper. The questions raised by today's movements are not trivial. They are about survival of the entire planet. We must build a movement that does more than offer charity while preserving the status quo. We must transform ourselves, our organizations, our communities, and our world.

After more than twenty years of both participating in and reporting on social movements, many of the most inspiring organizers I've seen recently are teenagers who already have a deep understanding of the systemic change that is needed. The changes we fear are impossible are already on their way. We can build a better world as long as we don't fall into traps of reform that leave out those who are most in need. If we listen to those who have the most to lose, and stand in principled struggle with those on the bottom, everything is possible. In the words of Assata Shakur again:

It is our duty to fight for our freedom
It is our duty to win
We must love and protect one another
We have nothing to lose but our chains.

Acknowledgments

In writing this book, I am indebted to the analysis of countless scholars and movement leaders. I lean heavily on the work of INCITE! and women of color feminists in general. I have learned from Black Panthers, civil rights movement veterans, sex workers, lawyers, artists, organizers, students, researchers, teachers, and many more.

I would especially like to thank the many people I interviewed for this book and the many more that I spent hours in conversation with, and many others who have influenced me with their writing. All of them helped me think about the ideas that later developed into this book. This long list includes Alexandra Lutnick, Alicia Garza, Andrea Ritchie, Andrea Smith, Angela Davis, Anna Saini, Berkley Carnine, Boots Riley, Caitlin Beedlove, Charhonda Cox, Clare Bayard, Craig Willse, Curtis Muhammad, Dean Spade, Deon Haywood, Derek Roguski, Elizabeth Falcon, Emily Danielson, Emily Ratner, Hannah Sadtler, J. M. Kirby, Jaclyn Moskal-Dairman, Johnshell Johnson, Kai Lumumba Barrow, Kate Mogulescu, Katie Seitz, Kelli Dorsey, Leah Lakshmi Piepzna-Samarasinha, Manissa McCleave Maharawal, Manju Rajendran, Max Rameau, Maxine Doogan, Melissa Gira Grant, Molly Crabapple, Molly McClure, Monica Jones, Nelini Stamp, Nicole Daro, Norris Henderson, Nyx Zierhut, Opal Tometi, Patrisse Cullors, Penelope Saunders, Rachel Luft, Sandy Nurse, Shana griffin, Shira Hassan, Sonny Singh, Sophie Lucido Johnson, Suheir Hammad,

Tara Burns, Tracie Washington, and the members of the organizations Alternate Roots and Critical Resistance. Also thanks to the many excellent journalists, producers, and editors I have collaborated with over the past several years, including Andréa Schmidt, Anjali Kamat, Christof Putzel, Laura Flanders, Jonathan Klett, Leila Garcia, Mat Skene, Melisa Cardona, Michael Okwu, Mira Oberman, Sanya Dosani, Sebastian Walker, and Sweta Vohra. And, always, thank you to my mom for inspiring me and teaching me.

I'm also grateful to the many people who read all or part of this book and gave feedback, including Aaron Schneider, Adrienne Goss, Amber Stephens, Amin Husain, Amy Barker, Chris Nayve, Garrick Ruiz, Gulnaz Saiyed, Hannah Galloway, James Lamar Gibson, Jayeesha Dutta, Jennifer Glick, Kat Aaron, Kimberly Joy Chandler, Laurie King, Leora Harlington, Lydia Pelot-Hobbs, Mike Duncan, Monica Tarazi, Sam Boskey, Sarah Jenny, Shawn Chollette, Suzanne-Juliette Mobley, and Tanya Gulliver-Garcia. Thank you also to everyone at AK Press, for all of your feedback, support, and patience—including Dana Williams who also read and gave feedback. With all of this brilliant support, clearly any mistakes are solely my own.

Notes

Foreword

1 Viet Thanh Nguyen, *Nothing Ever Dies: Vietnam and the Memory of War* (Cambridge: Harvard University Press, 2016), 272.

Introduction

1 My conversations with Brandon Darby relayed in this book are based on personal memory. With, in some cases, the help of recollections of others who were there or heard about them at the time.

Chapter One: The History of Saviors

1 All Breedlove quotes are from interview with the author. Throughout this book, unless otherwise noted, quotes are from interviews with author.

2 Caitlin Breedlove and Paulina Helm-Hernandez, "Willing to be Transformed: A Nine Year Queer, Cross-Race Work Marriage," *Caitlin Breedlove* (blog), September 24, 2015, https://medium.com/@caitlinbreedlove/willing-to-be-transformed-a-nine-year-queer-cross-race-work-marriage-33dd247d0bd5#.h6kgarv2m.

3 This phrase has been used in multiple places, including by Chris Boeskool, who writes on his blog that he has searched but can't find who originally said this. Chris Boeskool, "When You're Accustomed To Privilege, Equality Feels Like Oppression," March 5, 2016, http://theboeskool.com/2016/03/05/when-youre-accustomed-to-privilege-equality-feels-like-oppression.

4 Robert the Monk, one of several reports of the pope's speech written after the fact, in *The Norton Anthology of English Literature*, Norton Topics Online, https://www.wwnorton.com/

college/english/nael/middleages/topic_3/clermont.htm.

5   From Columbus's diaries, Early Americas Digital Archives, http://mith.umd.edu/eada/html/display.php?docs=columbus_journal.xml.

6   Andrea Smith, *Conquest: Sexual Violence and American Indian Genocide* (Cambridge: South End Press, 2005), 23.

7   Richard H. Pratt, "'Kill the Indian and Save the Man': Capt. Richard H. Pratt on the Education of Native Americans," History Matters, http://historymatters.gmu.edu/d/4929.

8   Noam Chomsky, *The New Military Humanism: Lessons from Kosovo* (London: Pluto Press, 1999); Michael Wines, "Double Vision: Two Views of Inhumanity Split the World, Even in Victory," *New York Times*, June 13, 1999.

9   "Radio Address by Mrs. Bush, November 17, 2001," American Presidency Project, www.presidency.ucsb.edu/ws/?pid=24992.

10   Phyllis Chesler and Donna M. Hughes, "Feminism in The 21st Century," *Washington Post*, February 22, 2004.

11   Jane McManus, "Talkin' Baseball and Diplomacy," *ESPN*, April 11, 2014, espn.go.com/new-york/columns/mlb/story/_/id/10766849/yankees-fan-henry-kissinger-red-sox-fan-samantha-power-talk-baseball-diplomacy.

12   Harsha Walia, "Reimagining Feminism on International Women's Day," *Rabble*, March 4, 2015, rabble.ca/columnists/2015/03/reimagining-feminism-on-international-womens-day.

13   Robin DiAngelo, "White Fragility," *International Journal of Critical Pedagogy* 3, no. 3 (2011): 58.

14   Dean Spade and Hope Dector, *Queer Dreams and Nonprofit Blues: Understanding the Nonprofit Industrial Complex*, videos, http://sfonline.barnard.edu/navigating-neoliberalism-in-the-academy-nonprofits-and-beyond/dean-spade-hope-dector-queer-dreams-and-nonprofit-blues-understanding-the-npic/#sthash.teM916T8.dpuf.

15   Ibid., 54.

16   Ruth Wilson Gilmore, *Golden Gulag: Prisons, Surplus, Crisis, and Opposition in Globalizing California* (Berkeley: University of California Press, 2007), 28.

17   Sarah Schulman, *The Gentrification of the Mind: Witness to a Lost Imagination* (Berkeley: University of California Press, 2013), 27.

18   Ibid., 52.

19   From an interview I produced with *The Laura Flanders Show*,

aired June 20, 2015.

20   Peter d'Errico, "Jeffrey Amherst and Smallpox Blankets," University of Massachusetts, www.umass.edu/legal/derrico /amherst/lord_jeff.html.

21   Handbook referenced in David Huyssen, *Progressive Inequality: Rich and Poor in New York, 1890–1920* (Cambridge: Harvard University Press, 2014), 65. Charity Organization Society of the City of New York, *Hand-Book for Friendly Visitors Among the Poor* (New York: G.P. Putnam's Sons, 1883), 6, available via Google Books, https://books.google.com /books?id=lbE0tIdF3AgC.

22   This analysis comes from Ruth Wilson Gilmore, "In the Shadow of the Shadow State," in *The Revolution Will Not Be Funded: Beyond the Non-Profit Industrial Complex*, eds. INCITE! Women of Color Against Violence (Cambridge: South End Press, 2009), 46.

23   Jay-Z, *Decoded* (New York: Spiegel & Grau, 2011), 220.

24   Derwin Dubose, "The Nonprofit Sector Has a Ferguson Problem," *Nonprofit Quarterly*, December 5, 2014, nonprofitquarterly.org/2014/12/05/the-nonprofit-sector-has -a-ferguson-problem.

25   See, for example, Jo Freeman (aka Joreen), "The Tyranny of Structurelessness," *Second Wave* 2, no. 1 (1972), www.jofreeman .com/joreen/tyranny.htm.

26   Gabriel Winant, "American Philanthropy and its Discontents," *Jacobin*, May 2014, https://www.jacobinmag.com/2014/05 /american-philanthropy-and-its-discontents.

27   Paulo Friere, *Pedagogy of the Oppressed* (New York: Bloomsbury Academic, 2000), 45.

28   Janet Poppendieck, *Sweet Charity? Emergency Food and the End of Entitlement* (New York: Penguin Books, 1999), 6.

29   Gilmore, "In the Shadow of the Shadow State," 42.

30   Poppendieck, *Sweet Charity*, 8.

31   Ibid., 5.

32   Bob Dreyfuss, "Grover Norquist: 'Field Marshal' of the Bush Plan," *Nation*, April 26, 2001, www.thenation.com/article /grover-norquist-field-marshal-bush-plan.

33   I make a similar point about foundations and quote some of the same sources in my book *Floodlines: Community and Resistance from Katrina to the Jena Six* (Chicago: Haymarket Books, 2010).

34   Andrea Smith, introduction to INCITE! Women of Color Against Violence, ed., *The Revolution Will Not Be Funded*, 8.

35   Spade and Dector, *Queer Dreams and Nonprofit Blues*.

36   Gara Lamarche, "Is Philanthropy Bad for Democracy?," *At-
      lantic*, October 30, 2014, www.theatlantic.com/politics/
      archive/2014/10/is-philanthropy-good-for-democracy
      /381996.

37   Dean Spade, *Normal Life: Administrative Violence, Critical
      Trans Politics and the Limits of Law* (New York: South End
      Press, 2011), 67.

38   Ibid., 127.

39   Credited to Hagi in multiple sources, including Bronwyn
      Isaac, "Must Buy: 'Lord, Give Me the Confidence of a Me-
      diocre White Man' T-Shirt," *Frisky*, December 22, 2015,
      www.thefrisky.com/2015-12-22/must-buy-lord-give-me-the
      -confidence-of-a-mediocre-white-man-t-shirt.

40   Paraphrased from Schulman, *The Gentrification of the Mind*,
      30.

41   Thomas Carlyle, *On Heroes, Hero-Worship, and the Hero-
      ic in History*, 1840, www.gutenberg.org/files/1091/1091-h
      /1091-h.htm.

42   "Neither slavery nor involuntary servitude, except as a punish-
      ment for crime whereof the party shall have been duly convict-
      ed, shall exist within the United States, or any place subject
      to their jurisdiction." U.S. Constitution, Thirteenth Amend-
      ment, Legal Information Institute, https://www.law.cornell
      .edu/constitution/amendmentxiii.

43   Karl Marx, *A Critique of the German Ideology*, Progress Pub-
      lishers, 1968. First published, 1932. Marxists Internet Archive,
      https://www.marxists.org/archive/marx/works/download
      /Marx_The_German_Ideology.pdf.

44   Howard Zinn, *Howard Zinn Speaks: Collected Speeches, 1963–
      2009* (Chicago: Haymarket Books, 2012), 299.

45   David Rising, "Germany Increases Reparations for Holocaust
      Survivors," *Times of Israel*, November 16, 2012.

46   Francis Butler Simkins, Spotswood Hunnicutt, and Sidman P.
      Poole, *Virginia: History, Government, Geography* (New York:
      Charles Scribner's, 1964), a state-mandated seventh-grade Vir-
      ginia history textbook. Sourced via Ned Sublette.

47   "The Atlantic slave trade between the 1500s and the 1800s
      brought millions of workers from Africa to the southern United
      States to work on agricultural plantations." Manny Hernandez
      and Christine Hauser, "Texas Mother Teaches Textbook Com-
      pany a Lesson on Accuracy," *New York Times*, October 5, 2015.

48   David Amsden, "Building the First Slavery Museum in Ameri-

ca," *New York Times Magazine*, February 26, 2015.

49   Public Enemy, "Can't Truss It," on *Apocalypse 91 . . . The Enemy Strikes Black* (Def Jam Recordings, 1991).

50   Amsden, "Building the First Slavery Museum in America."

51   Sarah M., "Just Say No: Why You Shouldn't Study Sex Work in School," *autocannibal*, September 24, 2013. https://autocannibalism.wordpress.com/2013/09/24/just-say-no -why-you-shouldnt-study-sex-work-in-school.

52   Marina Sitrin, "Walking We Ask Questions: An Interview with John Holloway," *Left Turn Magazine*, February 1, 2005 http:// www.leftturn.org/"walking-we-ask-questions"-interview -john-holloway.

53   Ngọc Loan Trần, "Calling IN: A Less Disposable Way of Holding Each Other Accountable," *BGD*, December 18, 2013, www. blackgirldangerous.org/2013/12/calling-less-disposable-way -holding-accountable.

Chapter Two: We Are the World, We Are the Children

1   Teju Cole, "The White-Savior Industrial Complex," *Atlantic*, March 21, 2012, www.theatlantic.com/international/archive /2012/03/the-white-savior-industrial-complex/254843.

2   Binyavanga Wainaina, "How to Write about Africa," *Granta* 92 (Winter 2005), http://granta.com/How-to-Write-about-Africa.

3   For example: Karen Rothmyer, "A Radical Alternative To Peace Corps," NPR, March 2, 2011, www.npr.org /2011/03/02/134194082/the-nation-a-radical-alternative -to-peace-corps.

4   For example: Jean Friedman-Rudovsky and Brian Ross, "Peace Corps, Fulbright Scholar Asked to 'Spy' on Cubans, Venezuelans," ABC News, February 8, 2008, abcnews.go.com/Blotter/ story?id=4262036.

5   Robert Keating, "Live Aid: The Terrible Truth," July 1986. Reprinted for the thirtieth anniversary, *Spin*, July 13, 2015, www. spin.com/featured/live-aid-the-terrible-truth-ethiopia-bob -geldof-feature.

6   "Prof. Mahmood Mamdani and John Prendergast, 'The Darfur Debate,'" at Columbia University, School of International and Public Affairs, April 14, 2009, https://www.youtube.com/ watch?v=yGOpfH_5_pY.

7   Ibid.

8   Ibid.

9   Marc Gustafson, "The 'Genocide' in Darfur Isn't What It Seems," *Christian Science Monitor*, August 19, 2009.

10   Philip Gourevitch, "Alms Dealers," *New Yorker*, October 11, 2010, www.newyorker.com/magazine/2010/10/11/alms-dealers.

11   Joshua Keating, "Joseph Kony Is Not in Uganda (and Other Complicated Things)," *Foreign Policy*, March 7, 2012, foreign policy.com/2012/03/07/guest-post-joseph-kony-is-not-in-uganda-and-other-complicated-things.

12   Rosebell Kagumire, "My Response To KONY2012" lybio.net/rosebell-kagumire-my-response-to-kony2012/people. Found via: Robert Mackey, "African Critics of Kony Campaign See a 'White Man's Burden' for the Facebook Generation," *Lede*, March 9, 2012, thelede.blogs.nytimes.com/2012/03/09/african-critics-of-kony-campaign-hear-echoes-of-the-white-mans-burden.

13   Rajiv Chandrasekaran, "Kony 2013: U.S. Quietly Intensifies Effort to Help African Troops Capture Infamous Warlord," *Washington Post*, October 28, 2013.

14   Vijay Prashad, "The Konyism of Samantha Power, US Ambassador to the United Nations," *Jadaliyya*, August 15, 2013, www.jadaliyya.com/pages/index/13584/the-konyism-of-samantha-power-us-ambassador-to-the.

15   Meena Hart Duerson, "Kony 2012 Filmmaker Jason Russell on Naked Meltdown," *New York Daily News*, October 8, 2012.

16   Jessica Testa, "The End of Invisible Children," *BuzzFeed*, December 15, 2014, www.buzzfeed.com/jtes/the-end-of-invisible-children#.thp4x6XzK3.

17   Gourevitch, "Alms Dealers."

18   Rafia Zakaria, "The White Tourist's Burden," *Al Jazeera America*, April 21, 2014, america.aljazeera.com/opinions/2014/4/volunteer-tourismwhitevoluntouristsafricaaidsorphans.html.

19   Dorinda Elliott, "Giving Back: A Special Report on Volunteer Vacations," *Conde Nast Traveler*, January 15, 2013, www.cntraveler.com/stories/2013-01-15/volunteer-vacations-rewards-risks.

20   Tracy Kidder, "Country without a Net," *New York Times*, January 13, 2010.

21   Dan Coughlin and Kim Ives, "WikiLeaks Haiti: Let Them Live on $3 a Day," *Nation*, June 1, 2011, www.thenation.com/article/wikileaks-haiti-let-them-live-3-day.

22   "The Caracol Industrial Park: Worth the risk?," *Haiti Grassroots Watch*, March 7, 2013, http://haitigrassrootswatch.squarespace.com/haiti-grassroots-watch-engli/2013/3/7/the-caracol-industrial-park-worth-the-risk.html.

23   Kathie Klarreich and Linda Polman, "The NGO Republic
      of Haiti: How the International Relief Effort after the 2010
      Earthquake Excluded Haitians from Their Own Recovery,"
      Nation, October 31, 2012, www.thenation.com/article/ngo
      -republic-haiti.
24   Ibid.
25   Justin Elliott and Laura Sullivan, "How the Red Cross Raised
      Half a Billion Dollars for Haiti and Built Six Homes," *Pro-
      publica*, June 3, 2015, https://www.propublica.org/article/
      how-the-red-cross-raised-half-a-billion-dollars-for-haiti-and
      -built-6-homes.
26   Michael Maren, *The Road to Hell: The Ravaging Effects of For-
      eign Aid and International Charity* (New York: Free Press,
      2002), 116.
27   See, for example, Ben Casselman, "Microloans Don't Solve
      Poverty, but Research Might Reveal What Will," *FiveThirty-
      Eight*, December 8, 2015, fivethirtyeight.com/features
      /microloans-dont-solve-poverty.
28   Associated Press, "SKS under Spotlight in Suicides," *Wall
      Street Journal*, February 24, 2012.
29   Jessica Hoffman, "Beyond Borders: An Interview with Haneen
      Maikey of Al Qaws," *make/shift* magazine 17 (Summer/Fall
      2015).
30   Ghaith Hilal, "Eight Questions Palestinian Queers Are Tired
      of Hearing," *Electronic Intifada*, November 27, 2013, https://
      electronicintifada.net/content/eight-questions-palestinian
      -queers-are-tired-hearing/12951.
31   From unpublished document supplied by Berkley Carnine and
      Liza Minno Bloom.

Chapter Three: The Death of Riad Hamad

1   Quoted in Greg Szymanski, "New Orleans Residents All over
      the Country Should Be Put on Red Alerts," *Rense.com*, http:
      //rense.com/general69/neoconsdevelopers.htm.
2   Later, crow and others would say that Darby was not a founder
      of Common Ground, but during his time as part of the leader-
      ship he was often described as a founder.
3   Diana Welch, "The Informant: Revolutionary to Rat: The
      Uneasy Journey of Brandon Darby," *Austin (Tex.) Chronicle*,
      January 23, 2009.
4   Rachel Luft, "Looking for Common Ground: Relief Work in
      Post-Katrina New Orleans as an American Parable of Race and
      Gender Violence," *NWSA Journal* 20, no. 3 (Fall 2008), pp 5–31.

5   From the film *Better This World*, quoted in Josh Harkinson, "How a Radical Leftist Became the FBI's BFF," *Mother Jones*, September/October 2011, www.motherjones.com/politics /2011/08/brandon-darby-anarchist-fbi-terrorism.

6   "[Episode] 381: Turncoat," *This American Life*, May 22, 2009, www.thisamericanlife.org/radio-archives/episode/381 /transcript.

7   Welch, "The Informant."

8   "COINTELPRO 101," film produced by the Freedom Archives, 2011.

9   "Who's That Weird Guy at Your Anarchist Meeting?" *AJ+ video*, June 17, 2015, www.facebook.com/ajplusenglish /videos/574875542653957.

10   Trevor Aaronson, "The Informants," *Mother Jones*, September/October 2011, http://www.motherjones.com/politics /2011/08/fbi-terrorist-informants.

11   Peter Eichenberger, "The Second Battle of New Orleans," *IndyWeek*, December 2005, www.indyweek.com/indyweek/the -second-battle-of-new-orleans/Content?oid=1196446.

12   Welch, "The Informant."

13   "Witness to Betrayal: scott crow on the Exploits and Misadventures of FBI Informant Brandon Darby," December 19, 2013, *Toward Freedom*, www.towardfreedom.com/29-archives/activism /3388-witness-to-betrayal-scott-crow-on-the-exploits-and -misadventures-of-fbi-informant-brandon-darby.

14   In his interview with *This American Life*, Darby says he met Riad while planning Critical Response and contacted the FBI about him soon after. "[Episode] 381: Turncoat," *This American Life*, May 22, 2009, www.thisamericanlife.org/radio -archives/episode/381/transcript.

15   Josh Harkinson, "How a Radical Leftist Became the FBI's BFF," *Mother Jones*, September/October 2011, www.motherjones .com/politics/2011/08/brandon-darby-anarchist-fbi-terrorism.

16   Courtney Desiree Morris, "Why Misogynists Make Great Informants," *make/shift* magazine (May 2010), https://inciteblog. wordpress.com/2010/07/15/why-misogynists-make-great- informants-how-gender-violence-on-the-left-enables-state -violence-in-radical-movements

17   "Early-Career Awards Fast Track Studies on Poverty and Health," Stanford Medicine News Center, September 24, 2015, med.stanford.edu/news/all-news/2015/09/early-career -awards-fast-track-studies-on-poverty-and-health.html.

18   Greg Moses, "Salamat, Riad Hamad," *Counterpunch*, May 3,

2008, www.counterpunch.org/2008/05/03/salamat-riad-hamad.

19   For a full description, see Greg Moses, "Take One: The Riad Hamad Memorial," *Texas Civil Rights Review*, December 2008, http://texascivilrightsreview.org/0005/12/08 /take-one-the-riad-hamad-memorial.

20   Thomas Hintze, "What Informs an Informant?," September 11, 2013, *Waging Nonviolence*, wagingnonviolence.org /feature/the-real-untold-story-of-brandon-darby.

21   Quoted in Welch, "The Informant."

22   Katie J. M. Baker, "Ethics and the Eye of the Beholder," *Buzz-Feed*, May 20, 2016, https://www.buzzfeed.com/katiejmbaker /yale-ethics-professor.

Chapter Four: Batman is the Problem

1   Roger Ebert, "Watching Rocky II with Muhammad Ali," *Chicago Sun-Times*, July 31, 1979.

2   From a talk at Comic Con International in San Diego, reported by Karl Kelly, "Frank Miller Reigns 'Holy Terror' on San Diego," July 26, 2011, Comic Book Resources, www .comicbookresources.com/?page=article&id=33550.

3   Quoted in Michael Cavna, "Frank Miller on Occupy Movement," *Washington Post*, November 4, 2011.

4   Schulman, *The Gentrification of the Mind*, 82.

5   See, for example, Syd Field, *Screenplay: The Foundations of Screenwriting* (New York: Dell, 1979).

6   Katharine Trendacosta, "Reminder: Rudyard Kipling Was a Racist Fuck and *The Jungle Book* Is Imperialist Garbage," April 4, 2016, *io9*, io9.gizmodo.com/reminder-rudyard-kipling -was-a-racist-fuck-and-the-jun-1771044121.

7   Rebecca Keegan, "The Atticus Finch Effect at the Movies: Do We Still Need a White Savior?," *Los Angeles Times*, July 15, 2015.

8   David Sirota, "Oscar Loves a White Savior," *Salon*, February 21, 2013, www.salon.com/2013/02/21/oscar_loves_a _white_savior.

9   For example, Jennifer Schuessler, "Depiction of Lyndon B. Johnson in 'Selma' Raises Hackles," *New York Times*, December 31, 2014.

10   Scott Feinberg, "Oscar Voter Reveals Brutally Honest Ballot," *Hollywood Reporter*, February 18, 2015, www.hollywood reporter.com/race/brutally-honest-oscar-ballot-2015 -773902. Brackets in original.

11   Gary Leupp, "A Racist and Insulting Film: 300 vs. Iran (and

Herodotus)," *Counterpunch*, March 31, 2007, www.counter
punch.org/2007/04/01/300-vs-iran-and-herodotus.

12   Dana Stevens, "A Movie Only a Spartan Could Love,"
Slate, March 8, 2007, www.slate.com/articles/arts/movies
/2007/03/a_movie_only_a_spartan_could_love.html.

13   Mark Moring, "'Machine Gun Preacher' Under Heavy Fire,"
Christianity Today, September 22, 2011, www.christianity
today.com/ct/2011/septemberweb-only/machinegunpreacher
.html.

14   Ian Urbina, "Get Kony," *Vanity Fair*, May 2010, www.vanityfair
.com/news/2010/04/christian-vigilante-201004.

15   *Dominican Today* Staff, "Danny Glover's Haiti Film Lacked
'White Heroes,' Producers Said," *Dominican Today*, July 26, 2008,
www.dominicantoday.com/dr/people/2008/7/26/28807
/Danny-Glovers-Haiti-film-lacked-white-heroes-producers
-said.

16   "Panther: An Interview with Mario Van Peebles," *Tikkun*,
July/August 1995, via FrontPageMag.com, http://archive
.frontpagemag.com/readArticle.aspx?ARTID=22287.

17   *MADtv*, season 12, episode 15, aired February 24, 2007 on
FOX.

18   Walidah Imarisha, introduction to *Octavia's Brood: Science Fiction Stories from Social Justice Movements*, ed. Walidah Imarisha and adrienne maree brown (Oakland: AK Press, 2015), 3.

19   Ibid., 4.

Chapter Five: Nicholas Kristof Saves the World

1   Schulman, *The Gentrification of the Mind*, 47.

2   Rebecca Solnit, "To Break the Story, You Must Break the Status Quo," *Literary Hub*, May 26, 2016, lithub.com/to-break
-the-story-you-must-break-the-status-quo.

3   Matt Taibbi, "Hey, MSM: All Journalism Is Advocacy Journalism," *RollingStone*, June 27, 2013, www.rollingstone.com
/politics/news/hey-msm-all-journalism-is-advocacy-journalism
-20130627.

4   Pamela Newkirk, "The Not-So-Great Migration: From the
Black Press to the Mainstream—and Back Again," *Columbia
Journalism Review*, May/June 2011, www.cjr.org/feature/the
_not-so-great_migration.php.

5   Leonard N. Moore, *Black Rage in New Orleans: Police Brutality and African American Activism from World War II to Hurricane Katrina* (Baton Rouge: Louisiana State University Press,
2010), 45.

6   Alex T. Williams, "Why Aren't There More Minority Jour-
     nalists?," *Columbia Journalism Review*, July 22, 2015, www.cjr
     .org/analysis/in_the_span_of_two.php.

7   Howard W. French, "The Enduring Whiteness of the Ameri-
     can Media," *Guardian*, May 25, 2016.

8   Quoted in Ibid.

9   Ibid.

10   Jarvis DeBerry, "Newsman's Silence on Henry Glover Case Is
     Troubling," *Times-Picayune*, December 19, 2010.

11   David Carr, "Journalism, Even When It's Tilted," *New York
     Times*, June 30, 2013.

12   Nicholas Confessore and Karen Yourish, "Measuring Don-
     ald Trump's Mammoth Advantage in Free Media," *New York
     Times*, March 15, 2016.

13   Nate Silver, "How Trump Hacked the Media," *FiveThirtyEight*,
     March 30, 2016, fivethirtyeight.com/features/how-donald
     -trump-hacked-the-media.

14   Solnit, "To Break the Story, You Must Break the Status Quo."

15   Judy Richardson, "The Way We Were: The SNCC Teenagers
     Who Changed America," *Women's Voices for Change*, Febru-
     ary 26, 2015, http://womensvoicesforchange.org/the-way-we
     -were-the-sncc-teenagers-who-changed-america.htm.

16   "Nicholas Kristof, Covering Conflict." Institute for Re-
     ligion, Culture, & Public Life, http://ircpl.org/nicholas
     -kristof-covering-conflict. "Edited transcript from the public
     discussion Kristof had with Sheila Coronel . . . at the Columbia
     Journalism School."

17   Jon Krakauer, *Three Cups of Deceit: How Greg Mortenson, Hu-
     manitarian Hero, Lost His Way* (New York: Anchor, 2011).

18   Nicholas Kristof, "'Three Cups of Tea,' Spilled," *New York
     Times*, April 20, 2011.

19   "What to Make of Kony 2012," *On the Media*, March 16,
     2012, http://www.onthemedia.org/story/192713-what-make
     -kony-2012/transcript.

20   Nicholas Kristof, "Viral Video, Vicious Warlord," *New York
     Times*, March 14, 2012.

21   Kate Crawford and Amanda Taub, "The Exclusive Club of
     Moral Authority: From Nick Kristof to Kony 2012," *At-
     lantic*, April 24, 2012, www.theatlantic.com/international
     /archive/2012/04/the-exclusive-club-of-moral-authority
     -from-nick-kristof-to-kony-2012/256287.

22   "Cambodia: Sex Workers Face Unlawful Arrests and Deten-
     tion," Human Rights Watch, July 20, 2010, https://www.hrw

.org/news/2010/07/20/cambodia-sex-workers-face-unlawful
-arrests-and-detention.

23   Aliya, "Cambodia: MTV No EXIT Campaign Indirectly Sup-
      ports Abusive Anti-trafficking Law," *SWAN*, June 22, 2009,
      swannet.org/node/1521.

24   Anne Elizabeth Moore, "Here's Why It Matters When a Hu-
      man Rights Crusader Builds Her Advocacy on Lies," *Salon*, May
      28, 2014, www.salon.com/2014/05/28/heres_why_it_matters
      _when_a_human_rights_crusader_builds_her_advocacy
      _on_lies.

25   Ibid.

26   Ibid.

27   Elizabeth Bernstein, "Militarized Humanitarianism Meets
      Carceral Feminism: The Politics of Sex, Rights, and Freedom
      in Contemporary Antitrafficking Campaigns," *Signs: Jour-
      nal of Women in Culture and Society* 36, no. 1 (2010): 65,
      traffickingroundtable.org/wp-content/uploads/2012/07/
      Militarized-Humanitarianism-Meets-Carceral-Feminism
      .pdf.

28   Ibid.

29   Elena Shih, "Humanitarian Investments or Filial Remittances:
      Moral Economies of Life After Trafficking in China and Thai-
      land," conference presentation, "Globalization, Gender and
      Development," University of Oregon, October 24, 2014.

30   Gerry Mullany, "Activist Resigns amid Charges of Fabrica-
      tion," *New York Times*, May 29, 2014.

31   Quoted in ibid.

32   Maggie McNeill, "An Example to the West," *Honest Cour-
      tesan*, April 3, 2012, https://maggiemcneill.wordpress
      .com/2012/04/03/an-example-to-the-west.

33   *Melissa Harris-Perry Show*, MSNBC, January 25, 2015.

34   Nicholas Kristof, "When Liberals Blew it," *New York Times*,
      March 11, 2015.

35   Cole, "The White Savior Industrial Complex."

Chapter Six: Is Teach for America Saving Our Children?

1   Sophie Lucido Johnson, "Unlearning 'These Kids Need You,'"
      Sophie Lucido Johnson (blog), April 10, 2014, http://www
      .sophielucidojohnson.com/blogblog/2014/4/10/unlearning
      -these-kids-need-you.

2   Ibid.

3   Milton Friedman, "The Promise of Vouchers," *Wall Street
      Journal*, December 5, 2005.

4   Nick Anderson, "Education Secretary Duncan Calls Hurri-
     cane Katrina Good for New Orleans Schools," *Washington
     Post*, January 30, 2010.

5   Robert R. Korstad and James L Leloudis, "Citizen Soldiers:
     The North Carolina Volunteers and the War on Poverty," *Law
     and Contemporary Problems* 62, no. 4 (Autumn 1999): 186,
     quoted in Danielson, "Volunteerism in Crisis."

6   Emily Danielson, "Volunteerism in Crisis: AmeriCorps as Di-
     saster Response," master's thesis, University of New Orleans,
     August 2010, http://scholarworks.uno.edu/cgi/viewcontent
     .cgi?article=2215&context=td, 11.

7   Gary Rubinstein, "Why I Did TFA, and Why You Shouldn't,"
     Gary Rubinstein (blog), October 31, 2011, https://garyrubin
     stein.wordpress.com/2011/10/31/why-i-did-tfa-and-why
     -you-shouldnt.

8   Alexandra Hootnick, "Teachers Are Losing Their Jobs, but
     Teach for America's Expanding. What's Wrong With That?,"
     Nation, April 15, 2014, https://www.thenation.com/article
     /teachers-are-losing-their-jobs-teach-americas-expanding
     -whats-wrong.

9   Eric Westervelt, "Teach For America at 25: With Maturity,
     New Pressure to Change," NPR, December 1, 2014, www.npr
     .org/sections/ed/2014/12/01/366343324/teach-for-america
     -at-25-with-maturity-new-pressure-to-change.

10   Video: "Chat with Nicholas Kristof & Wendy Kopp at World Eco-
     nomic Forum," https://www.facebook.com/teachforamerica
     /posts/103352449790207.

11   T. Jameson Brewer, "Teach for America's Biggest problem Isn't
     Green Teachers or Failing Schools. It's That It Can't Take Crit-
     icism," *Washington Post*, October 20, 2015.

12   T. Jameson Brewer and Sarah Matsui, "Taking on TFA: Disil-
     lusioned Teach for America Alumni Are Striking Back at the
     Organization's Neoliberal Narratives," *Jacobin*, October 2015,
     https://www.jacobinmag.com/2015/10/tfa-wendy-kopp
     -corporate-education-reform-new-orleans.

13   George Joseph, "Teach for America Has Gone Global, and Its
     Board Has Strange Ideas About What Poor Kids Need," *The
     Nation*, July 1, 2016, https://www.thenation.com/article/
     teach-for-america-has-gone-global-and-its-board-has-strange
     -ideas-about-what-poor-kids-need.

14   Dana Goldstein, "Teach for America Has Faced Criticism for
     Years. Now It's Listening—and Changing," *Vox*, September 5,
     2014, www.vox.com/2014/9/5/6079493/teach-for-america

-criticism-changing.

15   Sarah Matsui, *Learning from Counternarratives in Teach for America: Moving from Idealism towards Hope* (New York: Peter Lang, 2015). Excerpt quoted at www.learningfromcounter narrativesintfa.com.

16   Alexandra Hootnick, "Teachers Are Losing Their Jobs, but Teach for America's Expanding. What's Wrong With That?"

17   Diane Ravitch, "Public Education: Who Are the Corporate Reformers?," *Moyers & Company*, March 28, 2014, billmoyers .com/2014/03/28/public-education-who-are-the-corporate -reformers.

18   Paul Buchheit, "4 Ways Privatization Is Ruining Our Education System," *Salon*, February 19, 2014, www.salon. com/2014/02/19/4_ways_privatization_is_ruining_our _education_system_partner.

19   Jessica Huseman, "These Charter Schools Tried to Turn Public Education into Big Business. They Failed," *Slate*, December 17, 2015, www.slate.com/blogs/schooled/2015/12/17/ for_profit_charter_schools_are_failing_and_fading_here_s _why.html.

20   "Timeline: NOPD's Long History of Scandal," *PBS Frontline*, www.pbs.org/wgbh/pages/frontline/law-disorder/etc/cron .html

21   Matthew Cunningham-Cook, "Why Do Some of America's Wealthiest Individuals Have Fingers in Louisiana's Education System?," *Nation*, October 17, 2012, www.thenation. com/article/why-do-some-americas-wealthiest-individuals -have-fingers-louisianas-education-system.

22   Alexandria Neason, "The Color of School Reform," *Slate*, June 5, 2016, www.slate.com/articles/life/tomorrows_test /2016/06/new_orleans_needs_more_black_teachers_and _knows_it_why_is_progress_so_slow.html.

23   Corey Mitchell, "Death of My Career," *Education Week*, August 19, 2015, neworleans.edweek.org/veteran-black-female -teachers-fired.

24   Mia McKenzie, "The White Teachers I Wish I Never Had," *BGD*, June 2, 2014, www.blackgirldangerous.org/2014/06 /white-teachers-wish-never.

25   Neason, "The Color of School Reform."

26   Brittney Cooper, "She Was Guilty of Being a Black Girl: The Mundane Terror of Police Violence in American Schools," *Salon*, October 28, 2015, www.salon.com/2015/10/28/she _was_guilty_of_being_a_black_girl_the_mundane_terror

_of_police_violence_in_american_schools.

27   Kenyatta Collins, "New Orleans Charter Schools Shouldn't Treat Students like Prisoners," *Time*, May 16, 2014, time .com/101440/new-orleans-charter-schools-shouldnt-treat -students-like-prisoners.

28   Catherine Michna, "Why I Stopped Writing Recommendation Letters for Teach for America," *Slate*, October 9 2013, www.slate.com/articles/life/education/2013/10/teach_for _america_recommendations_i_stopped_writing_them_and _my_colleague.html.

29   Gregory Childress, "DPS Ices Relationship with Teach for America," *Herald-Sun* (Australia), August 30, 2014.

Chapter Seven: The World's Oldest Excuse for Male Violence

1   Melissa Gira Grant, *Playing the Whore: The Work of Sex Work* (New York: Verso, 2014), 6.

2   Emi Koyama, "Rescue Is for Kittens: Ten Things Everyone Needs to Know about 'Rescues' of Youth in the Sex Trade," *Eminism.org* (blog), September 20, 2013, eminism.org/blog /entry/400.

3   Thank you to Alexandra Lutnick, author of *Domestic Minor Sex Trafficking: Beyond Victims and Villains* (New York: Columbia University Press 2016) for her advice as I was thinking about these issues.

4   Henry Mayhew, *London Labour and the London Poor* (London: George Woodfall and Son, 1851), 215, quoted in Laura María Agustín, "Helping Women Who Sell Sex: The Construction of Benevolent Identities," Rhizomes 10 (Spring 2005), www.rhizomes.net/issue10/agustin.htm.

5   Agustín, "Helping Women Who Sell Sex."

6   Ibid.

7   Joanne McNeil, "The 'White Slavery' Panic: Anti-Prostitution Activists Have Been Equating Sex Work with Slavery for Over a Century," review of Karen Abbott's *Sin in the Second City*, *reason.com*, April 2008, reason.com/archives/2008/03/13 /the-white-slavery-panic.

8   Karen Abbott, *Sin in the Second City: Madams, Ministers, Playboys, and the Battle for America's Soul* (New York: Random House, 2008), 31.

9   McNeil, "The 'White Slavery' Panic."

10   Marlene D. Beckman, "The White Slave Traffic Act: The Historical Impact of a Criminal Law Policy on Women," *Georgetown Law Journal* 72 (February 1984): 2.

11   "A Brief History of the FBI," Federal Bureau of Investigation, https://www.fbi.gov/about-us/history/brief-history.

12   Marlene D. Beckman, "The White Slave Traffic Act: The Historical Impact of a Criminal Law Policy on Women," *Georgetown Law Journal* 72 (February 1984): 1111–42.

13   Remarks to the Washington Conference on International Narcotics Control. September 18, 1972 www.presidency.ucsb.edu/ws/?pid=3578.

14   Robyn Maynard, "#Blacksexworkerslivesmatter: White-Washed 'Anti-Slavery' and the Appropriation of Black Suffering," *Feminist Wire*, September 9, 2015, www.thefeministwire.com/2015/09/blacksexworkerslivesmatter-white-washed-anti-slavery-and-the-appropriation-of-black-suffering.

15   Ibid.

16   International Labour Organization report: "21 million people are now victims of forced labour, ILO says," www.ilo.org/global/about-the-ilo/newsroom/news/WCMS_181961/lang--en/index.htm.

17   Benjamin L. Corey, "Why Sex Still Dominates Christian Focus on Human Trafficking," *Patheos*, August 11, 2015, www.patheos.com/blogs/formerlyfundie/why-sex-still-dominates-christian-focus-on-human-trafficking.

18   Glenn Kessler, "Why you should be wary of statistics on 'modern slavery' and 'trafficking,'" *Washington Post*, April 24, 2015.

19   Glenn Kessler, "The false claim that human trafficking is a '$9.5 billion business' in the United States," *Washington Post*, June 2, 2015.

20   Ta-Nehisi Coates, "The Black Family in the Age of Mass Incarceration," *The Atlantic*, October 2015, www.theatlantic.com/magazine/archive/2015/10/the-black-family-in-the-age-of-mass-incarceration/403246.

21   Bernstein, "Militarized Humanitarianism Meets Carceral Feminism."

22   Ibid.

23   Victoria Law, "Against Carceral Feminism," *Jacobin*, October 17, 2014, https://www.jacobinmag.com/2014/10/against-carceral-feminism.

24   From biography at http://www.revolvy.com/main/index.php?s=LauraLederer.

25   Camerin Courtney, "A Q&A with Laura Lederer," *TCW*, January 2008, www.todayschristianwoman.com/articles/2008/january/1.17.html.

26   "INCITE! Critical Resistance Statement," *INCITE!*, www

.incite-national.org/page/incite-critical-resistance-statement.

27   Coalition Against Trafficking in Women, http://catwinterna
     tional.org/Content/Images/Article/621/attachment.pdf.

28   Rachel Vorona Cote, "Celebrities Have Vital Opinions about
     Decriminalization of Sex Work," *Jezebel*, July 27, 2015, jezebel
     .com/celebrities-have-vital-opinions-about-decriminalization
     -1720495904.

29   Quoted in Emily Shire, "Prostitutes Tell Lena Dunham to Stop
     Grandstanding About Sex Work," *Daily Beast*, July 29, 2015,
     www.thedailybeast.com/articles/2015/07/29/prostitutes
     -tell-lena-dunham-to-stop-grandstanding-about-sex-work
     .html.

30   Ibid.

31   Grant, *Playing the Whore*, 38.

32   Quoted in Emily Bazelon, "Why Amnesty International Is
     Calling for Decriminalizing Sex Work," *New York Times*, May
     25, 2016.

33   Amnesty International, "Human Cost of 'Crushing' the Mar-
     ket: Criminalization of Sex Work in Norway," *Amnesty Inter-
     national*, May 25, 2016, www.amnestyusa.org/sites/default/
     files/norway_report_-_sex_workers_rights_-_embargoed_-
     _final.pdf.

34   Ariel Wolf, "So These Sex Workers Walk into a Human
     Trafficking Conference," *Tits and Sass*, October 15, 2014,
     titsandsass.com/so-these-sex-workers-walk-into-a-human
     -trafficking-conference-red-umbrella-project-at-the-toledo
     -international-human-trafficking-conference.

35   Quoted in Elizabeth Nolan Brown, "The War on Sex Traf-
     ficking Is the New War on Drugs," *Reason*, November 2015,
     https://reason.com/archives/2015/09/30/the-war-on-sex
     -trafficking-is.

36   Emi Koyama, "Pimping Does Not Equal Enslavement:
     Thoughts on the Resilience of Youth and Adults Who Have
     Pimps," November 14, 2011, *eminism*, eminism.org/blog
     /entry/284.

37   Alexandra Lutnick, *Domestic Minor Sex Trafficking: Beyond
     Victims and Villains* (New York: Columbia University Press
     2016), 27.

38   Emi Koyama, "Pimping Does Not Equal Enslavement: Thoughts
     on the Resilience of Youth and Adults Who Have Pimps."

39   Ibid.

40   Young Women's Empowerment Project, *Girls Do What They
     Have to Do to Survive*, (Chicago: Young Women's Empow-

erment Project, 2009), https://ywepchicago.files.wordpress
.com/2011/06/girls-do-what-they-have-to-do-to-survive-a
-study-of-resilience-and-resistance.pdf.

41   Grant, *Playing the Whore*, 5.

42   Jody Raphael and Deborah L. Shapiro, *Sisters Speak Out:
      The Lives and Needs of Prostituted Women in Chicago* (Chica-
      go: Center for Impact Research, 2002), www.healthtrust.net
      /sites/default/files/publications/sistersspeakout.pdf.

43   Tracy Clark-Flory, Matan Gilat, and Leigh Cuen, "Sex Work-
      ers More Worried about Cops than Dangerous Johns," *Voc-
      ativ*, October 23, 2015, www.vocativ.com/news/239316
      /national-blacklist-for-sex-workers.

44   Grant, *Playing the Whore*, 6.

45   Melissa Gira Grant, "'The Red Light and the Cloud': A His-
      tory of the Future of Sex Work," *Red Light and the Cloud*,
      December 24, 2013, https://medium.com/@melissagira/the
      -red-light-and-the-cloud-9a936daaddb8#.k0d2m8vc8.

46   FBI press release, https://www.fbi.gov/denver/press-releases
      /2013/federal-and-local-law-enforcement-crack-down
      -on-prostitution-and-human-trafficking-in-colorado.

47   All figures from Matt Sedensky and Nomaan Merchant,
      "Hundreds of Officers Lose Licenses over Sex Miscon-
      duct," *Big Story*, November 1, 2015, bigstory.ap.org/article
      /fd1d4d05e561462a85abe50e7eaed4ec/ap-hundreds
      -officers-lose-licenses-over-sex-misconduct.

48   Ibid.

49   Tara Murtha, "Activists Campaign against Philadelphia Judge
      Who Ruled Rape as Theft," *Rewire*, October 30, 2013, https://
      rewire.news/article/2013/10/30/activists-campaign-against
      -philadelphia-judge-who-ruled-rape-as-theft.

50   Maggie Lange, "Texas Says It's OK to Shoot an Escort If She Won't
      Have Sex with You," *Gawker*, June 6, 2013, gawker.com/texas
      -says-its-ok-to-shoot-an-escort-if-she-wont-have-s-511636423.

51   Brown, "The War on Sex Trafficking Is the New War on
      Drugs."

52   Ibid.

53   Ibid.

Chapter Eight: Monica Jones versus Dr. Dominique

1   "Article IV: Offenses Involving Morals; Division 1: Prostitution
      and Fornication," Phoenix City Code, www.codepublishing
      .com/AZ/Phoenix/frameless/index.pl?path=../html/Phoenix
      23/Phoenix2352.html.

2   From Project ROSE emails received via a Freedom of Informa-
        tion Act (FOIA) request by the ACLU of Arizona.

3   Young Women's Empowerment Project, *Girls Do What They
        Have to Do to Survive.*

4   From Project ROSE emails.

5   Dr. Stéphanie Wahab and Meg Panichelli, "Ethical and Hu-
        man Rights Issues in Coercive Interventions with Sex Work-
        ers," *Affilia* 28, no. 4, aff.sagepub.com/content/28/4/344.refs.

6   Kate Mogulescu "The Super Bowl and Sex Trafficking," Janu-
        ary 31, 2014 *New York Times*.

7   Chris Hall "Is One of the Most-Cited Statistics About Sex Work
        Wrong?" *The Atlantic*, September 5, 2014, www.theatlantic
        .com/business/archive/2014/09/is-one-of-the-most-cited
        -statistics-about-sex-work-wrong/379662.

8   Brown, "The War on Sex Trafficking Is the New War on Drugs."

9   Tara Burns, "People in Alaska's Sex Trade: Their Lived Expe-
        riences and Policy Recommendations," sextraffickingalaska
        .com/pdfs/AKSWR.pdf.

10   I am indebted to Tara Burns for her extensive research on these
        laws and on individual cases.

11   Burns is funding her research online via patreon.com/
        TaraBurns.

12   "I'm Katha Pollitt's 'Highly Educated' Leftist—And A Sex
        Trafficking Victim," Tits and Sass, May 22, 2014, titsand-
        sass.com/im-katha-pollitts-highly-educated-leftist-and-a-sex
        -trafficking-victim.

13   Grant, *Playing the Whore*.

14   Shamik Bag, "The New Rhythms of Sonagachi," *Live Mint*, Feb-
        ruary 24, 2012. www.livemint.com/Leisure/zc6wRB1Jmjj9c
        JKrSCLlWP/The-new-rhythms-of-Sonagachi.html.

15   SANGRAM/VAMP Team, *The VAMP/SANGRAM Sex
        Worker's Movement in India's Southwest* (Association for
        Women's Rights in Development, 2011), www.awid.org/sites/
        default/files/atoms/files/changing_their_world_2_-_vamp_
        -sex_workers_movement_in_indias_southwest.pdf.

16   Editorial, "Homeland Security's Peculiar Prosecution of Rent-
        boy," *New York Times*, August 28, 2015.

17   Compiled at https://storify.com/WassailingGirl/notyourres
        cueproject.

18   Elizabeth Nolan Brown, "A&E Cancels Prostitution 'Reality'
        Series *8 Minutes*," *Reason*, May 6, 2015, https://reason.com
        /blog/2015/05/06/ae-pulls-8-minutes-sex-work-show.

Chapter Nine: Demanding the Impossible

1   Unless otherwise noted, most quotes in this chapter are from interviews by the author or interviews by Sebastian Walker for *History of an Occupation*, a documentary I produced with Sweta Vohra for the program *Fault Lines* on Al Jazeera English, which aired March 2012.

2   Yasmine Ryan, "The Tragic Life of a Street Vendor," *Al Jazeera*, January 20, 2011, www.aljazeera.com/indepth/features /2011/01/201111684242518839.html.

3   Quotes and ideas from a talk I attended at American University in Cairo in the summer of 2011.

4   Onkwehón:We Rising, "Decolonization Is Not a Metaphor: The Basics of a Genuine Anti-Colonial Position," *Onkwehón:We Rising*, May 16, 2016, https://onkwehonwerising.wordpress .com/2016/05/16/decolonization-is-not-a-metaphor -the-basics-of-a-genuine-anti-colonial-position.

5   Eric S. Blake, Todd B. Kimberlain, Robert J. Berg, John P. Cangialosi, and John L. Beven II, National Hurricane Center, "Tropical Cyclone Report: Hurricane Sandy, 22–29 October 2012," National Hurricane Center, February 12, 2013, www .nhc.noaa.gov/data/tcr/AL182012_Sandy.pdf.

6   Jay-Z, *Decoded*, 220.

7   Josh Dawsey, "In a Pinch, Aid Workers Go Upscale," *Wall Street Journal*, November 13, 2012.

8   Allison Kilkenny, "Occupy Sandy: One Year Later," *Nation*, October 28, 2013, https://www.thenation.com/article/occupy -sandy-one-year-later.

9   Evan Hill, "One Year after Sandy, the Flood of Occupy Volunteers Recedes," *Al Jazeera America*, October 27, 2013, america .aljazeera.com/articles/2013/10/27/one-year-after-sandythe floodofoccupyvolunteersrecedes.html.

10   Febna Caven, "Being Idle No More: The Women Behind the Movement," *Cultural Survival*, https://www.culturalsurvival. org/publications/cultural-survival-quarterly/being-idle-no -more-women-behind-movement.

11   Imani Altemus-Williams, "Idle No More—No More Is It Just for Canada," *Waging Nonviolence*, January 10, 2013, wagingnon violence.org/feature/idle-no-more-no-more-just-for-canada.

12   Quoted in ibid.

Chapter Ten: Black Lives Matter

1   Alexis Pauline Gumbs, "an archeology of freedom," *Left Turn Magazine*, November/December 2008.

2   "A General Conference of Freedom's Prophets: AME's Re-
     working Trails to Freedom," panel discussion, Philadelphia,
     April 8, 2016.

3   Jason Fagone, "The Serial Swatter," *New York Times Magazine*,
     November 24, 2015, http://www.nytimes.com/2015/11/29
     /magazine/the-serial-swatter.html.

4   Ibid.

5   Peter Gelzinis, "What Looked Like a Sure Thing Became Any-
     thing But," *Boston Herald*, July 14, 2013.

6   Unless otherwise noted, quotes and background by Cynthia
     Garza, Patrice Cullors, and Opal Tometi are from a combination
     of interview with author, Facebook and social media records,
     public events, their own writing, and interviews I produced with
     Garza, Cullors and Tometi for *The Laura Flanders Show*.

7   Thandisizwe Chimurenga, "Integrity Matters: An Inter-
     view with Black Lives Matter Co-founder Patrisse Cullors,"
     Daily Kos, November 27, 2015, www.dailykos.com/story
     /2015/11/27/1454572/-Integrity-matters-An-interview
     -with-Black-Lives-Matter-co-founder-Patrisse-Cullors.

8   Waldo E. Martin and Patricia Sullivan, eds., *Civil Rights in the
     United States*, vol. 1 (New York: Macmillan, 2000), 58.

9   Patrisse Marie Cullors-Brignac, "We Didn't Start a Move-
     ment. We Started a Network," *Patrisse Marie Cullors-Brignac*
     (blog), February 22, 2016, https://medium.com/@patrisse
     mariecullorsbrignac/we-didn-t-start-a-movement-we-started
     -a-network-90f9b5717668#.hxkjdewx0.

10   Darryl Holliday, "The New Black Power," *Chicago Magazine*,
     March,2016,www.chicagomag.com/Chicago-Magazine/March
     -2016/black-leaders.

11   Arlene Eisen, *Operation Ghetto Storm: 2012 Annual Report
     on the Extrajudicial Killings of 313 Black People by Police,
     Security Guards, and Vigilantes*, updated ed. (2014), www
     .operationghettostorm.org/uploads/1/9/1/1/19110795
     /new_all_14_11_04.pdf.

12   Julia Carrie Wong, "The Bay Area Roots of Black Lives Matter," *SF
     Weekly*, November 11, 2015, www.sfweekly.com/sanfrancisco
     /san-francisco-news-black-lives-matter-alicia-garza-bart
     -black-friday-14-ferguson-racism-socialism-bayview-hunters
     -point-lennar-acc/Content?oid=4255090.

13   Radley Balko, "How Municipalities in St. Louis County, Mo.,
     Profit from Poverty," *Washington Post*, September 3, 2014.

14   Email communication with Jeff Ordower of Missourians Or-
     ganizing for Reform and Empowerment (MORE).

15   Cullors-Brignac, "We Didn't Start a Movement."

16   From interview produced by the author, aired on *The Laura Flanders Show*, March 25, 2015.

17   Wong, "The Bay Area Roots of Black Lives Matter."

18   Chimurenga, "Integrity Matters."

19   Barbara Ransby, *Ella Baker and the Black Freedom Movement: A Radical Democratic Vision* (Chapel Hill: University of North Carolina Press, 2005), 293.

20   Dani McClain, "The Black Lives Matter Movement Is Most Visible on Twitter. Its True Home Is Elsewhere," *Nation*, April 19, 2016, www.thenation.com/article/black-lives-matter-was -born-on-twitter-will-it-die-there.

21   Ibid.

22   Cullors-Brignac, "We Didn't Start a Movement."

Chapter Eleven: Decentering Privilege

1   "Culture Shifts," *Catalyst Project*, November 19, 2014, collective liberation.org/culture-shifts-2.

2   Marisa Franco, B. Loewe, and Tania Unzueta, "How We Make Change Is Changing," *Organizer Sandbox*, June 22, 2015, https://medium.com/organizer-sandbox/how-we-make -change-is-changing-part-i-5326186575e6#.5pxap5fe6.

3   Ibid.

4   Ibid.

5   Spade and Dector, *Queer Dreams and Nonprofit Blues*.

6   "Adaptation of Charles H. Kerr translation from the original, for The IWW Songbook (34th Edition)," Marxists Internet Archive, https://www.marxists.org/history/ussr/sounds/lyrics /international.htm. The original French lyrics are similar, translated as "There are no supreme saviors / Neither God, nor Caesar nor tribune / Producers, let us save ourselves / We decree common salvation!"

7   "Who We Are," Harriet's Apothecary, www.harrietsapothecary .com/who-we-are.

8   Richest 1% to Own More Than Rest of World, Oxfam Says," BBC, January 19, 2015, http://www.bbc.com/news/business -30875633.

9   John D. Rockefeller's Commission on Foundation and Private Philanthropy, "The Role of Philanthropy of a Changing Society," in *America's Voluntary Spirit: A Book of Readings*, edited by Brian O'Connell (New York: Foundation Center, 1970), 293. Quoted in Team Colors Collective, editors, *Uses of a Whirlwind: Movement, Movements, and Con-

temporary Radical Currents in the United States (Oakland: AK Press, 2010), 8.

10   Quoted in *The Media*, no. 41 (August 29, 2014), fvckthemedia.com/issue41/on-ferguson.

11   Ta-Nehisi Coates, "The Myth of Police Reform," *Atlantic*, April 15, 2015, www.theatlantic.com/politics/archive/2015/04/the-myth-of-police-reform/390057.

12   André Gorz, "Strategy for Labor," in *Theories of the Labor Movement*, ed. Simeon Larson and Bruce Nissen (Detroit: Wayne State University Press, 1987), 102.

13   Ibid., 116. Emphasis in original.

14   "The Challenge of Prison Abolition: A Conversation" ("A conversation between Angela Y. Davis and Dylan Rodriguez"), *History Is a Weapon*, http://www.historyisaweapon.com/defcon1/davisinterview.html.

15   Quoted in "The FBI's War on the Black Panther Party's Southern California Chapter," *MIM Theory*, no. 11 (October 30, 1999), It's About Time: Black Panther Party Legacy and Alumni, www.itsabouttimebpp.com/Chapter_History/FBI_War_LA_Chapter.html.

16   Spade, *Normal Life*, 33.

17   Ibid.

Index

AK Press is small, in terms of staff and resources, but we also manage to be one of the world's most productive anarchist publishing houses. We publish close to twenty books every year, and distribute thousands of other titles published by like-minded independent presses and projects from around the globe. We're entirely worker-run and democratically managed. We operate without a corporate structure—no boss, no managers, no bullshit.

The Friends of AK program is a way you can directly contribute to the continued existence of AK Press, and ensure that we're able to keep publishing books like this one! Friends pay $25 a month directly into our publishing account ($30 for Canada, $35 for international), and receive a copy of every book AK Press publishes for the duration of their membership! Friends also receive a discount on anything they order from our website or buy at a table: 50% on AK titles, and 20% on everything else. We have a Friends of AK ebook program as well: $15 a month gets you an electronic copy of every book we publish for the duration of your membership. You can even sponsor a very discounted membership for someone in prison.

Email friendsofak@akpress.org for more info, or visit the Friends of AK Press website: https://www.akpress.org/friends.html

There are always great book projects in the works—so sign up now to become a Friend of AK Press, and let the presses roll!

Jordan Flaherty is an award-winning journalist, producer, and author. He has produced television documentaries and news reports for *Al Jazeera America*, *Al Jazeera English*, *tele-SUR*, *The Laura Flanders Show*, and *Democracy Now*. He was the first journalist to bring the case of the Jena Six to a national audience, and he has so far been the only journalist identified as a subject of the New York City Police Department's spying programs. His last book was *Floodlines: Community and Resistance From Katrina to the Jena Six.*